Pop Culture in America

Pop Culture in America

Edited with an Introduction by

David Manning White

 a New York Times Book

Quadrangle Books
CHICAGO

Library of Congress Catalog Card Number: 70-101077

The publishers are grateful to the contributors herein for permission to reprint their articles. "Rock As Salvation" by Benjamin DeMott appears in somewhat different form in *Supergrow,* copyright © 1968, 1969 by Benjamin DeMott, reprinted by permission of E. P. Dutton & Co.

Contents

3. Film and Stage

4. Music

5. Art

6. Books

Pop Culture in America

Introduction

No one ever went broke underestimating the taste of the American public.
—H. L. Mencken

Culture begets a dissatisfaction which is of the highest possible value in stemming the common tide of men's thoughts in a wealthy and industrial community; and which may save the future, as one may hope, from being vulgarized, even if it cannot save the present.
—Matthew Arnold

IT WAS Victor Hugo, I believe, who once said that all generalizations are false, including this one. Few, if any, of the phenomena of contemporary life produce as many fruitless generalizations as the relevance (or irrelevance) of popular culture in contemporary society. There are many who are convinced that the quality of their lives would be improved immeasurably if overnight every television and radio transmitter mysteriously imploded, all the presses that print our newspapers and magazines corroded into a rasping halt, and the word "best-seller" became an historical footnote. At least they think their lives would be better. But examine their disdain for the mass media more closely and you soon discover that their neo-elitism is showing at the intellectual seams. They are the same people who sigh when they contemplate the unwashed masses reading the *New York Daily News* and watching *Hollywood Palace* every Saturday night, salivating over *Naked*

Came the Stranger, or enjoying a Debbie Reynolds film like *The Singing Nun.* But it's all fitting and proper if the mass media provide the neo-elitists with their *New York Times,* which in turn alerts them to a smashing lecture on Etruscan artifacts on WNDT, the educational television station, to the latest Pasolini film at an East Side cinema, or to a paperback edition of a recent Nabokov, Barth, or Malamud novel.

Let's set the record straight: it isn't the mass media *per se* that trouble neo-elitists so much as the way other people with a lower cultural IQ use these media. Given time to reflect on the proposition, even the neo-elitist is not likely to wish us all back into the days of hand-illuminated manuscripts or an occasional troupe of players to perform the man from Stratford's latest comedy.

The Common Man, sometimes known as "the thirteen-year-old-mentality" target, history's *mobile vulgus,* doesn't begrudge his neo-elitist contemporaries the pleasures and usages *they* choose to extract from the mass media. For the most part, the Common Man couldn't care less for their solicitude about his cultural poverty; he continues to laugh heartily at the all-too-familiar antics of a Jackie Gleason when he ought to be savoring the performance of an Orson Welles as an equally obese Falstaff. It is easy to become embroiled in a feckless debate about cultural tastes concerning how or why we should make all men cultural *fraters.* But we shall serve ourselves better if we can begin to understand why we have the kinds of mass entertainment that flourish in this society today.

There is a very high correlation between a man's occupation, his socio-economic status, and what he reads, what kind of music appeals to him, what kind of cinema is likely to get his patronage, and so forth. Of course, we have known many exceptions to this generalization, and who cannot call to mind a little hunchbacked lathe operator in Sandusky, Ohio, who spends all of his leisure hours listening to the Beethoven Quartets in the public library's music room, or a Ph.D. chemist from MIT who collects only Eddy Arnold records and reads the latest Harold Robbins novel with a joyous visceral reaction?

Education alone is no assurance that an individual will prefer Bartok to Hoagy Carmichael (personally, I like both of them, depending on my mood and other circumstances), but in the aggregate it is quite likely that those who are more highly educated will appreciate and enjoy Bartok. Even today, when college populations have more than doubled since the end of World War II, the median number of years of school completed by Americans twenty-five years and older is less than twelfth grade for male whites, and eighth grade for nonwhites. Only about 20 per cent of our work force fall into those categories designated (1) Professional, technical, and kindred workers, and (2) Managers, officials, and proprietors. These are the categories of people with greater income, education, and, I suspect, an interest in the more subtle and "artistic" of the popular arts. But there are roughly 80 per cent who are clerical and sales workers, craftsmen, operatives, laborers, service workers, private household workers, farmers and their hired hands. Only when we accept these demographic facts of life in our democracy can we appreciate how utterly naive it is to tear our togas over the low-to-middle-brow level of our popular culture and to chastise the mass-media industries for debasing the national taste. Mass entertainment in this country is a business, and the object of any business is to show a profit (the larger the better) by getting people to patronize it. The critics of the mass media are certain that the mediocre quality of most television programs, popular magazines, or films is due to some cabal on the part of the media managers. The gatekeepers of the media, on the other hand, often with the futile grimace of a Pontius Pilate, rationalize their products by insisting that they are giving the public what it wants. How do they know what the public wants? Easy. The proof is in the cash box, and in a country where Mammon is a very potent god, money talks in clarion tones.

Would we have a "better" (i.e., less homogenized) brand of popular culture if the people wished it? If it could produce revenue in sufficient terms, why not? I have known scores of writers, television producers, and publishers and had long talks with many of them. Most of them are cynical about the public's taste, but few are openly contemptuous. Some are ashamed of the product they say the public demands from them. Indeed, I know a perfectly delightful, urbane, compassionate television producer whose eyes dim with tears when he ponders the latest episode of a weekly situation comedy produced under his aegis. A sip of sixty-year-old brandy to settle his Chateaubriand does wonders for such attacks of artistic conscience.

If the public at large is dissatisfied with the quality of mass entertainment, it can show its malaise where it counts, at the box office. Often it does that very thing. 20th Century–Fox almost bankrupted itself by putting $40 million into *Cleopatra*, the 1963 release starring Elizabeth Taylor. Although about half this sum was spent in advertising and publicity, the whole venture was a perfect example of Gresham's Law, and the Great Audience was far more interested in the much-documented romance between Taylor and Richard Burton than the opulent pageantry of the film. *Cleopatra* brings home a point: the more money invested in a particular mass-media product, the more limited the creative options become.

Other film spectacles that bombed out, despite the most skillful and expensive of promotion campaigns, were *The Agony and the Ecstasy* (1965), another 20th Century–Fox fizzle, and *Lord Jim* (1965), based on Joseph Conrad's novel. Each year the television networks spend millions on new series, but two or three months after the September fanfare, most of them are replaced. The Great Audience speaks through the dreaded "ratings," and account executives in Madison Avenue swallow another tranquilizer. A point to be considered is simply that the public *does show* preference for one popular-culture product over another. The media managers, in spite of their casuitrous speculation and planning, can never be certain they are "on target." The neo-elitist critic of our popular culture would say that it doesn't really make any difference, because the public will switch channels from one banal television show to another equally mediocre program.

II

The seemingly insatiable appetite of 200 million Americans for the varieties of popular culture means that many hundred thousand people are employed in this continuous quest for salable and satisfying products. Television, for example, begins its competition with other media for the consumer's attention with the youngest tots. A statistically minded chap (whether pro television or con is not certain) has concluded that by the time a child graduates from high school he will have spent fifteen thousand hours in classrooms, but *eighteen thousand hours* in front of a television set. Those who feared in 1947, when television first became a real competitor for leisure time, that the other media would wither away from lack of attention were being unduly pessimistic. As we enter the 1970's, for example, we find the book-publishing industry as vigorous as any time in our history. There are more than sixteen hundred publishers who issue one or more titles each year, although approximately 60 per cent of our books are published by fewer than ninety publishers. 1969 saw almost thirty thousand new titles published, totaling nearly one billion copies. An industry that sells more than $1.5 billion of its products is far from moribund.

The newspaper, although its primary purpose is to inform, must also be considered an agency of popular culture. The trend since 1945 has been toward concentration of ownership among the daily newspapers in this country. As Dr. Raymond B. Nixon has pointed out, newspapers in 97 per cent of the nation's seventeen hundred cities with dailies now have a local "monopoly," and nearly half are owned by some group or national chain. Yet with the emergence of television and the resurgence of radio, competition for the reader's time and the advertiser's dollar has never been keener.

The past two decades have witnessed the death of several well-known dailies, such as the *Traveler* and *Post* in Boston, and such New York stalwarts as the *Herald Tribune, World-Telegram,* and even the tabloid *Mirror.* But the number of daily newspapers remains fairly constant, fluctuating from about 1,750 to 1,760, and nearly 63 million copies are sold every day. If we assume, conservatively, that each paper is read by poppa, momma, and at least one of the kids—although each may seek different rewards from his reading—that would give us a daily newspaper reading audience in excess of 180 million. A popular comic strip in any newspaper may be read by as much as 70 per cent of all of its readers. The comic-strip *Peanuts* probably has fifty to sixty million readers every day of the year. This kind of readership cannot be matched even by the most fervently watched television programs. The newspaper industry is still the titan of advertising revenue, with a total annual income of more than $4.5 billion.

Magazines in the United States today serve all tastes. Some fifty of them have a circulation of one million or more, but there are literally thousands of magazines which emerge from approximately 2,600 magazine publishers. In 1965 alone, sixty new magazines appeared, including Igor Cassini's *Status,* aimed at sixty thousand of the Beautiful People, *Arts and Antiques, Sportsfishing, Dare, Tiger,* and *Penthouse.* Very few American activities, from dieting to collecting cars, are not represented in a journal of their own.

Money alone cannot ensure that a magazine will flourish, as evidenced by *Show,* which cost Huntington Hartford $7.5 million in less than five years and suspended publication in 1965. Moreover, some magazines which were once enormously popular and financially strong came upon bad days after World War II, notably *American, Collier's, Liberty,* and the *Saturday Evening Post.* The *Post* had been the magazine *par excellence* of the American middle-class family, but in 1950 television began to replace it as the family's main source of entertainment. Advertisers began to move their money elsewhere, and though the magazine still had six million subscribers in 1968, its demise was inevitable. After losing more than $60 million since 1961, and after several attempts to change the magazine's format and slant in a vain effort to revitalize its appeal, the *Saturday Evening Post* died quietly in its sleep on February 8, 1969.

When any of the mass-media products fail there is always a complex set of reasons, and it is too simplistic to sweep all failures into a general basket labeled "The public didn't go for it." A case in point was the death of *Reporter* magazine, a highly literate and thought-provoking journal throughout its nineteen shaky years of existence. If there was (and is) a readership for the *Nation* and *New Republic* throughout the postwar years, surely there were enough Americans (one subscriber out of every 2,000 people in the United States would have given the journal a healthy 100,000 list) to keep the *Reporter* alive. So one would have to look for other reasons for its inability to be a viable entity, and perhaps we would find the cancerous growth in management, or perhaps in other variables.

The ultimate reason why a television serial that looks so great among the pilot programs in April is a dead duck by November, or why a new musical with a $400,000 investment dies on the road before the New York opening, is that it doesn't make any rapport with the public. But the back-of-the-scene turmoil, the artistic tempers that flare out like sunspots, lack of communication between the writer and the director, the editor and the production man, the publisher and the editor—these are also major causes why the public was given a product that was moldy and foredoomed even before they saw it.

If television influenced all the mass media since 1945, the one whose form and content it probably affected most was the film. First of all, television furnished "free" what has to be paid for at the movies (though it is surprising how many televiewers do not know or wish to know that the cost of advertising is part of the price they pay for a bar of soap or a new sewing machine). Since millions of American had gone to the movies regularly for years, almost by habit, it was not terribly difficult to supplant one viewing habit with another. For those who had accepted whatever flickered on the silver screen with equal enthusiam/apathy, and to whom the movies' prime purpose was to kill time or fabricate an innocuous fantasy world, a change of allegiance to television involved no great decision.

Hollywood reacted in a number of ways, and though its perspective has changed radically during the past twenty-five years the film industry is still a major force in our popular culture. Some studios, such as Republic, which produced "B" pictures exclusively, no longer exist; the day of the double feature, one or both of "B" stature, is passé. Besides, television offers a substitute for the old "B" pictures. A product that is guaranteed to offer no intellectual, emotional, or aesthetic experience is TV's interminable series dealing with cowboys, doctors, or police officers. These are the perennial favorites of the Great Audience—at least the network moguls think so. In fact, many of these banal series are filmed on the lots of MGM, Universal, and 20th Century–Fox. After a few years of tearing their hair as theater after theater closed down during the early fifties, Hollywood got hep and joined the electronic interloper with the small screen. At the same time the moviemakers began to concentrate on sex-and-sand spectacles with wide screens and super-sound systems, products clearly beyond the capacity of a twenty-three-inch tube.

Today there are still six large studios, not to mention a substantial number of independent producers in the American movie industry. True, many of the neighborhood theaters in our large cities have been converted to supermarkets and bowling alleys, or are boarded up, but there are still more than sixteen thousand theaters, and they are attended by nearly sixty million Americans every week. The fact that these patrons are willing to spend about $1.5 billion a year bespeaks a certain vitality for the film industry. As we look back at the best productions that have come out of Hollywood since 1945, the list is impressive. Take John Huston's *Treasure of Sierra Madre* (1948), or some of the films of Elia Kazan during the early fifties, such as *A Streetcar Named Desire* (1952) and *On the Waterfront* (1954). Other notable films of the 1950's include George Stevens' *A Place in the Sun* (1951), *The African Queen* (1951), *Sunset Boulevard* (1950), *A Star Is Born* (1954), *An American in Paris* (1951), *Moulin Rouge* (1952), *High Noon* (1952), *Friendly Persuasion* (1956), and *The Bridge on the River Kwai* (1957). The sixties had its own share of first-rate cinema conceived and produced in Hollywood—films like *Elmer Gantry* (1960), *The Hustler* (1961), *The Miracle Worker* (1962), *Judgment at Nuremburg* (1961), *Dr. Strangelove* (1964), *Who's Afraid of Virginia Woolf?* (1966), *Sound of Music* (1965), and *West Side Story* (1961).

There were, of course, many other excellent and enduring films produced and distributed during these years, and I have probably chosen my own favorites. I wouldn't think of describing such a list as Hollywood's typical product, knowing full well that for every *Elmer Gantry* or *Miracle Worker* there were dozens of films like *Beach Party, The Sandpiper,* and *Love Me Tender,* and that such films clearly appeal to a great number of Americans. *Love Me Tender* was an Elvis Presley vehicle which was among the fifteen top-grossing films of its year, as were *Beach Party* and *The Sandpiper.* The noteworthy aspect of the films I remember as well worth seeing is that *each* of them, too, was among the top-grossing films of their respective years. Deduction: the Great Audience will patronize a lot of junk, but it will also recognize some of Hollywood's more artistic attempts. Another interesting thing about the list of films that I picked almost at random from those I remembered kindly is that every one of them except *The African Queen* either won the Academy Award as the best picture of the year or was a close runner-up. Deduction: the industry itself can delineate between garbage and filet mignon. One final correlation from my list is worth noting.

The National Board of Review committee consists of some 175 public-spirited men and women who have an interest in films as well as a recognized sense of social responsibility. Again, except for *The African Queen,* they picked every one of the pictures on my list. (I still love Huston's *African Queen* even if it didn't win a prize. Actually, Humphrey Bogart did win the Best Actor award for his portrayal of Charlie Allnut, and Kate Hepburn might have won the Oscar for the Best Actress for the same picture, except that Vivien Leigh gave an unforgettable performance as Blanche DuBois in *Streetcar Named Desire.*) Deduction: well-made films can be successful at the box office, can please the critics and be recognized by the people in the industry as something to be proud of. That such films could and did come from Hollywood, along with the swill the same studios offered the Great Audience, is a point we sometimes forget.

Perhaps more than any other of the mass entertainment media, with the exception of popular music, the motion picture in the past twenty-five years has felt the impact of a *young* audience. Two-thirds of the audience for films today consists of people under twenty-five. Because this generation is more sophisticated, more highly educated, and in many ways more liberal-minded than their parents, since 1945 we have seen a growing interest in the foreign film. The best work of a Fellini, Renoir, Truffaut, or Bergman is analyzed and discussed on every campus from Stanford to Slippery Rock. At Dartmouth, for example, more than thirteen hundred of the college's three thousand students belong to a film society that shows one hundred films a year. Film appreciation courses are given in hundreds of colleges, and most of the sixty thousand students enrolled can become ecstatic about De Sica's *Bicycle Thief,* but are completely turned off by a Cecil B. DeMille epic. In the past quarter-century we have seen a phenomenal growth in the number of so-called "art" movie theaters, not only in our larger cities but in places like Pine Bluff or Toledo as well.

I have a friend who attended the University of Georgia and became a film buff with a special affinity for the work of Michelangelo Antonioni. He is now a chemical engineer working in Atlanta, where he regularly attends the cinema of his choice; obviously that choice is a far cut from the Cary Grant cum Rock Hudson cum Doris Day brand of situation comedy that used to attract his mother and dad to the movies on Saturday night. There is little doubt that the *young* audience is already affecting Hollywood releases by its conviction that social realities are not incompatible with entertainment. Two of the biggest hits of 1969 (both at the box office and in terms of critical response) were *Easy Rider,* Peter Fonda's idyll of the "turned-on" generation, and *Midnight Cowboy,* whose script would have been turned down immediately by any major studio not even a decade ago.

Let's turn to still another major source of mass entertainment in postwar America: radio, the medium whose obituary was written too soon. As Robert Hilliard has aptly pointed out, when national network television became a reality in the early 1950's, the word spread fast that radio would soon die. Such predictions looked good when radio net profits, which in 1952 had reached $61 million, dropped to $32 million in 1961. Then suddenly the tide changed for radio, possibly because a young audience responded with almost frenzied devotion to rock, folk rock, and soul music. By 1965 profits were up to more than $77 million. Radio had passed the test for survival and had learned to live with its half-brother, television. At the end of World War II there were approximately 950 stations on the air, and only five years later, in 1950, the number had proliferated to 2,900. Today there are more than six thousand radio stations in the United States. Ninety-seven out of every one hundred American homes have one or more radios, and it is estimated that there are more than a quarter of a billion sets in use, if we include automobiles and public places. Because a radio station is relatively inexpensive to establish, as compared with a television station, and can be operated with a smaller staff than a newspaper, we have a great many stations that focus on one aspect of popular culture, whether it be hard rock music, country western and blues, show music and standard jazz, or classical music. The listener who opts for such stations knows pretty much what to expect, for in fact the station is focusing on his expectations.

In some cities there are radio stations that have no music at all, only news or talk. Topics of the day—local, regional, national, or international—are discussed by a "talk-master" at the studio and whoever feels like telephoning him. The level of discourse is something short of a Socratic dialogue, and Plato would have closed down all radio stations within the hour if he were subjected to some of the fustian and blather that ensue. But Plato didn't put much faith in the libertarian notion that anyone can speak his mind and that good and truthful ideas will prevail over lesser minds in the marketplace of thought.

In any case, today there is radio programming for every taste, and it is estimated that the average time spent each week per person listening to radio is between twenty and twenty-five hours. If that seems like too high an estimate, remember that from five o'clock Friday afternoon until 8 or 9 A.M. Monday morning virtually 200 million Americans are not in school or on a job. (Housewives, of course, must do their routine thing over the weekend, but they are heavy users of their kitchen radios, which dispel some of the daily ennui of preparing meals, washing dishes, and so forth.) There are sixty-four "leisure" hours alone over the weekend, and even if twenty-four of them are spent sleeping, and six more in eating and brushing your teeth, there are still many hours to fill. Radio is a deceptively seductive time-filler. Bear in mind that whether you are listening to Rasputin and the Freaked Out Monks' latest ear-splitting disk, or to a performance of the Boston Symphony from Tanglewood, you are still filling time. If we use radio to hear the best of classical and contemporary music, provocative discussions such as *Meet the Press* or *Capitol Cloakroom,* or the news of the hour, we tell ourselves that we are using radio for cultural enrichment, information, and even possibly for enlightenment. Properly speaking we are doing that, but it is nevertheless *our* way of filling time, rather than building a rock garden, reading Spinoza or Ian Fleming, walking with our kids in the countryside, or any other way we choose when we are not earning a living.

Today the American Broadcasting Company has more than four hundred affiliated stations, the Columbia Broadcasting System about 250, the National Broadcasting Company slightly less, and the Mutual Broadcasting System claims over five hundred affiliates. But network radio is hardly the same as it was immediately after World War II. In 1949 the nation still tuned its radio sets in the evening to hear Jack Benny, Charlie McCarthy and his friend Edgar Bergen, Fibber McGee and Molly, Amos 'n' Andy, or the Inner Sanctum. And a very popular Arthur Godfrey. Walter Winchell was "must" Sunday-night listening for twenty or thirty million people. Amos 'n' Andy were still going strong, and so was a comedian named Bob Hope. By the mid-fifties time was running out for night network programming, as millions now turned on their television sets to *see* as well as hear *I Love Lucy,* Jackie Gleason, and Ed Sullivan. Some of the top stars of radio, like Benny, Hope, and Godfrey, made the switch to television easily.

The extraordinary speed with which television became the dominant purveyor of popular entertainment was due largely, of course, to the versatility and novelty of the medium. In 1947 if an American owned a television receiver he probably would have been the only one in his block, for there were only 75,000 throughout the entire country. Some twenty years later there were 55 million television-serviced homes in the United States (95 per cent) with more than six hundred commercial stations and 156 educational stations to provide the programming bill of fare. There were critics in 1950 who, after an evening of watching Milton Berle, or Ed Sullivan's musical potpourri (which juxtaposed Robert Merrill singing the *Largo al Factotum* with a trained seal playing "Goodnight, Sweetheart, 'Til We Meet Tomorrow"), swore that the public would soon tire of such banalities. Twenty years later, Ed Sullivan, with his face a little more lined, looking more like the adulated subject of an Irish wake than a celebrity, is still enticing the natives with the same format, the same jugglers and magicians. Chautauqua for Mencken's latter-day booboisie.

According to the Nielsen polling organization, whose statistics can mean life or death to anxious men in Radio City, Burbank, and all points between, the average American home watched television 6.75 hours a day in January 1968. There is every reason to believe that the figure exceeds seven hours a day now, since the average time spent in front of the set has increased almost every year. As people became willing to abdicate more and more of their leisure hours to television, the program producers were pressed to invent more and more time-fillers. More than any other medium, television wore out, ate up, and downright devastated most of the creative talent that was attracted to it. Where are yesterday's shows that had such delightful spontaneity and pace as Sid Caesar's merry antics with Imogene Coca, Danny Kaye's ebullience, *Have Gun Will Travel, I Spy,* and *The Man from U.N.C.L.E.?* For a brief interlude these programs had their moments of rapt attention and the interest of millions of viewers. But after one or two TV seasons, the creative team of producer, director, and performers grows a little stale. The pressure of thirty-six consecutive weekly productions takes its toll, and gradually the viewer who last season couldn't bear to miss an episode of *I Spy* finds an inexorable sameness about the series. Apathy sets in; the people at *I Spy,* who by this time are bored with doing the show, sigh with resignation and relief; and the network looks for a replacement. As long as people continue to watch the "tube" more and more hours, the networks really aren't concerned whether *I Spy* sells soap or whether another show will hopefully grab the public's fancy, especially when it grabs it away from the competing network's offering during the same time slot.

The American nation, if one is to judge them by their mass entertainment preferences, are quite a sentimental people. We cherish a gentle tug at the heartstrings when Fred Astaire goes through his nimble steps even in his seventies, singing the same ditties we heard him croon to Ginger Rogers in *Top Hat*—the medium has changed, but, dear Dr. Marshall McLuhan, the message is the same. One contemplates with awe those viewers in 55 million homes watching seven hours a day of old class "B" movies exhumed from the vaults of RKO and Universal, the Broadway veneer and coyness of a Johnny Carson, the ersatz excitement of twenty-two giant boys mauling each other for the dear old Dallas Cowboys and the Green Bay Packers (Nero, old chap, you think *you* had gladiators?), tears of nostalgia in their eyes as Bing Crosby sings "I'm Dreaming of a White Christmas" for the 11,402nd time. 420 million hours a day to be entertained and sold, sold, sold. Show me an American who doesn't know that you can take Salem out of the country, but you can't take the country out of Salem. What would Henry David Thoreau have to say about his countrymen today when most of the rooftops of his beloved Concord have di-pole antennae? Would he amend his statement that most men lead lives of quiet desperation to "most Americans lead lives of quiet, habitual narcotization by soap-sellers and mind-ticklers"?

Now, I have nothing against soap *per se*. I merely wonder what has happened to a country where in 1967 Procter and Gamble alone spent more than $200 million for advertising, almost all of it for television. It says something about the sensibility of a nation that requires *eight times* the amount paid by Thomas Jefferson for the entire Louisiana Purchase to persuade us that Ivory Soap is 99.44 per cent pure.

Why has the national advertising budget risen so fast, from about $3 billion in 1945 to nearly $20 billion today? The noted wit, Mr. Stan Freberg, in a seminar conducted at the University of Kansas in 1968, came very close to the answer, despite his tongue-in-cheek discourse. Freberg believes that the consumer (and to the marketing geniuses of Madison Avenue every man Jack of us is a viable, statistically verifiable, stratified consumer) has reached a point of commercial saturation. What follows is a sort of Hegelian thesis, antithesis, and synthesis, with the big corporations having to spend more and more money to snag the attention of us consumers. Our antithesis is to build more immunity, "in the interest of sanity," says Freberg, and, in turn, Procter and Gamble develops newer and costlier ways to wash our rebellious minds with soap—and the triad begins again. Freberg wonders if it really takes "a $19-billion sledge-hammer to drive a 39-cent thumbtack."

III

Earlier in this Introduction I said I had no desire to become engulfed in yet another useless drawing-room argument over whether popular culture in America is a noisome weed or a strangely enduring kind of flower. A number of distinguished critics believe that mass culture should be considered something like a bubonic plague of the modern mind. If one leans toward this position and desires reinforcement, he will find such arguments stated forcefully by Dwight Macdonald, Irving Howe, Ernest van den Haag, Bernard Rosenberg, and Hannah Arendt, to name but a few. It is difficult to find anyone from academe who will say a few kind words, let alone be a St. George for the side of popular culture; but there are a few such intrepid souls who at least try to understand this phenomenon without caressing it. The noted sociologist Edward Shils is perhaps the most conspicuous "semi-champion" of this point of view, but one also can find cogent arguments from the pens of Gilbert Seldes, Raymond Bauer, Leo Rosten, and, to an extent, Bernard Berelson.

The public, in general, neither digs Messrs. Macdonald, Howe, or van den Haag, nor Professors Shils, Bauer, and Seldes, mainly because the "mass culture" controversy is limited to magazines like *Dissent* or the *New York Review of Books* or to ponderous discussions on educational TV stations, or to seminar rooms at several hundred colleges and universities. But even the walls of academe offer no sure sanctuary, for most college students are also heavy users of the available mass media, and there is considerable research evidence that college graduates select most of the same mediocre television programs as their noncollege contemporaries.

My own view of the role of popular culture in American life will not endear me to either of the opposing sides, for I can see some merit at both ends of the argument. Does it do any good to tell ourselves that our mass culture is appreciably less violent than the *circus maximus* of Nero and his contemporaries? Or that Shakespeare's company competed with the bear-baiting pits a hundred yards away in Elizabethan London, and that today Shakespeare still is being performed, whereas bear-baiting has been discarded as suitable entertainment? Will it give us solace to realize that 99 per cent of the television programs, and perhaps only 97 per cent of today's novels, films, essays (including this one), and popular music from Irving Berlin to Lennon and McCartney probably will be completely forgotten or else be a matter of bewilderment or sniggering to our grandchildren's children?

On the other hand, can we be sure that just because something is enormously popular it will not endure? Robert Burns's poems and songs belonged to the people of his day long before the literary coterie in Edinburgh lionized and eventually ruined the poor man. Bob Dylan's poetry, if it has enduring relevance, need not be vitiated even though four or five million kids buy his albums and play them half the night. John Huston's *Treasure of Sierra Madre,* like Chaucer's "Pardoner's Tale," makes the point *radix malorum est cupiditas.* I suspect that a hundred years from now our descendants will be able to recognize both of these works as concise, masterful statements of the human condition. It really won't matter to them that Huston's "Pardoner's Tale" came out of Hollywood. By that time Hollywood may be only a footnote in the continuing saga of mass entertainment.

I suppose what most offends the bitter antagonists of the Great Audience culture is that each of the mass media, with their potentially enormous number of consumers, can *vulgarize* the arts so much faster than was possible a hundred years ago. Popular culture is not only a pervasive, salable, and ever-proliferating product; it is a natural consequence of our highly industrialized society. As the working week has diminished from seventy to sixty hours during our grandfathers' time to little more than half that for most workers today, the question of what to do with our leisure hours has become increasingly germane.

If we could take an instant audit of what every American over twenty-one was doing during any of his leisure hours we would find a broad spectrum of activity. We might find 100,000 or more of them reading the banal, pseudo-erotic novels of Harold Robbins, whose art is, generously put, neo-troglodyte, and whose work epitomizes what I mean when I refer to popular culture as a "product." Perhaps 100,000 are building cobbler's benches or canoes in their basement workshops, while 300,000 are playing golf, tennis, or just walking in the woods. Many millions, of course, are just sitting in front of their television sets with a can of beer in their hand, a little like the people in Plato's cave. The workday has been boring or tedious or nerve-wracking, and the television set is a good sugar-tit.

My point is that you can find our population doing many things to relax and trying to forget the exigencies of the working day. To be sure, most of what is going on between 5 P.M. any day and 9 A.M. the next has little if any social value. Yet, would we prefer the Orwellian specter of *1984* as practiced in its current version in mainland China, where hundreds of millions of Chinese spend their nonworking hours listening to or reading the state-controlled media-dispensed propaganda? This clearly is *one* socially ameliorative way to spend leisure time; at least the state thinks it is. It may be that Chairman Mao is merely applying the strict rules on the dangers of popular art that Plato espoused so strongly in the tenth book of the *Republic*. Plato happens to be an excellent example of a self-appointed arbiter of the public's taste. He intended to ban Homer and Hesiod because they sometimes portrayed the gods as immoral, death as fearful, and the relationship of reward to merit as quite fortuitous. These are ideas from which youth must certainly be shielded, according to Chairman Plato. Or Chairman Mao, for that matter.

I find myself far more in sympathy with Plato's pupil, Aristotle, who states clearly in the *Poetics* that it is not the only purpose of art to edify or teach us a moral lesson. This is not to say that Aristotle had anything against our being edified as a consequence of an artistic experience. But he thought art was under no aesthetic obligation to give us enjoyment of the "higher" sort, whatever that might be. We recognize, as did Aristotle, that the greatest art stimulates and invigorates our minds and hearts alike. But Aristotle intuited long before the days spent by millions upon millions of Americans, in factories and foundries, in punching IBM cards or selling anti-perspirant in cluttered drugstores, that man needs recreation as well as serious endeavor.

In Aristotle's book, the lower classes, too, who for a number of reasons are less likely to appreciate art of the more serious sort, are entitled to forms in which they find entertainment and even repose. His reasoning: better that they should enjoy art of some kind than be cut off altogether from aesthetic pleasure.

Aristotle might have winced, as many of us have, to watch a Metropolitan Opera Company diva perform a Puccini aria on a television variety show, followed immediately by an advertisement for mouthwash and a merry band of acrobats standing on each others' heads. The Platonist would demand that the televiewer watch the entire opera, dreary recitatives and all, or watch nothing; the Aristotelian would shrug his shoulders and hope that the Puccini aria might intrigue the chap whose aesthetic tastes had been limited to jugglers and magicians to desire more familiarity with Puccini or Mozart. I am not so naive that I expect a massive leap away from Harold Robbins, Mickey Spillane, Ian Fleming, Norman Rockwell, and their ilk because the Great Audience occasionally gets exposed to a more demanding art, and then only in bits and pieces. But there are signs that our popular culture has risen, albeit slowly, and is continuing to rise. We should be patient. Any elitist worth his salt knows that it took the masses thousands of years to get as vulgar as they are.

It really is no skin off my nose if my neighbor prefers a re-run of *Peyton Place* at 8:30 P.M. while I decide to go to one of nearly a dozen "art" cinema houses in Boston to see Fellini's *La Strada* for the third or fourth time. I may, somewhat smugly, consider myself a bit more "cultured," but if my neighbor derives enjoyment and surcease from his workaday anxieties by watching *Peyton Place,* I have no more right to take him away from it than he has to enter my art theater and yell "Culture Vulture!"

I would and do have the right to protest loudly if somehow my tastes cannot be satisfied merely because there are not as many of me as there are of him. As I have tried to point out, however, it doesn't take a very large percentage of the available audience to make a viable market. That is why we have some specialized magazines that can make money for their publishers with fewer than fifty thousand subscribers, or about one out of every four thousand people in the United States. It also explains why we now have thousands of paperback book titles to choose from. Granted, a Leon Uris novel like *Exodus* sells millions, but it is also economically feasible to publish paperback editions of less spectacular sellers like David Riesman's *Lonely Crowd* or Hesse's *Siddartha*. I shall never forget overhearing a conversation some years ago between a middle-aged gentlemen, whose diction and grammar were far from Oxonian, and a clerk in a paperback book store. The customer said he had recently purchased one helluva good war story by a writer named Homer, and he asked if Mr. Homer had written any new books for him to read. Without batting an eye, the heroic clerk said, "Yessir, we just got a new one by him that I think you would like. It's called the *Odyssey.*" The man went out of the store, caring little whether he was reading one of the world's masterpieces. He would read a fast-moving prose translation of a timeless story that night. I wonder what the clerk told him when he came in for the third novel by Mr. Homer. "Sorry, sir, he was traveling in Greece and he died unexpectedly."

IV

If somehow we could devise a meaningful scale of cultural measures, the mean would be higher today than in 1945, though the rise is not dramatic. For example, study the list of best-sellers, both in fiction and nonfiction, since 1945, and you will see that the level remains fairly constant. Best-sellers right after the war included *Forever Amber,* Lloyd Douglas' *The Robe,* and *The Razor's Edge* by Somerset Maugham, all of which were made into mediocre films, as was Remarque's *Arch of Triumph.*

Adventure stories by Thomas Costain and Frank Yerby pop up on the best-seller charts continuously. But the lists occasionally offer titles that are still worth reading today, such as Mailer's *Naked and the Dead,* Thornton Wilder's *Ides of March,* Marquand's *Point of No Return,* and A. B. Guthrie's *The Way West.* Even Nelson Algren hit the 1949 best-seller list with his *Man with the Golden Arm.* But most of the time it was a flash-in-the-pan novel like *Raintree County,* or the *Egyptian,* or *By Love Possessed.*

In nonfiction since 1945, the tradition of good old middle-class American values was reinforced by Norman Vincent Peale, except for those Jewish readers who were seeking *Peace of Mind* with Rabbi Liebman. The mere fact that excellent, enduring books can become best-sellers does not *ipso facto* mean that a cultural revolution has occurred. For if only one out of ten of the, say, ten million who buy serious books had bought *Dr. Zhivago,* for example, that alone would have elevated it to the best-seller list. (Hollywood managed to botch *Zhivago* up, too.) There is a kind of "bandwagon" effect that occurs when a novel sells 100,000 copies, so that we think *everyone* is reading it when in truth only one person out of two thousand has bought it.

Perhaps the finest book to achieve the best-seller status, if only briefly, was George Orwell's *1984,* which appeared in 1949 with its hopeless view of where our century was heading. Best-sellers of recent years have, if anything, failed to match the level of such novels as Waugh's *Brideshead Revisited,* or even O'Hara's *A*

Rage to Live. Recently we have seen books like *Valley of the Dolls,* Harold Robbins' *The Adventurers,* or Gore Vidal's tutti-frutti *Myra Breckenridge* hover near the top, although serious works of art like Barth's *Giles Goat Boy* or Bellow's *Herzog* also made the list for a while. Since 1955 it would appear that most of the best-sellers offer the Great Audience a more explicit peek through the transom of Sex, that topic that used to be fit only for pornographic imports from Paris. But the throng who bought Nabokov's *Lolita* found they had gotten more than they bargained for, namely, an encounter with one of the most brilliant and demanding literary minds of this century. His subsequently published books, although adding to his reputation, are no longer making the best-seller lists.

What is the course of popular culture as we begin the seventies? Frankly, I do not look for any dramatic changes, simply because the media managers will continue to accommodate what they perceive to be the *taste* of the majority of their consumers. If the normal bell curve of the country's consumers is satisfied with *Bonanza,* Elvis Presley, and Irving Wallace, then everything one standard deviation from that mean (or at least two-thirds of our media products) will be just as intellectually and emotionally stimulating. There will still be room at the top of the bell curve for educational television, although one hopes that it might become less pedantic, less self-conscious of its mission to save the world from the Philistines, and frankly a little more entertaining. (Or is there a rule that edification must be slightly musty and boring?) The top 5 per cent of our population in terms of education, occupations, and so forth, will still constitute the more than ten million potential consumers of books by Samuel Beckett and Vladimir Nabokov, films by Truffaut and Godard, and magazines like *Commentary* and *Fortune.*

The Book-of-the-Month Club, with its uncanny know-how in finding the pulse of socially mobile upper-middle-brows, will continue to disseminate hundreds of thousands of books each year, ranging from popular mishmash like Updike's *Couples* and Rod McKuen's ballads to more substantial works like Solzhenitsyn's *Cancer Ward* and Harrison Salisbury's brilliant account of the siege of Leningrad, *The 900 Days.* Other book clubs have flourished and then gradually faded away in the quarter-century since

World War II, but the Book-of-the-Month has become an American institution, as safe and predictable as a good blue chip on the Big Board. If, God forbid, the revolutionary tactics of a small but determined group of young people in this country lead to terror in the streets, I can visualize thousands of homes in suburbia where the perplexed middle-brows will bolster their walls with hundreds of unread Books-of-the-Month instead of sandbags.

The dominant form of popular culture in this country for the next decade will continue to be television. Not only does it usurp the greatest number of leisure hours, but it affects other aspects of the entertainment complex. Professional football, for example, was a relatively minor sports activity until the networks discovered it. With its enormous capacity for "status conferral," television made Vince Lombardi a national hero, and when he moved from Green Bay to Washington, D.C., every seat in a huge stadium was sold out for the season, despite the fact that the Washington Redskins hadn't been title contenders in twenty-five years.

As long as CBS and NBC continue to log a substantial corporate profit each year, we can expect little difference in the patterns of their programming. ABC will also continue to scramble for its slice of that $2.5 billion advertising pie by continuing to appeal to the under-thirty "music scene" audience with such programs as *Tom Jones* and, expectedly, *The New People*. Yet ABC's most popular program over the past decade has been the apotheosis of squaresville, the indestructible (thanks to Geritol?) Lawrence Welk. To those who place their hope for improvement of television on more channels, stations, networks, and programs, ABC is palpable evidence that an increase in program choice does not necessarily bring an improvement in program quality.

Does all this mean that the next quarter-century of television will be a video-tape replay of the past? Without being overly optimistic, there may be some improvement. This may come about because of new communications technology, such as cable-TV, pay-TV, and satellites, whose effects are beginning to become apparent. Pay-TV has finally been authorized by the Federal Communications Commission in the larger metropolitan areas. More channels may result in a "fragmenting" of the mass television audience; television stations, like many radio stations, may well program for only specialized minority groups. Just as we now have radio stations in many of our large cities whose target audience is the black minority, it is quite likely that a future UHF television station will also serve this specialized group. Indeed, the new communications technology, especially wired-television, may bring into the home a great deal of specialized information and services.

New sources of program distribution may also develop new sources of program production; at least one might hope for this. The independent TV program producer, like the rising independent film producer, may find more "playing time" for his product on cable television, pay-TV, and perhaps educational stations. On the other hand, with so many electronic mouths to feed, where are we suddenly to find so many more good programs and series when today we are hard put to find any the caliber of *Mark Twain Tonight* and *East Side, West Side?* Where are the talented writers, the skilled performers, the directorial geniuses to come from? There is a somber possibility that the expanding communications technology, rather than opening new programming horizons, may promote a situation even more onerous than in the quarter-century since 1945—a kind of mass-mass culture.

In the realm of film there is every reason to believe that Hollywood is facing a financial crisis greater than that of the early fifties, when television challenged its hold on the Great Audience. In the next decade the major studios will be primarily financial midwives, renting their studio facilities to independent producers in return for distribution rights to the finished product. This trend is already in evidence at Warner Brothers, Columbia, and Paramount.

This is not to suggest that the American film will lose its dominance of the world box office. The film industry is as resilient and fabulous an invalid as its high-brow cousin, the legitimate theater. American motion-picture financiers are now the heaviest investors in international film-making ventures. Federico Fellini's newest film, *Satyricon,* was financed largely by United Artists, as was Truffaut's *Stolen Kisses.* There is almost an ironic twist in seeing Karel Reisz, who some years ago was the archtypical anti-Hollywood kind of director, being backed by Universal for his latest film, *Isadora.* Two excellent films, *Oh, What a Lovely War* and Zeffirelli's *Romeo and Juliet,* each had heavy

American backing and were released in this country by Paramount. And MGM supplied more than travel expenses for Antonioni's film-making at Zabriskie Point, U.S.A. If the old Hollywood—with its star system and factory-like sound stages, its cultural America Firstism—is nearly dead, another, more international, celluloid phoenix is arising.

There will, of course, be plenty of the same kind of commercial entertainment films that carry the usual Hollywood stamp, and one envisions (thanks to advanced cosmetic art) an eighty-year-old Cary Grant romancing a mere sixtyish Sophia Loren. There will, however, be an increasing number of films we now associate with the anti-Hollywod, so-called Underground cinema. As film in some ways moves away from the masses, and as the number of art theaters increases, we can expect more offbeat films like *Coming Apart, Endless Summer,* Robert Downey's *Putney Swope,* and *Downhill Racer*. We will also see more experimental films from young, campus-trained film-makers, many of whom are being encouraged by the American Film Institute. For these young film-makers, "film is power." They embrace the film medium as a means of protest and of overturning the Establishment. As we might expect, Hollywood has not been loath to recognize a trend, so that films like Haskell Wexler's politically oriented *Medium Cool* are distributed by major companies (in this case, Paramount) to reach the young, dating-crowd audience.

If this Introduction has any one special point to make it is that despite the blight of commercialism, American popular culture since 1945 is not totally a wasteland. Good and enduring movies continue to come out of Hollywood; the giant book clubs often distribute novels and nonfiction of more than ephemeral worth; there are magazines to suit the most refined sensibilities; and television, while it has yet to recapture its Golden Age of entertainment and drama, nevertheless provides us with news and informational programs of great impact and immediacy. Indeed, television may well be forcing us to reconsider the demarcation between art and reportage. That such achievement, however less than perfect, is possible at all, given the circumstances of a cultural democracy, is in itself quite remarkable. The mass media in order to survive must reflect prevailing taste and cater to public demands. Despite the strictures placed upon them by the taste of the majority, innovative and daring media managers have been able to break away, now and then, from the expected mode.

Much of the encouragement for innovation has come from the Young Audience. Today in the United States, for the first time in our history, more than half of college-age youth are engaged in higher education. If education and exposure to diverse cultural experiences are the answer to raising the level of mass taste, there is reason for considerable optimism. In our universities and colleges today there may be developing the Great Audience of selectivity and discernment that Gilbert Seldes has long envisioned. One can hope that the enthusiasm and interest now being cultivated on hundreds of campuses will show up in future offices on Madison Avenue, at NBC, and at United Artists.

Whether the products of the mass media improve or deteriorate depends to a large extent on the future relations among American social, economic, political, and educational values. The mass media endemically mirror the prevailing social climate, so popular culture over the next quarter-century will be no better or worse than our society demands and therefore deserves.

Part 1

PANORAMA

They talk of the dignity of work. Bosh. The dignity
is in leisure.
—Herman Melville

Then the maiden Aunt
Took this fair day for text, and from it preached
A universal culture for the crowd.
—Alfred Lord Tennyson

IN 1883, Richard Jefferies wrote what at the time must have
seemed almost pure fantasy: "I hope that succeeding generations
will be able to be idle. I hope that nine-tenths of their time will be
leisure time; that they may enjoy their days, and the earth, and
the beauty of this beautiful world; that they may rest by the sea
and dream; that they may dance and sing, and eat and drink."
Since the late nineteenth century the work week has diminished
from seventy hours or more until today we have forty hours
or less. With automation proceeding apace in the next decades,
particularly through computer technology, it is not speculative fantasy to foresee a thirty-hour or even a twenty-five-hour work week
before the end of the century.

More and more, Americans will have to learn how to use their
leisure hours in a way that will afford them pleasure, repose, and
satisfaction. We have already learned that we pay a price for our

leisure. Automobiles, for example, get us places many times faster than the horse carriage of Melville's day, but they also pollute our atmosphere, help us to kill ourselves at a greater rate than most wars, and are party to a great deal of our malaise—particularly when one wants to go to the seashore and gets involved in bumper-to-bumper driving for two hours.

The social implications of our new leisure is the theme of Bruce Bliven's essay. Not only does he provide an excellent synopsis of the many ways we use our nonworking hours, Bliven also draws upon the insights of sociologists (David Riesman, for example) who have specialized in studying our leisure patterns. This first essay is a kind of blueprint for the many questions raised by discussions of mass culture, and the subsequent articles in this book attempt to answer them.

As we have stated in the Introduction, there are leisure activities for every *taste*. Our super-speed presses can as easily print a reasonably priced paperback edition of Thomas Mann's *Magic Mountain* as a pseudo-pornographic put-on like *Naked Came the Stranger* (written in 1969 as a hoax by some sardonic newspapermen, it quickly made the best-seller list). Often it would seem the mass audience enjoys being victimized by those who cater especially to their visceral needs. As long as the victims are willing to pay for their own banalization, there will be sleazy entrepreneurs to exploit such markets.

William Schumann, a noted American composer and former president of Lincoln Center for the Performing Arts, addresses himself directly to an especially germane question: are we a "cultured" nation? He finds that we are about halfway between those exclamations that the United States is going through a magnificent cultural explosion and those sighs that there is hardly an oasis on the horizon in our cultural desert. Schumann voices a concern shared by many Americans when he states that the "arts need a public laboratory (an audience) which does not evaluate every effort solely in terms of box-office returns." Entertainment has its place, and pleasure is not *ipso facto* a dirty word. Yet a truly "cultured" nation must have "artists and works dedicated to nothing less than the exploration of every conceivable nuance of revelation through the unique worlds of music, theater, and dance." The commercial realities of not only our mass culture, with its television audiences of millions, but even our Broadway theater too often lead us, says Schumann, to insist that art must at all costs please, at all costs be a success.

Marya Mannes, a brilliant commentator on American manners and mores, also finds herself in the middle of the debate on the worth of American popular culture. Miss Mannes welcomes the fact that there are more new orchestras, art galleries, and community theaters, all of these arts having shown substantial growth since the end of World War II. Yet she questions whether *attendance* at a play or concert is significant evidence that we are more cultured as a nation. Her thesis is that to have a true cultural democracy the Great Audience must truly understand something about the craft of music or sculpture or dance. She is properly leery of the sunshine patriots of the arts who may flock to the museum to see a recently acquired Rembrandt, mainly because the press has revealed that the painting cost the museum $2 million.

Howard Taubman, distinguished music critic, reiterates some of the arguments of both Schumann and Miss Mannes in his essay, a forceful plea for American support of the arts. In comparison with several countries in Europe (including the Soviet Union) whose governments help to sustain vigorous artistic activity, Taubman finds that the United States has much catching up to do—if indeed we have the will to do so.

A common theme of the essays in this section is that we must pay a price (and not only in dollars) if we really wish to achieve a high level of popular culture. We must begin with the cultural education of our young people from the earliest grades on, a task which public education has been unable to meet up to now. Just as today we have art supervisors, music supervisors, and so forth, in most of our school systems, tomorrow we must have supervisors who are trained as critics of our mass media.

How many millions of children have had their potential capacity to enjoy art ruined by an uninspired teacher? How long must we wait before our public schools begin to educate for enlightened leisure-time use of our mass media? Shakespeare has been taught for generations as if he wrote his lines on Mount Sinai instead of as a living, striving player/playwright in Elizabethan London. Small wonder that most students after their tenth-grade exposure to Portia or Puck content themselves with Red Skelton.

Benjamin Disraeli once said, "Increased means and increased leisure are the two civilizers of man." Since the gross national product of the United States will soon reach $1 trillion, and our leisure time will also expand, the prime ingredients are available. The questions become, then, how "civilized" do we want to become? How much are we willing to give to achieve it?

Using Our Leisure
Is No Easy Job

by Bruce Bliven

A HUNDRED years ago, the average work week in the United States was about 70 hours. Today, it is about 40 hours—and experts say that in the next decade or so it will be cut again, the predictions ranging from 37 hours or thereabouts down to 20 or even less. This reduction might come as a shorter work day, or fewer work days per week or longer—very much longer—vacations.

What shall we do with all that free time? Many people are profoundly troubled about this question. They feel that, far from being a blessing, the change may prove a catastrophe. Certainly, the growth of leisure time is an extremely serious matter that deserves far more attention than it is getting.

In the last few decades, leisure has brought about a profound alteration in the patterns of our society, although most people are not yet fully aware of it because it has come about so gradually. A hundred years ago, nearly everybody worked very long hours, six or seven days a week, and family vacations were almost unknown. Rich men might send their wives and children to the seashore or the mountains in the summer, but rarely joined them for more than a few hours a week at most. Poor people, the overwhelming majority, had no vacations—their free time consisting of holidays of one or two days' duration.

Men and boys went hunting and fishing, but this was more to get food than as recreation. On special occasions like the Fourth of July, there were athletic events like wrestling, three-legged races or chasing a young greased pig, but many watched and few participated. It is hard for us to realize that most of today's organized sports go back less than a century—except horse racing, which has been practiced since antiquity. Baseball did not really take hold in its present form until the eighteen-fifties, football and tennis until the eighteen-seventies, and golf and basketball until the eighteen-nineties. At the turn of the century golf and tennis were still considered the sports of the rich because of the cost of the equipment needed.

Today, we are seeing an astonishing "recreation explosion." We spend from $30 billion to $40 billion annually, perhaps as much as 20 times more per capita than we did in 1900. Max Kaplan, in his book, "Leisure in America," reports that in 1959, 33 million people went swimming at least once, fishing was enjoyed by 32 million, dancing by 32 million, bowling by 18 million, hunting by 16 million. Baseball, professional and amateur, regular or softball, is played by 18 million, golf by eight million and tennis by four million.

Other forms of outdoor recreation have also mushroomed. Skiing had not reached the United States in 1900, and water-skiing and scuba-diving had not been invented, but now millions participate in these sports. We spend more than $100 million annually on fishing and hunting licenses, and $1 billion on gardening equipment, seeds and plants. Vacation travel eats up $10 billion, three-quarters of it being spent on automobile trips within the United States.

Spectator sports have expanded similarly—far beyond the increase in population. Kaplan says that 28 million watch baseball annually, 23 million football, 18 million basketball and nine million horse racing. While hardly a sport, television is of course the most popular of all types of passive recreation. In less than two decades, it has grown to the point where people spend seven-eighths as much time watching it as they spend at work! Last year, Americans occupied nearly 300 billion person-hours in front of the screen—or at least, with their sets turned on.

Not only has recreation expanded enormously, but it has been upgraded culturally. In 1900 there were 10 symphony orchestras in the country; today there are about 1,200. We have more than 1,500 local theater groups, most of them amateurs. People spend $500 million annually on concert tickets. In 1934, 500 records of Beethoven's Ninth Symphony were bought, and in 1954, 75,-000. We expend $2.5 billion annually for musical instruments,

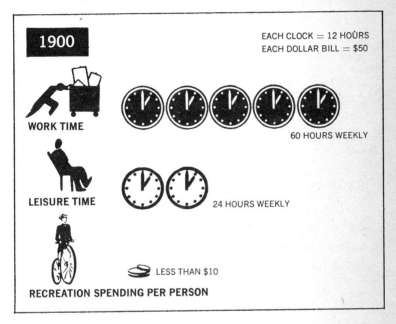

1900

EACH CLOCK = 12 HOURS
EACH DOLLAR BILL = $50

WORK TIME

60 HOURS WEEKLY

LEISURE TIME

24 HOURS WEEKLY

LESS THAN $10

RECREATION SPENDING PER PERSON

radios and TV sets. Twenty million of us play the piano, four million the guitar, three million the violin. There are two million "Sunday painters."

We buy more than a quarter of a billion paperbacks each year. True, many of them are at the level of the pulp magazines of a generation ago, but they also include almost every classic there is and in editions many times larger than ever sold before. Though much of television is mediocre, its audience is so huge that the good things it offers have a fantastic impact. A single performance of "Hamlet" on a national network, for instance, reaches more people than all the performances in theaters from Shakespeare's day to our own!

Sixty years ago, very few employers paid any attention to what their workers did in their spare time, though some did arrange an annual "company picnic." Today the picture is wholly changed. Many big firms maintain vacation retreats and often they provide playing fields for their employes. The Scrooges who ran most of the big companies in 1900 would be aghast at the universal coffee breaks today—sometimes guaranteed by union contracts.

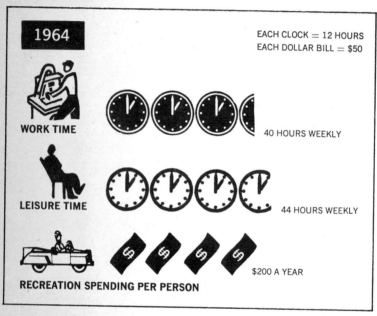

This increase in leisure and leisure-time pursuits has been made possible by the expansion in productivity per man-hour, which has trebled since 1900. Coupled with the growth of population, this has multiplied the production of goods by six times—which is lucky for us. As Gerard Piel, publisher of Scientific American, points out, if we were now turning out goods for a 1900 standard of living, we should have about 58 million unemployed. Looked at another way, we could maintain our present standard of living and still have 27 million unemployed if we worked the 60-hour week common at that time.

One important difference, however, is that in those days work was usually more satisfying spiritually. People were craftsmen who gratified their creative impulse by beginning something and carrying it through to the end. Today, in contrast, most work is fragmented. The man or woman on a beltline performs one operation over and over again and the clerical worker has usually become a cog in a big impersonal machine. Many students of human behavior believe that this change has led to profound frustration, and that the character as well as the amount of recrea-

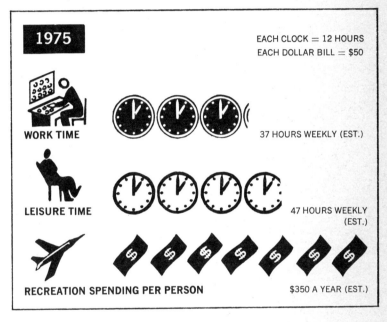

tion today represent an attempt by the individual to restore his psychological balance.

Georges Friedmann, a noted authority on the psychology of labor, believes that the character of work creates the character of play. Erich Fromm, the psychiatrist, thinks that the "do-it-yourself" movement, on which we spend $6 billion a year, has grown partly out of the yearning by today's workers for the exercise of a craftsman's skill. Indeed, he goes even farther and says in his book, "The Sane Society": "The mode of work is itself an essential in forming a person's character."

Ferdynand Zweig, another labor expert, believes that modern factory work creates a great yearning to get "back to nature," the sort of impulse that sends so many people camping in the mountains, and jams our national parks to bursting point every summer. Daniel Bell, the Columbia University sociologist, thinks that the great impersonal modern corporation sets up in its employes a profound, if frustrated, desire to become one's own boss.

Despite the obvious advantages of the tremendous flowering of leisure activities in recent years, however, students of human behavior fear that people simply will not know what to do with themselves if the work week is still further reduced. Certainly, present modes of recreation can hardly fill much greater periods of free time. Although so many Americans, and especially those engaged in beltline operations, are frustrated and discontented in their jobs, they also seem unhappy when they are *not* working. This is a fairly new phenomenon in the world's history, and even today is found only in a few industrialized countries—most of all, our own.

"Work," says David Riesman, the Harvard sociologist, in "The Lonely Crowd," "is considered more important than play. . . . In our society, consumption is defined as a means rather than an end. This implies we consume in order to achieve full employment." The factory worker comes home at the end of his shift and after a minimum of rest, plunges into some other activity. Most people say that even if they had an independent income they would still go on working, and most rich men's sons feel uncomfortable if they don't have a job. Sebastian de Grazia remarks, in the Twentieth Century Fund study, "Of Time, Work and Leisure," that the only Americans who have ever felt completely relaxed about not working have been the hoboes.

In pioneer society, everyone's labor was needed, and not working was regarded as immoral. Children used to be told, "Satan finds some mischief still/ For idle hands to do." Not until 1918 did the National Education Association pluck up enough courage to declare that learning good use of leisure was one of the cardinal aims of education. As late as 1926, the president of the National Association of Manufacturers could say, according to Harvey Swados in "Mass Leisure," "I regard the five-day week as an unworthy ideal. . . . It is better not to tamper with God's laws."

Among those who flout "God's laws" least are top business executives. While the general work week is about 40 hours, they average 55-60 hours. De Grazia says that two-thirds of them habitually take work home from the office. Half the industrial workers in the country now get three weeks' vacation annually, but this is not true of their bosses, who in theory could take as much time off as they pleased. Kaplan reports a survey which found that only a quarter of them took a month off, while one-third took three weeks and another third, two weeks. The remaining one-twelfth, presumably, were like George Bernard Shaw, who boasted he had never taken a vacation in 70 years.

Instead of adjusting in a relaxed fashion to the shorter work week, we seem to be going in the other direction. It is a commonplace to say that Americans "work hard and play hard," and that we don't know how to sit still and do nothing. Our tempo has speeded up to a feverish pace—Riesman says that we even play Bach and Mozart 10 per cent faster than was usual in their lifetimes. There is some truth in the old joke that after returning from a vacation filled from morning to night with organized activities, what one needs is a good rest.

Some authorities feel that the pressure, which extends even to children, can do much harm. Prof. Ronald C. Doll of Hunter College recently reported that children are expected to "be busy all the time," increasing the danger in later life of "heart attacks and nervous breakdowns." "When," he asks, "does the child have an opportunity to grow privately, quietly and independently to be himself?" This situation is characteristic of what Riesman calls the "other-directed" society, in which conformity to what someone else wants for you is the great objective.

What would people do if they had more leisure? Not necessarily what they say they would do. Business executives usually complain that they wish they had more time for reading and for cultural pursuits in general, but in fact they spend 80 per cent of their free time watching television or pursuing hobbies that can be called cultural only by stretching the term.

When large numbers of people were asked what they would like to do if they had more time, the biggest proportion said they would do more work around the house, and the second biggest, that they would spend more time with their families.

This agrees pretty well with their actual performance. When a typical sample was checked as to their most recent activities, it was found that after the omnipresent television, watched by about three-fifths of the total, some two-fifths just "visited" with friends or relatives, and one-third worked around the house and garden (many of course did two, or all three, of these things). Discouraging to the uplifters is the fact that self-improvement with lectures or classes engaged only one in a hundred—the same proportion that went to a play or concert.

Does labor really want a shorter work week? Riesman reports, in the symposium, "Mass Leisure," that when a sample of trade-union members was queried, the rank and file seemed much less interested than their leaders. Riesman thinks this is because their leaders are better educated and have wider interests. (It is also true, of course, that they hold their jobs by making more and more demands on management—including a shorter week!)

In some parts of the country as many as one-third of the labor-union members said that if they had shorter hours they would go out and get a spare-time job to help meet expenses. It is a startling fact that about four million Americans are already engaged in this "moonlighting"—just about equal to the number of able-bodied people who are fully unemployed.

Among both blue- and white-collar workers, many mentioned that more time off would mean more "honeydew" days. These are days when your wife calls you to endless disagreeable chores with requests that always begin the same way: "Honey, do you mind cleaning out the playroom?" "Honey, do you want to take out the garbage?"

Is the prospect of greatly increased leisure as perilous as the prophets of gloom predict? Clearly, it needs to be carefully explored. We should have a great national debate on this subject, from the local level up to Congress. I don't feel, however, that there is any need for panic. We have already survived a doubling of our free time in the past few decades, and the adjustment has been made so readily that most of us are hardly aware that we have had one. Change will be rapid in future, but it will not come overnight. The American people are highly adaptable, much less bound by convention and tradition than those of most other countries, and we have powerful weapons of mass communication that can be mobilized when necessary.

Viewed in the long perspective, it is ironic, if not fantastic, that easing the burden of toil should be viewed as a problem and not as a blessing. Since time immemorial, men's lives have been constricted by the need for exhausting labor, as they still are in many parts of the world. We should rejoice that technology is now freeing us from that burden. The transition will be difficult, but beyond it lies an era that means, in many ways, the fulfillment of man's fondest dreams.

Have We "Culture"?
Yes—and No

by William Schuman

OUR COUNTRY'S INTEREST and activity in the performing arts is clearly on the rise. Scores of centers for the arts are under way. Culture, as we like to refer to all these enterprises, is now a household word—well, almost. But I wonder whether we are generally aware of the considerations which alone can make of our centers more than the real estate ventures they are sometimes accused of being. These considerations raise questions which are apposite as today we celebrate the first anniversary of Lincoln Center.

To begin with, what is culture? It is a word we use in a variety of ways and for a variety of meanings. We use it in reference to soil, pearls, blood, beauty, penicillin, milk and in myriad other combinations to describe sociological and anthropological states of being. But in its broadest meaning culture delineates the entire gamut of our moral, spiritual, esthetic and intellectual nature; in short, the measure of our civilization. While this broad meaning of culture includes our political institutions and, indeed, nothing less than our social mores in general, history has bestowed upon it a quite specific reference to the arts.

Culture, then, is a word that commands respect. When we use it in relation to the arts, we have a sense of elevation. We fancy

From the *New York Times Magazine,* September 22, 1963, copyright © 1963 by The New York Times Company.

that we are above the mundane, materialistic considerations of everyday life and have entered the realm of pure esthetic sensibilities. In a very real sense this is so, yet any examination of the state of our culture as a nation will reveal that, far from escaping the verities of economic, social and political institutions and customs, culture is an integral part of them. Culture—the arts—like problems in plane geometry, must deal with the given.

What is the given? Accurately to define it would entail a complete description of life in twentieth-century America. Stated in capsule form and no doubt oversimplified, it is the economic and social conflict between the democratic ideal (the common man) and the basic autocracy of artistic standards imposed by works of art, by the artist (the uncommon man). This conflict is at once our greatest problem and most inspiring opportunity.

Democracy—majority rule—cannot exist as such in the actual practice of the arts. A play is not created by a committee. A symphony orchestra is not a democratic institution—if it were, each player would be given a chance to conduct and give his interpretation of the composition being performed. No, of necessity the orchestra is and must be an absolute monarchy—the conductor is king. And yet the arts in our society enrich life, not because of the limitations imposed by criteria for mass acceptability, but rather by the opportunities offered by mass exposure and education. A society which, for all its shortcomings, has the potential to insure accessibility to all of the riches of art and, at the same time, guarantee artistic freedom, is a dynamic society.

This is the key to true democracy of the arts. And I believe that this is the direction in which America has been moving. But what of now? Are we in fact a cultured nation? The answer is to be found in a series of yeas and nays, somewhere between the inflated cries of a "cultural explosion" and the counterclaims of a "cultural wasteland."

That we are making headway is, to my mind, beyond dispute. The performing arts have a place in our consciousness astonishingly different from that of only a decade or two ago. While this difference can be gauged in the tangible evidence of the facilities we are erecting all over the country to house our artists, the true measure of our advance stems from the reasons we are building such facilities. Over the years our composers, choreographers and playwrights have been producing the works which alone can form the basis of a national culture in the performing arts.

Without the creation of new works, the performing arts would become the exclusive domain of the past; there would be a lack of nourishment at the source and in consequence no expression from the men of our time. In America we have, in this respect, reason for increasing satisfaction. The creative aspect of our artistic life, despite many problems, is one of health. In music, the theater, the dance, the film, we have our high-level creators who can take their places with the most gifted of the world and, what is more, whose diversity of styles, techniques, esthetics are paralleled in no other country.

In music, our composers have long since established themselves as master craftsmen. This is even more impressive when one realizes that the arrival on the scene of the American composer no longer subservient to the European master is wholly of this century and, for all practical matters, a development since the twenties. To be sure, there were gifted American composers before that time, but not in any sense comparable with the riches we have today. American composers range from the most conservative, through the middle-ground creators, all the way to those employing the most advanced experimental techniques.

In education we have our great professional music schools and centers of high-level instruction in drama and dance. But our interest in education in the arts is not limited to professional training. Nowhere in the world are the arts so much a part of general education as in this country—from elementary school through the university. To be sure, the quality of instruction varies. At its best, and its best is on the rise, there is recognition that the arts are the stuff of general education, that instruction in their practices and exposure to their wonders is rightfully the domain of liberal education. There is conviction, despite the understandable emphasis these days on the sciences and mathematics, that the arts are meaningful in ways only to be discovered through direct experience.

In the choreographic world, we have our "modern dance" choreographers who have developed styles of their own, unprecedented in the world of dance "vocabulary." We also have our traditional ballet masters. And we have created jazz works that are wholly fresh. Our dance encompasses an enormous range, from the popular and inventive developments in our music theater to experiments that try the most liberal eyes (and ears).

In the theater and in the production of films, it is clear that only a small percentage of our efforts can be considered other than routine, commercially motivated enterprises. Yet America has produced some outstanding films and plays. In our theater, while our national literature is still limited, its best is of an extraordinarily high quality. Furthermore, we do have gifted writers today who are adding to this heritage. It is to be expected that as our interest in serious art continues to develop, efforts in the theater and in films of high artistic order will increase.

The skill of American performers is taken for granted, which is perhaps the greatest compliment that we can pay them. Yet we should realize that in music and dance, at least, our superb artists are of recent vintage. As for our leading symphony orchestras, they have few peers; the extent of our activities and developments in this phase of music is nothing short of sensational.

For all our progress, however, we often tend to assume that the grass is greener elsewhere. When we compare our achievements and institutions in the arts with those of other countries, we are liable to fall into two kinds of provincialism: the negative provincialism of the pseudosophisticate expatriate variety, on the one hand, and the excessive and chauvinistic claims that come from 100-per-cent Americanism on the other. We still look to Europe in ways unjustified by the facts of our artistic life. We must realize that our country, which for so many years looked abroad for its artists, has now become, artistically speaking, an export nation. Not only are American artists in every field highly regarded the world round, but large numbers of students from abroad now come to this country for their art education.

Yet we still reveal feelings of inferiority in the discrimination we often practice in this country against our own artists. Such discrimination—when it exists, for example, with the American conductor or performer who feels obliged to impress foreign audiences before he can be accepted at home—is not only unjustified, but inimical to the development of indigenous art.

One asks no special favor for the native artist, especially in a day when, more than ever before, we are seeking to minimize national barriers. (Certainly the arts have proved to be particularly well-suited to hasten this process.) However, the first responsibility for the development of artistic life begins in one's own community. And such recognition is in no way incompatible with an international point of view. We should compare our achievements with those of other nations, not in a sense of competition but for the enlightenment such comparison can shed. To be meaningful, this comparison must preclude emotional judgments. And this is exceedingly difficult because the arts are ammunition in the world's ideological struggle.

Because the arts have been injected into the cold war, we have a particular interest in comparing our own achievements with those of the Soviet Union and its satellites. We are struck immediately by the fact that in the Soviet Union the art is official and therefore controlled. This concept is abhorrent to us. We don't believe in official art or in official anything else. We believe that it is a terrible price to pay for artistic riches. We would all rather function within the limitations of our own constantly developing and emerging society than be given all the material support required for an abundant artistic life minus its most precious ingredient—freedom of expression.

Knowing that the riches of artistic life in totalitarian countries carry a price tag of control which we would never pay should not, however, blind us to the achievements of that art. Let us recognize that in the Socialist totalitarian countries the arts controlled by the state are also handsomely enriched by the body politic.

The artistic life is abundant and the opportunities in the major cities, at least, for the populace at large to attend artistic events at reasonable prices has been widely reported as far exceeding anything that we have in this country. The arts have an enviable place in the scheme of national importance. Paid education is guaranteed for all talented youngsters, as is employment for all artists, young and old. If we could, for a moment, overlook artistic control, all of this would seem paradise to any American artist— no economic problems and a place of honor in society.

But there are negatives attendant to artistic control which affect the arts themselves in a fundamental way. While the technical achievements of the Iron Curtain artists have been widely admired in this country and elsewhere, knowledgeable observers have all remarked on the lack of variety, the ignorance of movements, techniques and new forms flourishing in the healthy artistic turmoil existing in free societies.

If there are negatives in the Socialist totalitarian countries, we certainly are not without our own. Our finest achievements have come about despite a basic artistic problem that runs counter to our national thinking. For the arts require of democracy a freedom in addition to those we all cherish: the freedom to fail.

What an un-American thought! The free enterprise system was built on success, not failure. Why, therefore, should the arts require special consideration in our scale of things? But curiously, it is not special consideration, but similar consideration, which would give the arts freedom to fail. If we compare artistic life with corporate life, we see at a glance the similarity and the discrepancy. Our great corporations operate research divisions and even the smallest business seeks to develop new avenues of exploration. In business research, as in artistic creation, there is the same cycle of experimentation, frustration and, often, failure before ultimate success. But in business the product is not marketed until success can reasonably be predicted.

Here is the difference. The arts need a public laboratory (an audience) which does not evaluate every effort solely in terms of box-office returns. And what, one may ask, is wrong with the box office as a barometer? If the art being produced doesn't have a large enough audience to support it, why bother?

We must bother because our present circle is a vicious one. The new play is provocative, but a production cannot be arranged because there is scant chance of dollar success. The new symphony is by a brilliantly talented composer, but it better not be programed because the audience might become restive. Why engage the fine string quartet when a name soloist in a conventional program will be safer? But, wait a minute. What are we suggesting here: that the arts must be "far out," must lose money, need not please audiences? Yes and no. The parallel between the arts and business marketing procedures is valid, but only up to a point.

Just as business exists on staples consistently in demand, so do the arts have a great treasure house of widely acclaimed works and performers. But, as in business, there must be constant research for new products. In art, the new products may please (as some of the best do and always have) or may outrage (as some of the best do and always have) but, in any case, there must be ample opportunity for exposure. And, unlike the procedures of manufacture and distribution of new products which, having been carefully pretested, give promise of success, the arts can only be evaluated through actual performance.

This is a dilemma which is basic to the functioning of art in a society which does not forgive failure. There must be the courage to face even predictable failure if there is conviction of artistic worth. There are precious few artists, managers or laymen who are willing to meet this dilemma or who can afford to. Part of the problem stems from the show-business psychology which reaches into every facet of American life.

As everyone knows, "There's no business like show business." What is the problem? The problem begins when the criteria of show business are applied to activities which cannot be adjusted to such limiting requirements. The problem lies in the practice of evaluating worth in terms of mass acceptability. That this is so often the case in our entertainment-saturated society is no fault of our superb showmen, but of those who adopt its methods and judgments in enterprises extrinsic to its particulars.

In show business, the audience is the undisputed master. If the show doesn't go, there is no second chance, not this year or any other year. You either make it or you don't. The aim is quite simple: to give the audience what it wants. You can experiment to your heart's content, but if you go beyond pleasing your patrons you close. Some remarkable men and women have managed to produce works of astonishing originality and artistic worth within these terms—notably our gifted theater composers, choreographers and designers and several of our playwrights.

But compare this minority with the preponderance of the lowest common denominator appeal to which most mass entertainment is addressed. We do not realize, I believe, the extent to which constant exposure to the cheapest elements of the entertainment world has colored our national psyche, and the confusion of values it brings to the arts, not to mention education and even worship. By show business standards we cannot justify the arts.

If the standards of the artist were always limited to those of the show-business world he would, perforce, have as his ultimate goal entertaining his audience through the selection or creation of non-provocative works which would titillate rather than challenge, produced with techniques which would dazzle rather than probe. But, you ask, are not the serious performing arts entertaining—do not their techniques dazzle and are not their audiences pleased? Yes, of course. But there is a vast difference.

The goal is to supply more than entertainment, more than mere pleasure. The stuff of the performing arts, at their highest level, involves artists and works dedicated to nothing less than the exploration of every conceivable nuance of man's capacity for revelation through the unique worlds of music, theater and dance: worlds which cannot be geared solely to the values of show-business entertainment, for they encompass far more.

These worlds take us where the artists choose to lead, and whether this be comfortable or pleasing or even entertaining is beside the point. What matters is the integrity of the expression—the dictates of one man's imagination as expressed through the disciplines of his craft. As an audience we are free to accept or reject his work, but never to modify the creative act through pre-conditioning, through prior insistence, real or implied, that it must at all costs please, at all costs be a success. This is the realm of the artist.

Although there is, then, the undeniable dichotomy between commerce and art, we can, to a large extent, solve the problem through more imaginative reliance on individual initiative and responsibility.

The most pressing need for our institutions of the performing arts is broader lay leadership. While it is true that we have always enjoyed the devoted services of men and women interested in the arts, we now increasingly require others. We must have the most influential and respected leaders of our communities—in business, labor, education, law and, in fact, all principal areas—whether or not such persons are themselves devotees of the arts. These leaders will respond. They will understand the importance of the arts to their communities and they alone can command the support required from all segments.

The management of artistic enterprises would gain immeasurably from the guidance of experienced businessmen. If there is a minor shortcoming in the management of a profit-making endeavor, the resultant reduction in the profit, while regrettable, isn't fatal. A management mistake, however, in the deficit-financed, money-raising world of the arts can result only in an increase of red ink.

Too few men of affairs are actually involved in the running of our art institutions. That this is so is perhaps an off-shoot of the not-distant past when the arts were considered not quite manly, when the kid on the block did better to carry a football than a fiddle case. Something of this psychology persists, but it won't for long.

In planning the development of our institutions of the arts, we must recognize that even though their support be essentially that of private patronage and responsibility, they are, nevertheless, by the nature of their functioning at least quasi-public institutions. Governmental bodies at all levels must increasingly support the arts.

We are awakening to the realization that there can be government concern and responsibility in the arts without loss of the advantages of private enterprise and patronage, of individual initiative and responsibility. We have awakened to the fact that the argument of government control of the arts in this country is academic. No activity of the government thus far in the arts (and there has been more than most of us are aware) gives the slightest reason to fear interference. And if artistic control ever were threatened by the government, we would change it. We are the government.

For the government in this country to become involved at all in the arts, it is imperative that its activities be kept apolitical. This is just what is happening. There is no monopoly on the part of either major political party in pleading the cause of the arts. We know that, as with the last, the present Administration wishes to foster the arts and that there is in formation the Federal Advisory Council on the Arts. We know, too, that no fewer than 15 states have formed or are in the process of forming Councils on the Arts. Increasingly, local governments are accepting responsibility in this field.

Never before in our history has there been a more hopeful climate for the flowering of our performing arts. Those of us who are in positions of leadership in our art centers and other institutions must point the way by bold programs that maintain the highest standards, yet seek constantly to increase accessibility of the arts to all. While we have hardly begun to scratch the surface of the possibilities in such matters as the expansion of seasons, the diversity of offerings and economic support, we can note marked progress and much activity.

What does it all add up to, this increased awareness of the arts —the interest of business, of foundations, of patrons, the stirrings of government, the scores of art centers? Do they make it possible for us now to say that we are a cultured nation?

I hope that we never reach the day when we so proclaim ourselves. To be cultured is to recognize a process which, like education, is never ended. What we have achieved is a greater understanding of our potential, of our weaknesses and our strengths. This means that if we continue to move forward our opportunities will multiply and we will cope with our problems. Ultimately, we can demonstrate that there is no discrepancy between artistic excellence and the democratic ideal; that, on the contrary, no form of societal organization relies more heavily on the full development of the talents of its citizens than democracy.

They're Cultural, But Are They Cultured?

by Marya Mannes

IN THE CHRONIC self-examinations which have come to be our national sport, one area of comfort, one beachhead of satisfaction seems to hold against the tide of doubt. We are getting more and more cultured all the time: the figures say so. More people go to symphony concerts than to baseball games. More people go to museums than ever before, more people read paperback classics and serious little magazines than ever before, more housewives paint more pictures than ever before, and the art galleries are booming.

There are, of course, the professional denigrators, the intellectual nit-pickers who claim that our mass media have debased culture by swamping it with trivia or spreading it too far and too thin, or by distracting people's minds from real art by slick counterfeits and commercial intrusions. To them and to us the voices of the mass media say proudly: who else brings Shakespeare and Churchill and Leonard Bernstein to millions? It is one of the blessings of democracy (cultural democracy, some call it now) that these same millions can, thanks to Ed Sullivan or magazines like Playboy and The Ladies' Home Journal, be given intravenous doses of culture along with the fun.

I find myself somewhere in the middle of this debate and full of questions. For one thing, exposure is not acceptance. For another, I profoundly distrust quantitative evaluations. They are one of the major curses of our society, nowhere more evident—and more misleading—than in television ratings. By several methods it is possible to estimate that thirty million people were looking at a certain program at a certain time. But as yet no method has been able to tell you how many of these thirty million were actively watching and enjoying it, how many were talking through it, eating through it, or sleeping through it and how many had the set turned on in an empty room while they foraged in the icebox.

You cannot, in other words, measure the quality of attention or the depths of impact. If, as the American Symphony Orchestra League estimates, only 2 per cent of our population is an audience for serious music, that is still a lot of people—three and a half million. But does that mean that we have three and a half million people who know about music? I was brought up in concert halls, watching my uncle, Walter Damrosch, conduct and my father, David Mannes, play violin as concertmaster and later conduct his own orchestra; and I watched the audience, too.

I knew then, as I know now, that people go to concerts for many reasons. Lots of lonely women go to lose themselves in vague emotions, drifting in large tides of melancholy or elation. Lots of men go because their wives make them, or because it is a civic duty. If you could look into the brains of many of these people you would find that they were thinking of anything but music: Shall I buy that hat I saw in the window yesterday? Shall I put money in that venture? Oh, there's Mrs. Brooks in Box 26!

I know people who have gone to concerts every week of their lives and say they love music, but most of them can't tell Bach from Haydn or know what a grace note is. Are they cultured?

Let's wander among the art galleries where, presumably, millions of Americans now wander. They file through, looking at the great classics of the past, and some of them—like some of the concertgoers—get that stab of pleasure, that sudden rush of enlightenment that signifies true contact between the giver and the receiver. But what strikes me most about the people who shuffle past pictures is the deadness of their eyes—the untrained eyes. They look, but they do not know what to look for. They see, but they do not feel.

Given no measure of judgment, no knowledge of craft, they will spend as much time before a huge pigmented convulsion which they are told is art as they do before a Goya which they know is a classic. Knowing nothing of the craft of painting, they are unaware of its absence. Their eye is arrested by a violent explosion of ego, but misses the quiet statement of an inspired observer. Are they cultured?

Let's go to a play on Broadway. How many of the audience go because they love the theatre enough to learn about it? How many have ever read plays, cared about the craft of acting, know the director's name, notice the strengths and weaknesses of the script or the performance? How many went to the play in the first place not because a certain writer wrote and certain actors play it, but because it's a hit?

Attendance, then, at a cultural event is alone not evidence of culture. Many more people than ever before have the money and leisure to avail themselves of such pleasure, but I am tempted to wonder whether this means that a greater *proportion* of our people cherish the arts than used to.

The availability is, of course, wonderful. Every new orchestra in a town that had none before is to be celebrated. Every new gallery is to be welcomed. Every new community theatre is an extension of human experience that we must salute and encourage. But none of them will make us a cultivated people unless we bring to them the knowledge and acquaintance which can weave them into the actual texture of our lives.

For culture is not an acquisition. It is not an ornament. It is not a luster. It is not a vocabulary. It is the product of need, effort and intimacy—as important a part of our mind and spirit and body as food and drink and work and love and breathing. It must live in us, not outside us. And I will not believe that we are a cultured people until we consider the Arts as the Art of Living, without which life has little meaning and less savor.

I believe that no human being can be called civilized, let alone educated and cultured, unless his senses are developed to their highest capacity: to hear, see, taste, smell and touch with knowledge and judgment. This development should start as early as possible in a child's life and should continue as long as possible. He should know, feel and try musical instruments, for until you learn how to play on one, no matter how simply, you cannot know music.

A generation of ears taught to listen not only to sound but to silence would never tolerate the whining inanity of rock 'n' roll on radio or the primitive caterwauls of pop singers who earn millions from the pockets of primitive adolescents. Nor, I think, would the educated ear permit this endless and meaningless murmur of music that surrounds us now in lobbies and elevators and stores and plants. These are all adulterators or pacifiers, having nothing to do with music.

As for the eye, I think a child should be taught to observe by drawing what he sees, and at the risk of being called a crypto-Victorian or, more simply, a black reactionary, I think our instructions should revert to certain strict disciplines by which a child attains humility before the fact of nature, and craftsmanship as the essential tool of expression.

The cult of self-expression without discipline has reached grotesque proportions in these decades, in which to qualify as a painter it is enough to reflect chaos in the largest possible space. I would rather a child copied one leaf with understanding than smeared his little ego in an acre of pigment. This he need not be taught.

I think to make art a part of life, certain attitudes in our society must be changed, and one of them is the feeling that artistic expression is unmanly and that a boy who wants to be a dancer or a poet or a sculptor or a musician should be discouraged, not only for economic reasons but because these are not proper professions for a man. Only we and the British seem to feel this way, and I cannot see that our societies have benefited from it. The Soviets, who can hardly be accused of effeminacy and decadence, not only venerate such talents in men and women but provide enormous incentives to develop them. So, I may say, have those past civilizations in which the arts have reached their highest form.

Yet American parents are proud when their sons become lawyers and apologetic when they choose to be actors—the same parents, mind you, who would claim they loved the theatre, went to art shows and adored ballet. But the practice of art is a last resort.

I think all young Americans should be taught the basics of architecture, decoration and city planning. For if they were taught these, the new generation could not tolerate the proliferating ugliness of their towns and cities. I know of no other so-called civilized society that has so blighted its land as we have.

Nearly every main street in America is an affront to the senses, with its poles and wires and neon lights and jumble of signs and planless clutter—a testament to haste and greed, to the absence of human dignity and the simple amenities of living. A testament, indeed, to the kind of paradox in which a city can support a splendid art museum and opera house, but permit its periphery to remain hideous with car dumps, billboards, hot-dog stands, and all the marks of a rootless and artless society. As for most of our public statuary—it is, quite literally, for the birds. The pigeons know bad art when they see it.

No, art doesn't mean just galleries or concerts or plays: it means cities where people can live in long perspectives, gaze into clear fountains and sit in the shadows of trees. It means daily pleasures of the eye and ear and touch, a constant awakening of the senses to the excitement of living. But these senses must first be trained to awareness.

Nor does art, or culture, mean only the professional training of an increasing number of artists, actors, musicians or poets, desirable as this might be. What we must, as Americans, get into our heads once and for all is that there is in all men a strong creative instinct and that this instinct can be turned to infinite good if it is recognized and freed.

A man familiar with poetry can write a better business report than the man who is not, for he possesses a sense of cadence, rhythm and clarity which can persuade. A public servant familiar with theatre and acting can bring a wider range of tone and greater emphasis to his speeches. A woman with a musical ear can bring to the teaching of English, for instance, common principles of form and direction which are invaluable. I cannot think of any human occupation which cannot be made more significant and more effective through the enlarged perceptions which acquaintance with art nourishes.

I myself owe whatever virtue I have as a writer to the fact that my first sixteen years were steeped in music as well as poetry. I try to sustain a musical line in everything I do, whether it is a sentence, a paragraph or a book, for the principles of theme, counterpoint, development and resolution are the same: what makes a good orchestral score makes a good novel.

In another area, a love of sculpture and considerable practice in it has made me conscious of the hidden structure in everything I see and of the visible surface of everything I touch. Through these awarenesses my daily living is heightened.

It must be evident by now that I hold to certain truths, that I believe in certain standards that are as timeless and immutable as the basic laws of nature and the composition of matter. It is fashionable today—particularly for certain professors who have become performers, and who have mastered the art of pleasing many rather than instructing the few—it is fashionable to deny the existence of such principles in the arts, and to claim that what is accepted by the many is right for the moment.

Public taste, they say, is the only valid criterion, and it is perfectly all right to say Winston Tastes Good Like a Cigarette Should because that's the way the language crumbles. Never mind about grammar—it no longer applies. Neither, it seems, does euphony. If there were no other way to determine good usage of language, proof lies in the ugliness of bad usage. Is it possible for an ear not to wince at a sentence like "She looked like she was sick"?

No . . . Taste changes, fashion changes, and the face of beauty changes from age to age. But the laws that govern creation, whether of matter or of man or of art, do not change. To maintain that there are no fixed standards in the arts, no points of reference, no guiding lines, is to excuse the lazy, to comfort the confused, and to abdicate responsibility.

I don't know whether we have a cultural democracy or not. I

am still not even sure what it means. But I do know that an awareness of the fundamental patterns of life is the measure of any real culture. Science can greatly increase this awareness. But only art can awaken it and sustain it in each of us. Without it we are blind—and deaf—and dumb.

Who Should Pay the Bill for the Arts?

by Howard Taubman

THE ANNOUNCEMENT not long ago that the Italian Government had granted a subsidy of about $16,000 to Chicago's Lyric Opera Company was, to say the least, startling. One was touched by the graceful gesture, and one could appreciate the explanation that the Italians had taken a practical step to insure that a market for an Italian commodity—performers as well as operas—would remain open. Since it is more blessed to give than to receive, one sympathized with the Italian wish to be on the giving end. Nevertheless, as an American, one was appalled.

The second largest city in the richest country in the world needed to accept what amounts to a handout from a nation which could easily put the money to use at home, if not to solve urgent social problems, certainly in its own opera houses. Here was a glaring example of the discrepancy in government attitudes toward the arts, for in the United States there is no direct federal assistance for artistic institutions. Here, too, was a striking reflection of a fundamental difference between the attitudes of Europe and America toward the arts, for in Europe they are regarded as an essential element of civilized life while in the United States

From the *New York Times Magazine,* December 7, 1958, copyright © 1958 by The New York Times Company.

they are still treated in too many places as a chic ornament that shows off social position.

But don't we maintain thirty major orchestras and hundreds of others, professional, semi-professional and amateur? Don't we have hundreds of university and civic theatres and dozens of opera workshops? Don't we support scores of museums? Don't we have an abundance of conservatories and art schools? Don't our foundations dispense largess to individuals and institutions? Haven't we signalized our respect for a triumphant musician by giving Van Cliburn a ticker-tape reception up Broadway just as if he were a conquering general, a daring aviator or an athletic hero?

We have these things and we do these things, and many of them represent progress. But they do not add up to a widespread, deeply felt national commitment. They bespeak the concern and goodwill of some segments of our population and some of our communities. They indicate that if enough of a hoopla is whipped up, we can be stirred by an unusual artistic accomplishment— and also be taken in by empty and passing sensations. But they do not establish that, as a people and a nation, we have yet accorded the arts the status they occupy in Europe.

Wherever you travel in Europe, you can discern the high valuation put on art. You see it in the principle of Government subsidy, which is practiced everywhere. You observe it in the efforts of the small towns as well as the great centers to organize their own institutions. You hear on the radio and see on television a far higher proportion than we do in the United States of fine music, opera and theatre, and good, civilized exchange of ideas.

Let us make a quick tour of Europe, pausing in some of the lands of West and East to see how the arts are situated. Begin with Great Britain, on whose institutions and concepts so many of ours are modeled. Here there was a long tradition of private patronage. But during World War II, when all the energies and resources of the empire had to be marshaled to wage the struggle, it was discovered that danger and hardship could be better endured if there were the solace and encouragement to be had from great art. The Government discovered that it was wise to support such enterprises as music and theatre.

When the war was over, the people would not let the Government retire from this field of activity. The theory that Parliament should appropriate funds for the arts won approval from both Conservatives and Labor. With characteristic ingenuity, the British devised the scheme of an Arts Council, a body of distinguished private citizens with knowledge of the arts, which was appointed to distribute the money without political strings. The Arts Council has been in existence for more than a decade, and though it may be criticized on details, its philosophy is rarely questioned. It helps major companies like the Royal Opera and Ballet with large grants. It assists orchestras, repertory theatres, museums, painters, sculptors and composers. It has even backed stage productions in the West End theatres where plays with noncommercial themes would not otherwise get a hearing.

There is a ferment in the British creative world. New young voices are raised in the theatre, music and graphic arts. Sometimes they are angry and derisive; sometimes they probe quietly. They are a source of stimulation and provocation.

This trend may even be noted in Britain's commercial television. The companies which got the rights to administer the programs on the channel open to advertising have made big profits, and they have recently been announcing gifts that total more than $250,000 to opera companies, ballets, theatres and art galleries.

On the Continent, public support of the arts has long been a fixed procedure. National, provincial and municipal governments make regular contributions as a matter of course. No one argues the merits of this method of cherishing artistic enterprise. The only differences between one country and another are in execution.

In France the Opéra, Opéra Comique and Comédie Française are national institutions with glamorous histories. In recent years they seem to have fallen on unadventurous, flabby days. This may be a reflection of the shakiness and uncertainty of the French political system in the last decade, and it is possible that the artistic institutions will develop new fiber now that a more determined Government has taken power.

Does the French experience indicate that Government support of the arts is not always a blessing? No doubt this system has its dangers, just as any system has if it falls into the wrong hands. But the French must ask themselves whether their historic theatres would continue to exist if there were no Government subsidy.

The chances are not. The next question must then be: Can more rigorous artistic standards be made to prevail when the state is the patron of the arts? The situation in other countries proves that the answer is yes.

In Germany one can discover the other side of the medal—that a prosperous economy and a stable, purposeful government are reflected in the vigor with which the arts are pursued. New opera houses have been constructed in a number of cities. Theatres are thriving. Experimental work in the arts is encouraged. Advanced music, for example, is cultivated with the help of regional, Government-owned radio stations. The Federal Government proudly distributes to foreign critics imposing collections of scores and recordings of contemporary works so that foreigners may be informed of what is going on creatively. Mark you, these are not pretty, flattering works. One may suspect that Government officials do not admire them, but they mirror our time's creativity and they are accepted. For art has a high estate.

Indeed, the arts have become one of the sharpest weapons employed in the competition for German minds between the Western-oriented Federal Republic and Communist-controlled East Germany. Berlin is a major battlefield in this contest. West Germany has brought the distinguished *régisseur* Carl Ebert, who had a notable record of refusing to compromise with the Nazis, to preside over its opera house in the old capital. Walter Felsenstein, who is esteemed as one of the most gifted operatic producers of our era, has been persuaded by East Germany to direct the Komische Oper, and there are lavish resources placed at his disposal, even though living standards are low.

In Bayreuth the Wagner festival, which even in the palmiest days of the redoubtable Cosima, widow of the composer, ran only two out of every three years, now has become an annual fixture. It has assumed a new importance because of the boldness of its experimentation in staging and lighting. The freshness of ideas instituted by Wagner's grandsons, Wieland and Wolfgang, has won wide suffrage despite the opposition of traditionalists. The main thing is that the money needed to accomplish this reorientation has not been wanting. It has come from the Federal, Bavarian and Bayreuth Governments; there have also been donations from individuals and corporations. The art of Wagner is acknowledged as a national heritage, and there is no question that it must be preserved and strengthened.

Look in on Italy. There is, of course, national pride in a world-famous establishment like the Scala Opera of Milan, which receives generous sums from the nation as well as from Milan. But the nation's efforts are not confined to one or two great show places. In a small town like Spoleto, the community, led by, of all people, a Communist mayor, gives its heart and relatively meager resources to a new festival organized largely from the United States.

It is true that this Festival of Two Worlds, which was conceived by Gian Carlo Menotti, brought a host of performers and visitors to Spoleto and that there was profit in the occasion for local people. But local pride was unmistakable. The citizenry took a naive pleasure in thronging the streets and gaping at the swells from Rome as they arrived in their elegant cars and modish clothes for opening nights. But when one talked to the Spoletini, one found that their delight was not entirely simple-minded, that they rejoiced in the glory that opera and theatre and paintings assembled for the festival could confer on their hill town.

The situation is not much different in the smaller countries of Western Europe. Austria, with its glorious musical tradition, treasures the Vienna State Opera, the Vienna Philharmonic and the Salzburg Festival as if together they were a ball team which seldom failed to win the pennant. The Netherlands maintains one of the great orchestras of the world in the Amsterdam Concertgebouw, other ensembles in other cities, theatres, opera companies, and an agreeable festival. Belgium puts on an impressive international exposition in Brussels, and the arts become so spectacular a part of the competition between nations that they tend to overshadow other displays.

And what about Eastern Europe, beginning with the giant, the Soviet Union? It goes without saying that in Communist-controlled countries everything is decided and run by the Government. It is no surprise, therefore, to find that in the Soviet Union, as in Poland, Hungary, Rumania, Yugoslavia and the others, the arts draw all their support, save what funds are taken in at the box-office, from the Government. What is astonishing is the extent of the support lavished on the arts in Russia.

Consider the professional theatres. A Soviet book published last year summed up the number that existed in 1956: 32 with permanent opera and ballet companies, 355 devoted to drama and comedy, 20 with operetta troupes, and 101 dedicated to shows for children and young people. In view of the steady rate of artistic expansion, one must assume that the figures have since gone up. And for the next seven-year plan, more than 100 additional theatres with permanent repertory companies are blueprinted.

These are not all the theatrical troupes in the Soviet Union. The armed services, trade unions and large factories also maintain professional companies. And if one added the amateur units, the totals would be staggering.

No one, of course, produces anything that goes contrary to the party line, and much of what is presented by these companies is carefully designed for purposes of internal propaganda. But a great deal is performed for the same reasons as in the West—to expose people to the outstanding creations of the past and to enrich them emotionally and spiritually.

The classics, from the Greek tragedies and Shakespeare to Chekhov, are excitingly performed in the theatre. The great operas of the Russian, Italian and French repertory, though not many of the German, are presented with theatrical virtuosity. The orchestras play the works that reflect the full gamut of Western musical heritage, up to, but not including, the problematical music of our time. The living creative artist is bedeviled by official strictures and party surveillance, but the interpretive artist has opportunity to develop his craft, to grow and to be secure in the knowledge that he has a fixed and honored place in his society.

The public for the arts in the Soviet Union is immense. Living performances are available in all the major cities and virtually all of the smaller ones. An effort is made to bring live shows to the state and collective farms and to the small towns in the remotest sections of this vast land. Granted that this is done in part to provide relief and escape for a people who have labored hard and been denied much. The fact remains that millions upon millions are being exposed to some of the noblest visions of man, that they may develop taste and standards, and that in the end they may become one of the most cultivated people in history.

Compared with the Soviet effort in the performing arts, we in the United States are dragging our feet. There are, of course, cheerful items in our balance sheet. We have a growing public. A powerful foundation like the Ford has decided to pay some attention to the arts. An exciting enterprise like the Lincoln Center for the Performing Arts is under way, and it will give New York and the United States an exceptional show place. We have abundance of institutions and individual artists. But we fail to make the best use, let alone full use, of our cultural resources.

We are seduced by our wealth into acting thoughtlessly and wastefully, as we have done with some of our human potential in the sciences. We boast of all our orchestras, but how many of them give their players more than half a year's employment? We point with pride to our free and varied theatre in New York, but how many of our finest actors have the opportunity to broaden their range? An outstanding performer may have to play the same role for months—and consider himself lucky at that. A painter of recognized gifts may languish neglected because his style is temporarily out of fashion.

Let us consider Van Cliburn's case, which has provided us with so salubrious a tonic. He is the hottest box-office figure in the world of music today. He has drawn audiences of 20,000 and more for single concerts. He has been as successful as Liberace. A tall, lean kid from Texas, who has honest claims to being termed an artist, has been honored in his own land.

Wonderful for Cliburn. But would he have enjoyed the same happy history if he had not had the luck to polish off the top prize in a competition in Moscow? The answer is no. Thus, in Belgium, the Brussels Competitions, held under the patronage of Queen Elizabeth, have become pre-eminent among European contests. Among the winners in the past two decades have been great Soviet violinists like David Oistrakh and Leonid Kogan; their acclaim has been worldwide. In recent years, two Americans —Leon Fleisher, pianist, and Berl Senofsky, violinist—have triumphed in Brussels.

Did the United States hail them as it did Cliburn? Not at all. They had finished first against stiff Soviet rivalry, but unfortunately not in Moscow. Unlike Cliburn, they did not profit from a good political break.

Here, then, is a vital lesson for us. We must learn to appreciate our own artists on their merits. When I was in the Soviet Union last spring, the Russians gently reminded me that it took them to discover Cliburn. They added that he was undoubtedly unique. I replied that, while we were proud of the young Texan, we could point to a host of other fine pianists. The Russians scoffed. I said I could name ten Americans who were in, or close to, Cliburn's class. The Russians regarded me with polite sympathy, and suggested that I name them. I did. Well, then, why were they not established artists at home and abroad?

I knew the answer did not spell it out. We are still subject to the ancient failing of being overly respectful to the stranger with a foreign reputation. We are easily beguiled by publicity sensations. We rush to hear those about whom a big noise is made, forgetful that there are others who have a great deal to offer us. We buy names rather than art, though there are times when the two are joined.

Here we come to the most important lesson we have to learn. We must become convinced by cultivation and experience that the arts are a vital element of any civilized society. Only if we achieve this conviction and wisdom shall we go on to integrate the arts in the fabric of everyday living. Then we shall proceed to do the things that remain to be done.

We shall insist that our artistic institutions have continuity. We shall make sure that their fate does not depend on the fluctuations of business cycles or on the whims of individuals. We shall not allow them to go about hat in hand like beggars. We shall work out techniques, using Government or private initiative or both, to employ our artistic resources to the full, thus serving the artist and the community. We shall see to it that our creative and interpretive artists will have not only an honored place but a secure one. We shall continue to be generous in our acceptance of the best from abroad but shall learn to appreciate our own at their full deserts.

Our attitude toward the arts will undergo a change when we learn to admire whole-heartedly achievements of the mind that do not produce an immediate monetary gain, when a Trendex count is not used to thrust low-grade conformity on the bulk of what is presented on a mass medium like television. Let us learn from Europe—and from our neighbors to the south, as well—that some of our wealth and ingenuity should be employed to provide our people not only with the material comforts but also with the adventures of the heart and mind that bring compassion and exaltation into our lives.

Part 2

TELEVISION AND RADIO

To have great poets,
we must have great audiences, too.
—Walt Whitman

What they do, boys, is creep up on you,
And I don't mean Indians.
I mean Americans, over the radio.
—William Saroyan

Man, the individual man, recognizes that in using
these machines and adapting himself to their
techniques, he must assume their attributes. This
is the moment of terrible truth, for in gaining "the
sweet fruition of an earthly crown," the individual
risks submerging his humanity and becoming a
digit in a socio-cybernetic system.
—Aubrey Singer

THE ROLE that television plays in the lives of every American (even those who profess to loathe it) has elicited a virtual flood of comment, criticism, and research studies. In households in every community, much of the dinner-table conversation revolves around something related to television, whether it is an event seen and interpreted by Walter Cronkite or David Brinkley, or whether Junior (age nine) should be allowed to stay up till ten o'clock on a week night to see a James Brown "special." Clearly, television has changed the fabric of our society's leisure patterns, but whether for good or bad, or a mixture of both, is a controversial subject.

In the first essay in this section, Charles A. Siepmann, a pioneer in television programming with the BBC and subsequently a noted critic of the medium, indicts the television industry for not even living up to its own bromide: that it is giving the public what it wants. He cites a research study sponsored by CBS which indicates that the average viewer thinks television programs depict too much imitable violence. The same study reveals that the average respondent feels there are too many commercials. In fact, Siepmann points out, a national survey showed that 43 per cent would prefer to have no commercials, and 24 per cent found most commercials so repulsive that they would pay for television to get rid of them.

Not until the 1969–70 season, after being threatened with possible congressional legislation spearheaded by Senator John Pastore, did nighttime network television try to curb violence. The barrage of commercials, of course, remains at the same level of intensity. Siepmann is highly critical of a system in which the "interests" of the public have been subordinated to the interests of the sponsor." Unfortunately, the Great Audience is perceived primarily as "consumers" of salable products, not as 200 million separate human beings, each with a personality which can be affected by the way the world "outside" his head is brought to him. Siepmann does not exonerate the public from blame, either, for he sees our own faces (with minor distortions) mirrored in the video tube. Perhaps it is true that "television represents nothing more than the visible outcropping of an ugly seam that runs under the surface of our culture—alienation from our true selves through misplaced materialist preoccupation."

The distinguished British student of popular culture, Richard Hoggart, is not quite as pessimistic about the future of television as Siepmann. Hoggart suggests ways in which television could be a more effective medium, not just for selling girdles or pancake mix but for society's welfare. As one of the authors of the famous Pilkington Report in England, which examined the assorted planks in a platform for responsible broadcasting, Hoggart notes that he and his colleagues were accused of "grandmotherliness, authoritarianism, fascism, socialism, and restrictionism for our pains." The media managers still frown at the suggestions of men like Siepmann and Hoggart, but thousands, perhaps millions of concerned Americans are beginning to ask the same questions about television.

Whenever we consider what television is offering young children, another note of anxiety is sounded by those critics who worry about the medium's effect on society in general. Robert Saudek, who examines the validity of this fearful attitude, is a well-known television producer. His program *Omnibus* in the early fifties is remembered nostalgically as a Sunday afternoon gem from television's more golden days. Saudek is also the father of five children, and frankly he is discouraged by what television offers them. His survey of the available network offerings (during 1962) showed that less than 1 per cent of their programming was designed to stimulate or challenge young people. He offers some excellent advice on how this unhappy misbalance can be corrected. Yet, as we enter another decade and a second generation of youngsters are well along in their acculturation, little has been accomplishd. As long as a patched-up reel or two of the *Three Stooges* is available, why bother? That, it would seem, is the attitude of hundreds of stations. And as long as millions of parents use the television console as a cheap baby-sitter, the station managers will construe this as a mandate to feed the public what it wants (or deserves).

David Karp, another "insider," has written for many television series and films. In his essay, Karp provides a capsule history of the medium during its first twenty years (1947–1967); if he is not quite as dismal about what has happened, in no sense does he paint the past (or the future) in rosy hues. Even looking back at what some have termed television's "Golden Age" proved disappointing to Karp, who agrees with the title of a Thomas Wolfe novel, "You can't go home again." Is it a fact of media life that "television buries its great moments in electronic quicklime," and that it is a medium not only without conscience but also without memory? Karp thinks so, and expresses these convictions with wisdom and wit.

The last essay in this section deals with "the new sounds of radio." William Honan shows what happened to the radio industry when it faced the reality that television had permanently taken its place as "dispenser of general entertainment for the masses." Using case studies of three New York stations which took a fresh approach to programming, Honan explains how adaptability to audience needs has proved successful. He, alone of the authors represented in this section, is almost optimistic for the future. Radio's "fractionalization" merely copied what the print media have been doing quite some time. Honan believes that television will ultimately follow this pattern once the UHF stations begin to catch on. To him, the relevant aspect of this specialization may be that the mass media (often condemned as purveyors of a bland, homogenized sameness) may soon become a "vigorous force working for cultural diversity." But he wisely adds a caveat to his prediction, namely, that the level or quality of that diversity is, indeed, another question. Yes, a real $64,000 question.

What Is Wrong with TV—and with Us

by Charles A. Siepmann

AT A LUNCHEON meeting during the convention of the National Association of Broadcasters in Chicago the other day, a Congressional guest, Representative Walter E. Rogers of Texas, got a standing ovation. Why? Because he is the author of a bill designed to prevent the Federal Communications Commission from regulating the amount of advertising on the air, and the House had approved the bill, 317 to 43.

But does the public approve? What, in broadcasting, is the "public interest," and who shall determine it? What, in other words, would constitute a true national policy for broadcasting and how could it be implemented?

A national policy implies a national consensus—something that all of us can agree to. Personal preferences are here beside the point. Such a policy can only be defined by analyzing (1) the distinctive potentialities of the television medium and (2) the compelling needs of our society—meaning needs shared by us all, as individuals and as citizens.

Television is distinctive in its universal reach. No other medium can transport us all simultaneously to the scene of action anywhere on earth. This universal reach creates a corresponding dependence. This is why we all turn to television in times of common need as we did during the four days that shook the world last November. Television is distinctive also as a new language, a new art-in-the-making with extraordinary power to quicken the senses and focus the mind on reality.

Television, then, will be true to itself as it exploits these distinctive properties and reckons with their implicit cultural and moral obligations. Its universal reach gives it its opportunity—to serve the common interest. But this is also its limitation. For, given an audience comprising the whole nation, only shared interests can be served—and not even all of these. Even rough justice is possible only by providing programs that offer *variant exposure to the widest practicable range of commonly shared interests.* Hence the test of true service is not the size of the audience at a given hour, but the overall variety of interests provided for throughout a day or week.

But we are already in trouble as we unconsciously confuse the interests (tastes) of the public with the public interest, which is what broadcasting, under law, is charged to serve. For the public interest has little to do with our appetites and desires, however widely shared. It has everything to do with our needs, as human beings and citizens of this democracy. In both realms our whims and appetites must be subordinate to our needs and duties (to ourselves and others) if we are to survive.

Consideration of our needs, moreover, has this advantage: Tastes differ, and any policy that seeks fairly to reconcile the myriad conflicting tastes and interests of a nation is foredoomed to failure. But our needs can be defined, and in terms that are, surely, acceptable at the bar of reason. What, then, are they, and from what do they stem?

They stem from our common humanity—from the chance that nature offers each of us to become a human being, transcending the beast that lurks in each of us. This, I suggest, involves the endless refinement and exercise of our distinctively human, suprabestial faculties. Broadly defined, these needs would seem to be as follows:

(1) *The need for relaxation.* Laughter, amusement, even idle frivolity are legitimate needs because they are psychological necessities. They have always been so.

(2) *The need for expansion of our horizons of knowledge and*

awareness—of people, their condition and their interaction with one another, their arts and their inventions—the all-embracing world of knowledge in a contemporary sense. (As it equips us to vote responsibly, such service meets our civic as well as our individual needs.)

(3) *The need not only for knowledge but for experience in depth,* comprising all that invites our understanding of what lies below the surface of events and of all meaning, including the meaning of life itself. This, pre-eminently, is the realm of the artist, the philosopher, the divine. But it is essentially a dimension of experience common to us all, forced on us inescapably the moment we use our minds and our imaginations. Awe, suffering, love, ecstasy are elements of this experience.

(4) *Practical needs in our day-to-day living.* There exists a storehouse of knowledge and experience here which, if made the property of all, would transform the happiness and health of millions. The extent and variety of such knowledge is vast—the rearing of children, healthy diet, marital relations, mental health and medical services, at one end of the scale; and at the other, such relatively trivial needs as how to cook and fill out income tax forms—the infinities of "how to do it" knowledge.

If we aspire to be human beings and to pay more than lip service to democracy and its claims on us, these are the four necessary components of a humanistic diet. Exclude any one of them, and we risk intellectual and emotional pellagra.

Television, then, serves us well as it meets all of these four needs at various levels of understanding. And with three networks available, we have the physical facilities for *nationwide satisfaction of each of these needs for three-and-three-quarter-hours a night, seven days a week, between the hours of* 6-11 *P.M. alone!* (Actually, more is possible, for more than one need can be met in a single program. "The Merchant of Venice," for example, and "The Defenders" both offer relaxation *and* experience in depth.)

Apply this yardstick, and how does television measure up? People will differ widely as they appraise the worth of any given program. But if we apply the above criteria, consensus is surely possible on some patent defects of present service.

For a start, the time devoted to light entertainment, especially in evening hours, is wildly disproportionate, amounting to more than provision for all the other needs combined. Much of it is a great deal better than some critics are ready to admit, but the sheer amount of it precludes enjoyment of other interests for which millions are hungry and to which millions are entitled.

A network president has described present practice as cultural democracy. On the same principle we should presumably have economic democracy if department stores cleared their shelves of all but their best-selling lines.

Consider next, not content, but modes of communication. Age-old in its hold on popular imagination is the drama. Television drama is a distinctive art. Its power to portray the human situation, hold up a mirror to reality, communicate experience in depth has been proven again and again. Its quantity and, many claim, its quality have declined, and we are scarcely compensated for this by the spate of dated films now on the air, such enjoyment as they provide being heavily discounted by exasperation at the endless intrusion of crude commercials.

They are cheaper, of course, and in television it is revenue that counts. A distinctive art form of wide popular appeal has been virtually discarded in the interests of the profit ledger.

And what of news? For years it was conspicuous by its absence at convenient hours. The defect has recently been somewhat remedied—in terms of the time devoted to it. But what of its quality? In New York City the newspaper strike of 1962–63 forced readers to rely on broadcast news, and the experience resulted in reassessment of its worth. Before the strike 83 per cent of a sample interviewed thought it excellent. After 100 days without a newspaper people changed their minds. Only 16 per cent now thought it excellent. Sixty-eight per cent spoke of radio and television news as *poor*.

News apart, sustained analysis and comment on national and world events remain conspicuously absent. Many-sided discussion, representing the full spectrum of diverse opinion, is all but non-existent. Television apparently knows better than Jefferson who claimed that "a nation that expects to be ignorant and free expects what never was and never will be."

Of daytime dramas, with their distorted image of reality, the less said the better. But here again it is less their presence on the air that invites censure than the alternatives of useful service which, by their profusion, they crowd out. It is the unbalanced diet—*absence* of service in our four categories of need—that here again makes a mockery of television as a responsible service to the nation.

Television's performance warrants analysis on another count as well, that of hypocrisy. It has long and insistently claimed that it gives the public what it wants. Whether one thinks this constitutes service in the public interest or not, let us put the industry to its own test. There is known to be widespread dissatisfaction with television on two grounds, of which the first is the excess of murder and mayhem on the air. God knows we have our bellyfull of it, as the reader can verify by sampling any weekday's output of the networks.

Thus in one evening, picked at random, there were two horror shows, two war films, two Westerns, four crook stories and six murders. Yet an exhaustive study of television's audience, sponsored by C.B.S., shows that even the *average* viewer "thinks that programs depict too much imitable violence." Twenty-five per cent of parents think children would be better off without television; 66 per cent cannot think of any example where children have benefited from it; 29 per cent cite examples where it harmed them.

It is the *average* viewer, again, who claims that there are too many commercials. Forty-three per cent would prefer to have none, while 24 per cent so resent them that they would pay for television to be rid of them. Here are matters on which broadcasting has a clear mandate from the people to speed reforms— and has responded with contemptuous disregard.

And as for advertising, we now have the preposterous situation of an industry that has for years claimed freedom from regulatory interference (on the ground that it can regulate itself) protesting violently when the F.C.C. proposes to adopt and to enforce the generous limits of advertising time which the industry itself had formulated but has not bothered to enforce. Such is the cynical hypocrisy of TV.

But not all television is commercial. There is educational television, too, broadcast by stations undistracted and uncontaminated by the lure of money.

The first educational television station went on the air in 1957.

Today there are 85. Progress has been slow partly because ETV was assigned a majority of frequencies in the ultrahigh-frequency band to which most receivers cannot be tuned without the added cost of an "adapter." The stations are variously supported and operated by school systems, universities and by the local community. Mostly they perform local services and reflect local life and talent. All are in more or less desperate financial need—at least as they aspire to rounded program service of high quality over extended hours.

But, thanks to the Ford Foundation, local production resources are supplemented by five hours of program material a week supplied by the National Educational Television Center. For the next three years the center is to receive $6 million to produce programs of first-rate professional quality, at least half of which are to cover public and international affairs. Thus the imbalance of commercial television is partly redressed, and continuous exposure to experience in vital areas of need becomes available to an ever larger potential audience.

ETV is only now beginning to hit its stride. Critics continue to speak of it as dull and unimaginative and compare it unfavorably with commercial television in its professional standards of production. It is also criticized as lacking a unified philosophy with program output proportioned to the priorities of need.

But it has many superb programs already to its credit and it is young. In areas where it has become more or less established it has regular viewers ranging from 10 to 25 per cent of the population that its signals reach. Its need is for more money and for what money alone can assure in significant numbers—men of talent and imagination at its controls.

What, in the light of this analysis, are the broad outlines of the picture? On the commercial side (ETV is too young to appraise fairly) it is the picture of an industry rising intermittently to triumphant heights of responsible service but committed in its day-to-day operations to a warped and false philosophy—and a disingenuous philosophy at that—as it belies its own claim that it gives the public what it wants.

Television in the public interest does not mean coralling a peak audience for every hour on the air. Dragging or luring the horse to the water is not its business. Its function is to keep the well full and uncontaminated; let the horse drink as and when it wills. We get entertainment aplenty, though even here the range of interest is artificially confined by adherence to proven stereotypes of lowest-common-denominator tastes. But even if all of it were rich and varied, we get too much of it.

Programs suffer from a fatal disproportion, with the result that vital needs and varied competing interests shared by millions get short shrift. In all but entertainment we get spotty, intermittent service. Yet it is only by continuous exposure that we acquire new interests, new insights, new awareness. Television takes us as we are (and that in the mass aggregate) and thereby keeps us where we are, denying that which we have it in us to become.

The pride and supposed virtue of private enterprise is that it is enterprising and takes risks. Television plays it safe. Its short-term gains are writ large in its profit-and-loss account. What of the long-term consequences—to television and to our society? "Style is the last morality of mind"? The trouble with television's style is that it is vulgar.

What lies at the root of the trouble? It is in large part the unique role that advertising plays in broadcasting as its major source of revenue. This gives the sponsor a degree of control over programs that is near absolute—in marked contrast to his control over newspaper and magazine content.

Thus a disastrous distortion of our system of broadcasting has taken place. The interests of the public have been subordinated to the interests of the sponsor. Sponsored programs are programs designed to expose commodities to the largest number of potential buyers. The tail of merchandising wags the dog of programing in the public interest.

But this is only part of the truth. For broadcasters are not so much in thrall to sponsors as they claim to be. They are, at least in some measure, masters in their own house—as they plow back into programs of which sponsors fight shy some part of their enormous profits. It is the Midas touch that plagues the broadcaster. Not profits, but profits without limit, determine program policy—and profits derived from a source that makes merchandising, not programing, its primary objective. Admittedly, not all television stations make big money. But enough do to support the contention that men making private profit through privileged access to a public property have obligations to serve the public interest first and foremost.

The profits of the television industry are in fact staggering. Total revenues in 1962 were nearly half a billion dollars—up 12.7 per cent over 1961. In 10 years profits have risen 5½ times. In 1962, 81 per cent of V.H.F. (very high frequency) stations made a profit, and one-fourth of these earned over $1 million. As to networks, C.B.S. has topped all previous profits in each succeeding year but two since 1957. Its profits for the third quarter of 1963 nearly doubled those for the same period in 1962. Not even faintly comparable increase in varied service to our needs has followed.

What can be done about it all? Will the answer come from the broadcasting industry—through self-regulation? If it be true that "by their fruits ye shall know them," the prospect seems bleak.

Promise (as measured by speeches of industry spokesmen and publicity releases) and performance (as measured by the criteria we have applied) are too contradictory to warrant hope or confidence. Supposedly educated men seem, in television, to lose their standards of morality, taste, honor and responsibility somewhere between home and the office. "Am I my brother's keeper?"—the question that has troubled the conscience of mankind for centuries —gets from television the contemptuous answer, "No," as it conflicts with money-making.

Given the crisis of our times, the desperate premium on our society's collective intelligence and moral standards, the men at the controls of television are perilously near to fiddling while Rome burns. Reluctantly one concludes that in television private enterprise and true service in the public interest are incompatible.

Can the industry be controlled? The Communications Act provided that it should be, established the F.C.C. and gave it broad, discretionary powers. But in 30 years, only two chairmen have stood up like David to this Goliath. License renewal—even of stations in flagrant default on the program service they promised as applicants—has been the norm for years. Until appointment to the F.C.C. is removed from the political spoils system and goes to men of high intelligence coupled with proven integrity and devotion to the public interest, it is naive to hope for better things.

And even then we should not hope for too much. Prescription

by an agency of government of what should be broadcast (other than in terms as broad and permissive as our four basic needs of men) is undesirable and probably impracticable. At best, the F.C.C. can only protect the public interest by fighting a rear-guard action against flagrant violation of such regulation as it imposes. You cannot, beyond a point, legislate the morality of men whose perspectives blind them to the inescapable association of responsibility with power.

Can Congress act? It can, indeed. Some have proposed a statutory requirement that there be an hour or more, in each of the three major segments of the day, aimed at audiences other than those seeking light entertainment. Others propose a limit on profits —as quid pro quo for privileged use of facilities neither privately owned nor primarily intended as lubricants for the machinery of commerce. Sponsors, again, could be deprived, as in Britain, of any power to dictate program content, and limited to buying time on the air as they buy space in newspapers. These and similar brakes on the wheels of avarice are possible.

But *will* Congress act? Many of its members are parties of interest—as owners or shareholders of radio and television stations. More still are too beholden to the broadcaster (for providing free time to address their constituents) to risk forfeiting such patronage. Their sympathy is indicated by their votes on the Rogers bill on radio-TV advertising.

Is pay TV the answer? Why should it be? The lure of profit is as compelling here as in our present system. And pay TV would be exempt from even the nominal control of programs now vested in the F.C.C. For when viewers pay for what they get it is unthinkable that government should prescribe what they should be allowed to pay for.

What of educational television? Given financial backing, programing wholly devoted to our societal and cultural needs would be feasible and is in fact in the making. Educational television is a potential countervailing force. But the very notion of a palliative is ill-conceived, for only the concerted effort of *all* our mass media, combined with our educational resources, is likely to see us through the troubled years ahead.

Time is no longer with us, but against us. The price of social and cultural immaturity grows more disastrous by the day. And anyhow, is commercial television to be given a free hand, its record of always too little and too late to be rewarded by unconditional surrender of publicly owned frequencies?

What, finally, can be looked for from the public? Television has lulled it into a fatal complacency. Its perspectives reflect the patterns of "service" that it has been offered. Custom as much as conscience "doth make cowards of us all." It is incredible what we get used to. (Little more than 30 years ago the radio sponsor dared not intrude into our homes after shopping hours; at 7 P.M. all advertising on the air ended!) What, moreover, can we expect of a public 65 per cent of which condoned television's foulest hour—the quiz scandals?

Flaccid, indifferent and unaware (because not made aware), it accepts what it is given—what is easy on the eye and ear, what gives no offense. Unchallenged, unstimulated, offered no leadership, it drifts out on television's soporific tide toward the fog banks of the mind that obscure the realities that face us. Television has made non-think popular.

These are lugubrious conclusions. But they perhaps direct us to the heart of the whole matter. For in television's mirror, surely, we see our own faces reflected with only minor distortion. What is wrong with television (though this gives the broadcaster no alibi) is in large part what is wrong with us. The notion that anything goes for a fast buck, tolerance and even enjoyment of brutality gratuitously thrown on the screen, non-think—these and like characteristics are not peculiar to television, for all that it aids and abets them. They are part of the temper of the people.

Television represents no more than the visible outcropping of an ugly seam that runs from coast to coast under the surface of our culture—alienation from our true selves and our tradition through misplaced materialist preoccupations. The times cry out for a regeneration, a new commitment and a new morality in our society. It is to this alone that we can look for redirection of television in the public interest. "The fault, dear Brutus, is not in our stars but in ourselves that we are underlings."

Not So Popular As "Gunsmoke," But—

by Richard Hoggart

LONDON

I SUPPOSE the editor wasn't quite serious but wanted to goad me into controversy. Will you discuss, he asked when he suggested this article, whether educational television programs can ever hope to command as large an audience as "Gunsmoke"?

The answer, of course, is "No." They can't, and it would be a queer society in which they could; or in which gardening programs or book programs or hobby programs or current affairs programs or ballet programs—no matter how good they were— attracted anything like the audiences that a variety show gets.

If we approach the problems of broadcasting in that way, we are sure to end in excessive depression. It's self-defeating, as is our fascinated interest in that false antithesis: "Giving the people what the people want" versus "Giving the people what someone thinks is good for them." At this point I always think of a sort of allegory.

Suppose 20 men live in the same street or block, and suppose they are all at home most evenings. By the time they've washed and eaten and helped to do the dishes it's about 7 P.M. and they are free till about 10:30, when they start thinking about putting out the cat and seeing to the boiler. So those are their "peak hours"—their "prime time" in your language—7 to 10:30 P.M.

Like the rest of us, they are often tired in the evenings, and all of them spend about half of this free time "putting their feet up" —that is, simply relaxing. It follows that at any time 10 out of the 20 can be found doing just that: "Putting your feet up" has the highest audience rating (50 per cent) of all prime-time occupations in that block.

These same 20 men spend the other half of their free time on quite different things. For example:

Two work in the garden.

Two do elaborate carpentry in the basement.

Two listen to music.

Two work on photography.

Two read books.

(One can, of course, vary such a list enormously.)

They do these things with a lot of interest. At any one moment in prime time, a total of 10, that is to say, half, of the 20 men are doing such things. But only two of them are ever doing any *one* of these things, so the audience rating of any one of them is low: only 10 per cent, against 50 per cent for "Putting your feet up."

Suppose we used not just an audience measurement, a measurement of numbers, but also an *intensity* measurement. Plainly, in my imaginary block the intensity curve for evening occupations— the degree of interest with which various things are done—would be directly opposed to the audience ratings.

If anyone said to these men—using the language used by apologists for the present state of television programing in the States —that because "Putting your feet up" has such a high audience rating, then it must be five times *preferred* to the other occupations, they'd think he was a fool. They enjoy both, but know they are pleasantly amused and half asleep in the one, but alive and interested in the other. If the interviewer persisted and said that it is clear from the ratings that superabundant facilities for "Putting your feet up" are what almost everyone *really* wants almost all of the time—so that in future apartment planning no other facilities would be provided—then the 20 men would be likely to run him off the block.

This is a very rough allegory, I know. But I think it points to some of the main elements in any serious attempt to provide broadcasting in the public service, to plan programing democratically. Programing in prime time, that is—any knave or fool can claim to provide a comprehensive service if he takes care that programs which don't attract a unified majority audience are put on only at 6:30 A.M. or on Sunday afternoon. My allegory reminds us, too, that we don't have to worry—at least not for quite a time—about whether we have a due proportion of "highbrow" programs. There are simpler, unbrowed questions about the nature of responsible broadcasting to be cleared up first.

To begin with, there is the idea of range—or "balance," as it is likely to be called in Britain. Obviously, most programs in prime time will be—ought to be—entertaining in subject and relaxing in manner. But broadcasting should still offer a fair range of subjects, because many people do have a variety of interests, and shouldn't be expected to stay up late or get up early so as to have some of them catered to.

And there should be a range of manners, of approach and treatment, from the relaxing to the fairly demanding, because many people don't want *only* relaxation *all* the time. If broadcasters don't offer a range of subjects and manners, then the variety of human interests won't get a fair showing.

This matters much more in television than in the press. We can always subscribe to a minority journal—a hobbies paper or political review or gardening journal. But the number of television channels is physically, and severely, limited; the compensations of a free market do not operate here. Broadcasters have to build variety into the system or see commerce's natural tendency toward concentration (catering to us always as unified majorities rather than as—sometimes—interlocking minorities) reinforced by the medium's natural limitations.

Next is the idea of different *intensities* in viewing. Over here, this is recognized by the B.B.C. with audience research that uses both a numerical index and an appreciation index, but not by the commercial channels, who use only a numerical index (similar to those used in the States).

I've heard the idea of different intensities of viewing called undemocratic and The Economist calls it "arrogant." This is nonsense. It's surely more democratic to try to cater to different depths in viewing than to stick to a one-dimensional scale. There are always two kinds of democracy: high and low. "Low" democracy satisfies itself by counting heads and seeing people as a mass; "high" democracy isn't satisfied until it's done all it can to allow for the individuality of everyone.

If we accept the notion of different intensities in viewing, we are only admitting that we don't watch all programs with the same amount of interest. Some don't shock or challenge or worry or surprise us or make us strain our emotional muscles to feel a keen joy or sorrow; they relax us. There is nothing wrong in this, of course; we all want to relax a lot, as my allegory emphasized. Other programs speak to us as more discriminating individuals, expect us to come alive, challenge us so that we react with enthusiasm or anger. And between these two poles there are innumerable combinations of different degrees of interest.

Suppose that you were planning a television program with only one purpose: to be as fair and democratic as you could. There is only a single channel in your city. Which would best meet your purpose—to program all your prime time so as to keep pretty nearly all your audience in a state of pleasant somnambulism (it is possible), or to try to ensure that during *some part* of each evening you put on something which gripped, say, half your total audience, while perhaps boring or even annoying the other half, and at another time provided something which engaged that other half?

Democracies congenitally worry about the total sum of human happiness. But is it axiomatic that 12,000,000 people watching for an hour with mild mutual acceptance feel more happiness than the same 12,000,000 people after they have divided themselves into two groups of 6,000,000, each watching for half an hour with a great deal of interest?

Or if—an easier question—you have two channels, which is the more democratic—to put Westerns on both channels at the same time because "most people watch Westerns" and because you believe that direct competition for customers *automatically and always* produces good results, or to alternate the types of program so as to give the other interests of *most* people a chance?

There are, of course, minorities—intellectual or cultural minorities—and they have a right to some consideration at a reasonable hour of the evening. But, to begin with, broadcasters ought, I suggest, to think of the sort of minority implied in the twin notions of varied range and intensity that I have mentioned. (It should really be "minorities," those areas of interest—actual or potential—in most of us where we can be personally most engaged.)

Some things—an occasional comedy show or an even more occasional drama—can deeply amuse or deeply move the great majority of us. But *on the whole* we are most closely engaged by those things which rouse a more individual interest, for which we care as experts care, because we know and recognize standards (whether in fishing or pigeon-racing or carpentry or anything else).

I am being optimistic here, I admit—but only a little. But if broadcasters don't allow themselves that much optimism, they will find themselves going down a pessimistically steep slope. If program planning doesn't recognize that most people—like the men in my allegory—are for some of the time more discriminating than a simple audience rating would suggest; if planners are satisfied only to know (it's true but not a cause for depression or cynicism) that at any time at least half of us will watch an undemanding and relaxing item; if they consistently provide programs on those lines, they will gradually become convinced that we, their audience, are much more foolish than we are and will think increasingly of ways to keep more and more of us more and more quiet for more and more of the time. In the end, the only shock we will ever feel will be the eruption of a hard-sell commercial in a program break.

It is this, precisely, that is meant by the "driving down of standards." It starts not in some conscious Madison Avenue Machiavellianism, but in false (low) democratic theory buttressed by commercial pressure. Goethe once said that if you do not assume that we are all a bit better as individuals than we seem as a mass, you end by believing we're worse.

T. S. Eliot, when he gave evidence recently to the Committee on British Broadcasting, produced a contemporary version of the same idea: "Those who say they give the public what it wants begin by underestimating public taste and end by debauching it."

So—to come back to that opening question—no educational

program (or hobbies program or opera program, etc.), no matter how well it may be mounted, can attract an audience as large as a competent relaxing program. It would be against nature. But these items ought to have some place in prime-time programing (much more than they get now in the U.S.), because many people want some of them and because they are watched with particular interest.

If, as some people do, we put that question about education and "Gunsmoke" another way and ask: "Can good programs ever be popular?" we will obviously receive and deserve another resounding "No." For what we usually mean by that question is: "Can 'highbrow' or demanding programs ever command a majority audience?"

It would be very much better if we didn't really mean "highbrow" when we say "good." "Goodness" should not be a measure of brow-height, or a bow toward accepted status-marks in the arts. For democratic programing, another meaning serves better: that "goodness" in a program is decided by its vitality and honesty, the quality of the life in it, whether it is a comedy show or a political discussion.

This cuts through a lot of confusion—and cant. It shows that a conventionally "good" or "serious" program—say, a panel of half a dozen professors brought together to discuss the state of the nation or a specially mounted performance of an artistic work —may *or may not* be "good." Such programs may be: they may be professionally skilled and honest attempts to present important issues to a huge audience with mixed backgrounds and abilities, or they may use skill and integrity so as to recreate an author's imaginative art on the small screen. They are then trying to be good television.

Or they may be specimens of *kitsch,* processed culture-vulturing, vehicles for technical gimmicks—fancy camera angles and mobiles and artificial pace and personality—pushing displays of what one critic has called virtuosity without virtue.

And exactly the same may be true of a comedy or a variety show. The best light shows live in the same world as genuinely intellectual or deeply imaginative works. The worst light shows belong to the same phony world as gimmicky cultural programs. Their error is not that they are either too coarse or too demanding; it's that they are empty. The packaging is exciting, but there is nothing inside the package.

Any good television professional knows all this, knows it in his professional bones—though he may have had to get used to turning out merely glossy jobs because that's the way the industry is set up.

One point—the hardest—I've left to the last. I mentioned earlier the minorities, actual or potential, in most of us. The rub comes with that word "potential." But I think democratic programing requires broadcasters to accept it. Few of us will, on our own initiative, seek interests outside those most easily made available within our social group or to people who have had our particular level of education.

Whatever else it is, television can be a good gateway. If programing is decided by head-counting, it will, since channels are so few, predominantly work like this: it will provide almost exclusively for *existing* interests and only for the *massively* popular interests.

Take sport. In Britain, television would show almost exclusively football or cricket, according to season. But many sports in Britain have been restrictively identified with specific social classes (and their available money). Nowadays we are more prosperous and habits are changing. The B.B.C. seems to have postulated that more people might like more and different sports if they had a better chance to see what they were like; and so the Corporation broke the head-counting pattern in programing.

As a result, some sports—competition swimming and show-jumping are two—acquired solid and appreciative viewing audiences and a great many more actual exponents.

How do we know "what we want," in fact, until we see what it's possible to want outside our inevitably limited pattern of expectations? As Commissioner Newton Minow has said: "How do you know what people would have watched if you'd given them something better?" It follows, I believe, that democratic programing should include some provision, in prime time, for interests not yet known to many of us so that we may have a better chance to widen, and not merely to reinforce, our range.

I have insisted throughout that this range of interests is not primarily a matter of brows of different heights. But of course if we think that it is better to use our minds clearly rather than confusedly, and to use our imaginations honestly rather than indulgently, then—by the kind of democratic premises I've been working from throughout—any broadcaster will have to think hard about the extent to which these qualities should have a chance to show in his programs.

It's too easy for him to argue that he has no right *ever* to strain anyone, *ever* to demand more attention than most of us are used to giving. By those criteria, if television had been invented 400 years ago, he'd have filled *all* his prime time with bear-baiting, hanging-drawing-and-quartering and necromancy.

The sad thought is that it's the modern equivalents of those occupations which *do* fill much of his prime time today—all in the name of democracy. Broadcasters are at one of the pressure-points of responsible democracy (and responsible democracy is itself as much an aspiration as a fact). Your own broadcasting people in America say this themselves at celebratory dinners; but it isn't much reflected in their programs.

I've tried to name the essential planks in a platform for responsible broadcasting. We also named them in our Pilkington Report here—and were accused of humbug, grandmotherliness, authoritarianism, fascism, socialism and restrictionism for our pains.

But consider New York City's television in prime time. One would have thought—in view of the enormous range of different interests represented by some 8,000,000 people—that each of the commercial channels might for some of the time have branched out so as to provide varied services. But the schedules, as everyone knows, show an almost solid and continuous concentration on the tried and tested relaxers.

It's the logic of a competitive commercial system and it runs counter to the needs of responsible broadcasting. It's an odd kind of democracy which leaves so much in so many people so little catered to.

It will be argued that while it is easy for systems like the B.B.C. to live up to the principles of democratic broadcasting, since their one aim is to program in the public service, it is difficult for competitive commercial systems, since they must show a profit. There is great vested interest in keeping the United States system as it is, and the commercial pressures on Congress not to allow Mr. Minow to use his powers will be enormous.

But even if the United States does not succeed, the facts remain: These are the principles of democratic broadcasting and, if it so wills, a country can build them into a solvent commercial system.

But how? It is clear that Mr. Minow is taking things stage by stage. Can he do it? He has certainly *said* all the right things, and said them well. I hope he can really do something. If he does, if he makes any radical improvements, he will deserve his own monument on the shores of the Tidal Basin in Washington. He'll have made as big a contribution as some of the Founding Fathers to the strengthening of real democracy in the States.

Must It Be "Kookie" and "Ka-Pow"?

by Robert Saudek

"MR. WIZARD BROUGHT some spiders into our class," an eight-year-old neighbor of that TV scientist reported to me recently. "One was really cool. It's called a golden silk spider, and it had lots of egg sacs. He showed us a black widow and Jeff said we better get rid of its egg sac fast because it might hatch out. Only it takes about a month for them to hatch, so it wasn't really dangerous to have them. The egg sac was like a little ball about this big—."

Every Saturday, for thirty minutes, Mr. Wizard conducts one of the few children's programs in television that undertake something more than entertainment. His effect on inquiring young minds is reflected in this child's report. Yet, by the three national networks' own listings, less than 1 per cent of their programing is designed to stimulate or challenge young people.

This is the condition that prompted Chairman Newton N. Minow of the Federal Communications Commission to describe children's programs as largely "time-wasters"—particularly arid patches in what he called the "vast wasteland" of television. The storm that his remarks stirred up is still raging in the wake of a series of hearings before the F.C.C. in Washington.

Just what does "children's television" consist of? The networks' programs of all sorts run to 1,000 hours a month. Of these, some seventy-five hours are devoted to shows created specifically for children. I have gone through the listings and find this time divided as follows: 4.5 per cent, news; 4.3 per cent, science or other information; 13.1 per cent, straight drama or adventure; 78.1 per cent, straight entertainment—i.e., cartoons, magic acts, etc.

Stated another way, more than 91 per cent of children's fare was designed to make them laugh or cry ("Roy Rogers," "Lassie," "Matty's Sunday Funday," "Bugs Bunny," "Sky King," etc.) and less than 9 per cent was designed to make them think ("Update," "American Newsstand," "Mr. Wizard," "1-2-3-Go!"). Thus, of the 1,000 hours of monthly network programing, only about six-tenths of 1 per cent is designed to appeal to youngsters' minds.

Of course, not all television is supplied by the three networks. But a spot check of "children's television" on the local level indicates that here, too, entertainment and adventure programs overwhelm the children's schedule. Here we find such titles as "Kooky the Kat," "Superman" (reruns), "Fun-a-rama," "Crusader Rabbit," "Billy Bang-Bang Movies" and "The Three Stooges."

There is growing restlessness among some parents who have visions of a network-produced generation of laughing hyenas who will while away their lives ever waiting to be entertained. They question the quality of planning that must go into the 91 per cent of children's programs that are characterized by such dialogue as this, taken from a recent show:

"This is Willie the Musical Worm in the apple, boys and girls. He never needs a doctor. I don't know what that proves, but I guess it proves something or other. Let's give Willie a great big hand! [*Applause*.]"

Or this, which followed within the hour:

"Understand you've been asking questions about me. What's on your mind, mister?"

"Thought maybe you'd like to cut me in, that's all."

"On what?"

"You know what. I happen to know what became of those horses that strayed down to the Indians."

"You can't prove a thing about me."

"Am I in?"

"No."

"All right, you asked for it. [*Ka-pow!*]"

The total vocabulary of all such shows combined can hardly exceed that of a four-year-old child.

Do children really want such programs? If asked, they would doubtless express satisfaction with whatever they are getting—for popularity polls are based on making choices among existing alternatives. This is the catch in the argument advanced by one network executive in answer to criticism of television programing: "It is always the public that sets a trend, not the broadcaster."

The opposing argument has been stated by Mr. Minow: "Broadcasters have a positive obligation . . . to elevate, inform and uplift, as well as to entertain." He has also said that "it is not enough to cater to the nation's whims—you must also serve the nation's needs."

The public does not really lead, ever, in a progressive society. In architecture, a few leaders do; in science, research scientists do; in the theatre, daring playwrights, designers and producers do. History is filled with examples of leaders who would not wait for a tongue-tied public, and who would not accept the answer that the public is satisfied with whatever it has—whether it be a flat world, smallpox or slavery.

If leadership and inventiveness in children's television are suspect, then the notion that TV might ever address itself to children of unusual capacities must be heretical. Yet it is increasingly the nature of our society to take a special interest in those young people whose intellectual capabilities and qualities of leadership appear to mark them for important roles in their adult years.

For example, a leading university has recently undertaken an experimental "Operation Gamble," under which a limited number of students are admitted each year because they show remarkable ability, energy and alertness despite the indifferent quality of their scholastic preparation. The public did not set this trend, but the public may benefit by it.

As reports filter back from the Soviet Union of Russian children who study their country's unabridged literary classics before they reach high school, as language tests reveal the limited vocabularies of our high-school graduates, as law schools complain about the inability of their entering students to write good English, many parents feel a need to re-examine the influences to which American children are subject.

Schools, television, newspapers, magazines and books cannot be separated in this respect. If children grow up unchallenged by big words, big books, big programs and big ideas, how will they be prepared for the decisions which adult life will demand of them both as individuals and as citizens? The very fact that television has the proven capacity to reach 50,000,000 homes in the nation, and that it is a licensed institution, would seem to place special responsibility on licensees to greet the coming generation with a good deal more than those cute little cartoon animals and overcharged M.C.'s.

For gifted children, of whom the country must boast many thousands, television that challenges would be an oasis. It may be said that books are available to them—and so they are—but television must not shirk the burden unless it believes that the statutory "public interest" which it is licensed to serve does not include an obligation to encourage vigorous and intelligent leadership among the nation's youth.

We believe that television in the United States is "freer" than in nearly any of the other Western countries, where government has planted its feet rather heavily at the helm and steers television's course through what it considers to be either scenic or character-building waters. American television is more of a pleasure cruise, where paper hats and noisemakers abound and the stuffier passengers may consult the news ticker for any unpleasant information they may desire.

Yet a certain tedium might be relieved—at least for the young —by injecting a little bracing mental stimulation into the endless hours of unrelieved distraction. Not too much to mar gracious living, of course, but perhaps just enough to demonstrate that TV has more strength to show than that manifested by its everlasting display of rippling muscles and a well-flushed intestinal tract.

What should these injections include? For children I would suggest:

Music: Except for the rare appearances of Leonard Bernstein in his stimulating sessions on the anatomy of music, there is not a single program addressing itself to the subject in terms a child might understand.

History and Biography: No programs for children represent this lustrous field of interest, yet an educated nation must have a genuine sense of its heritage and civilization. Television could supply a view of history that would be a valuable corollary to textbooks.

Science: It is hard to believe that the medium most directly indebted to modern electronics should have disregarded its own birthright almost completely, leaving science in the capable hands of one individual called Mr. Wizard. Nonetheless, science is as visual as drama. The microscope, telescope, chemistry beaker, Bunsen burner and all the manifestations of the biological laboratory are waiting for new opportunities to expand young horizons.

Drama: Discrimination in drama is no more fostered by following Roy Rogers and Lassie than is art appreciation awakened by reading the comic strips. Yet the loftiest dramatic expression permitted in children's television is that of a dog rescuing its master from a blaze, or a monosyllabic exchange and a burst of gunfire in the corral. Somewhere among the "spell of dreams" there must be richer material than this for the little ones.

Government: One weekly children's program, "Update," carries lively and penetrating comments on politics—treated in even greater detail than are most adult news and commentary shows. Yet politics and diplomacy are the lifeblood of democracy, so my schedule would include enough to give young people a sense of their place in their lives.

City government would be a good place to start. Comparative political systems and some of the language of diplomacy would constitute preparation for the responsibilities of citizenship. The Constitution, the three branches of our Government and the anatomy of a trial have the kind of substance that adds to a child's maturation.

Entertainment: There is no shortage of this commodity in the present schedules. If this remains all that most children watch, there will, nevertheless, be those whose curiosity will prod them out of the bargain basement and up to the quality merchandise.

The ideals and vitality thus spread among the youth of the

country, if measured by the sale of acne cures, might leave something to be desired by the acne-cure people. But such television would be more like the kind Thomas Jefferson might create if he were among us.

This is not a world divided between eggheads and lovers of Westerns. It is a world with a wide variety of people and problems, challenges and "breakthroughs," and children have only a few years to catch up before they must bring their own force of character to bear on it.

Television has suffered from an excess of caution. It likes to move slowly, to make short-range plans and to stay in familiar territory. Like the old lady in Boston, it sees no reason for moving when it's already there.

But perhaps television will take courage from the retentive capacity of the same eight-year-old quoted at the outset of this article. This is his report on a TV commercial he had seen some months before:

"I remember a commercial that showed a big reflector and the sun gave it electricity, instead of batteries, so it wouldn't run out. All you need is the river and the sun. The sun comes down to this thing, it reflects up to another thing, which sends the electricity to the river and it pumps the water. It's really cool."

It is this tenacity of a new idea grasped by a young mind, this thrill of discovery, which can make children's television extraordinary. As long as the rating services are merely turnstiles for counting customers, we shall never be equipped to measure this priceless "retention factor" which spells the difference between the long, gray line of forgotten programs and the memorable children's shows that could unleash the power of the mind.

A Look Back into the Tube

by David Karp

GALUMPHING ABOUT my house is a 15¾-year-old son who stands 6 feet 1 inch tall, needs a shave almost every other day, wears his hair in what appears to be a modified version of a Bessarabian's caracul hat, listens to Ravi Shankar playing a hot raga on the sitar, and, the state of California's driving laws being what they are, will be behind the wheel in less than eight months. He is a child of television. Television will be four-and-one-quarter-years older than Ethan this year.

I can recall holding him, all 22 inches of him, inside a receiving blanket, over my shoulder, rubbing his small back to soothe his colic as I watched television. That was 1952. Ethan's colic is gone. Television's colic has simply grown worse.

Twenty years is a long time, however you want to figure it. It amounts, in human terms, to a generation. A television generation.

Consider first, as a sobering thought, that the 18-year-old boy or girl (the child of television's first generation) has seen 17,000 hours of television, 500 movies and spent only 12,000 hours in the classroom. The figures come from George Stevens Jr., one of the directors of the American Film Institute.

What has the television generation seen in 20 years? Technically, TV has zoomed from "line of sight" transmission to Telstar satellites. From muddy kinescope to sparkling TV tape. From a small, black, white and grainy picture to something large, colorful and flawless. It has gone beyond to theater-sized television, as George Orwell warned in his glumly prophetic novel, "1984." That it has not fulfilled Orwell's prediction that it would be used to "brainwash" citizens is simply due to the fact that brainwashing doesn't seem to have a ready sponsor to pay for the time.

But it has done something more threatening; it has, through closed-circuit television, provided solvent snoops with the tools to turn the television camera on all of us. Closed-circuit television not only watches the sealing of tin cans on assembly lines, it also enables apartment-house superintendents to observe the comings and goings of tenants and their visitors, reputedly is used in the women's dressing rooms of some department stores to prevent shoplifting, and most blatantly used by one large company to keep check on employes smoking and loitering in its toilets. The last invasion caused a union furor. While there does not appear to be anything terribly wrong with watching television, there is something terribly wrong when television starts watching the watchers and the unwary.

It has come to this, and it is at this point in TV's relentless technical progress that I began to empathize with the sculptor in H. G. Wells's "Shape of Things to Come" who cried out, in the accents of the late Sir Cedric Hardwicke, "Enough of progress! Stop! Stop it before it destroys us!" When closed-circuit television is linked to the computer and its memory cores, and both are fed to the recently developed C.B.S. Laboratories' video-cartridges, we are going to find that privacy, as a human right, is gone. Despots dreamed of such power since the dawn of man, and television, as a rather casual lagniappe, has handed it over in just 20 years without any urging from the Government.

Television as a news medium has acquired a peculiar and powerful status that no other medium has ever held. Marshall McLuhan, that high priest of "pop" analysis, has, in fact, classified television's on-the-spot "actuality" reporting of events-as-they-happen as a totally new form of communication. This form of reportage has, in McLuhan's view, transformed the "mere" reader into an electronic participant. The viewer is turned on to what is really happening as if he had an electrical umbilicus tied to the tube. In McLuhan's view, the television watcher has finally achieved the status of Aldous Huxley's "feelie" participant and damned high time it happened, too.

But TV has another power: to spread the news about politics and politicians in such a fashion as to "make" news about them. Perhaps you haven't noticed it, but politicians, who are swift to assess what is good for them and what is bad for them, knew all about the "umbilicus" before Marshall McLuhan told anybody.

Political parties now spend the bulk of their campaign funds on television. It is now a political truism that television either defeated Richard M. Nixon or elected John F. Kennedy in 1960. But there is no doubt that it was television which did it. Some analysts blame the configuration of Nixon's lower jaw, as seen on the television screen, as an important factor in his defeat. One show-wise observer commented, "Nixon looks like a sinister chipmunk." Others go on to predict that it does not much matter how Richard Nixon comes out in the primaries in New Hampshire or any place else, if something isn't done about that lower jaw, he can't get elected.

The television "image" of a politician is thus a determinant in his success. There are TV fanatics who insist that it is "the determinant and the current crop of Republican Presidential hopefuls is as telegenic a crowd as was ever assembled by a casting director. Whatever the merits of that argument, there is one indisputable and pitiless fact about television: Anyone subjected to it long enough gives up a precise and exact measurement of his soul, and the depth of his character. The small, ad lib, meaningless remarks which candidates utter after they have made their speeches or answered the questions of the press, while the cameras are still rolling, are often the most revealing and most damning statements they can make.

Newspapers charitably, and sensibly, omit the banal small talk and quips. Magazines, especially The New Yorker, feed on them with delicate malice. But TV, with its rather gaping, simple-minded staring, just does not know when to stop recording. And it is this mindless and unblinking attention to trivia which gives TV its power.

A small example of this power was afforded by the televised

Kefauver Crime Committee hearings of 1951. There were memorable closeups of the soft hands of Frank Costello, whose attorneys protested that a televised picture of their client's face "invaded his privacy." But an also unforgettable vignette in those hearings was the confrontation of a minor mobster, with a Spanish accent, and the late Senator Kefauver of Tennessee, who badgered him about his American citizenship. This hoodlum was vague about many things, but the one thing he knew was that as a Puerto Rican he was an American citizen by birth. It slowly became evident to the TV audience that Senator Kefauver wasn't aware of that fact. The witness became more confused as Kefauver pressed for information on his "naturalization." A committee aide finally leaned over and informed Senator Kefauver, in an elaborately covered whisper, that Puerto Rican birthright was as good as any you can find in Tennessee. The subject was dropped. The *gaffe* by the Senator might have been missed even by those sitting in the committee room. It was not missed on television.

The Army-McCarthy hearings did not, by themselves, destroy the power of the late Senator Joseph McCarthy. But their televised version, in 1954, certainly helped. Joe McCarthy, whatever you thought of him, was Hollywood's version of a heavy. The unshaven, heavy-lidded, strong features, the baldish head, the rasping, insistent, nasal voice, the bullying manner, the constantly swallowed belch, were all plainly in sight and sound of the TV cameras and audio equipment. When he attacked the patriotism of one of the late Joseph Welch's legal aides, Welch cried out, in real pain, "Senator, have you no decency? No decency at all?" The verdict, on Joe McCarthy, from the TV viewers who had had no prior opinions on the man, was in. The Senate's later decision to censure him was purely a legal certification of a public appraisal. Some say that McCarthy fell because he made his first powerful enemy when he took on the United States Army. There are other opinions that McCarthy fell because television viewers got a good look at him in a committee room and did not like the sight and sound of him.

The ability of television to subject human beings to a total, enveloping examination is not a quality which can be described as being "fair" or "unfair," and yet the effect of that capability does come down to such judgments. For instance, there were no crueler and more uncomfortable sessions than the televised press conferences of former President Eisenhower. Even the most worshipful of Ike's advisers and admirers recognized that the televised record of his fumbles, uncertainties and banalities in the rough and tumble of a press conference would eventually reduce a legitimate American hero to an old bore. Video coverage of the conferences was discreetly discontinued. Television was "unfair" to Dwight D. Eisenhower.

President John F. Kennedy, on the other hand, appeared in TV press conferences as eagerly as a seal in water and radiated charm, sparks, facts and figures. He was a demon debater with a brilliant smile. He not only knew his onions, he let you know he knew them and was insouciant about it. When historians assess John F. Kennedy, let them not ignore the television record. Unless they view the charisma of his television appearances, they cannot appreciate why he became the idol of most Americans.

Lyndon Baines Johnson may, on his domestic record, turn out to be one of our great Presidents, but he is as homely as you can get without being asked not to loiter. His change from old-fashioned "specs" to contact lenses was an attempt to improve his TV "image." He read from a TelePrompTer, went on a diet, and projected sincerity with every ounce of his being. But he is one of those unfortunates to whom TV is not kind. His major address on Vietnam in San Antonio saw him back to the old-fashioned spectacles, reading from a prepared speech on the rostrum and giving up any attempts to improve his TV "image" by the more obvious tricks.

He has also retired from the TV screen, where he used to be as ubiquitous as the "rather-fight-than-switch" commercial, or Ralph Bellamy's soggy reassurance that Geritol will put pep into tired, iron-poor blood. For all President Johnson's reputed "toughness" of personal character, he is a sensitive man who suspects that television appearances are going to hurt rather than help his image. For television will make or unmake politicians, comics, raconteurs and reputations, and until a public figure can pass the public test of television, it is uncertain whether he, or his platform, is going to be acceptable to the public at large.

Is it fair? Is it right? Is it rational? Well, it is television and it is with us. Twenty years with us and beyond. Harry Ackerman, one of the powers in charge of programing for Screen Gems (currently responsible for "The Flying Nun," "The Second Hundred Years," and "Bewitched," in addition to others), reported in a panel discussion that he asked William S. Paley, *the* power of C.B.S. back around 1950, what television would be like in 20 years. Mr. Paley was reported to have replied, "The mixture as before." Mr. Ackerman went on to explain that Mr. Paley meant that television programing would not resemble the nineteen-fifties, but would be a mixture of a different kind—but still a mixture. While I did not speak to William S. Paley in 1950 and, in fact, don't really talk to him now, either, I beg to differ with Harry Ackerman and think Mr. Paley meant exactly what he said: The mixture as before.

Some dour seer with limited prescience might have guessed what television was going to become when the first chick who pecked his way out of the shell in 1948 was Milton Berle with two blacked-out front teeth, short pants, a striped knee-length shirt, and a moon-sized lollipop. In 1948, Milton Berle starred in "The Texaco Star Theater," complete with four singing gas station attendants and a diamond-stickpinned pitchman named Sid Stone who rolled back his sleeves, spit on his hands and slapped them together as he confronted the suckers with, "Now, I'll tell ya' what I'm going to do for ya'!"

We do a time dissolve in entertainment programing, melting past the death of Stalin, the rise of China, the rise of Castro, the Berlin airlift, Korea, the second Arab-Israeli war, the Cuban missile crisis, the Kennedy assassination, the first march on Washington, three Presidential tenures, sputnik, the walk in space, the landing on the moon, the race riots, the Black Power crisis, the third Arab-Israeli war, and we zoom in on 1967. A fanfare of trumpets. And onto our screen, in color, in stereophonic sound, steps Jerry Lewis, with prop buck teeth in his mouth, a pair of thick, prop glasses, an acute adenoidal voice, his hair plastered down in front, and gives us his version of a professorial cretin. You see, Paley was right: the mixture as before.

But that is television. Never mind that there is a litter of comedians between Jerry Lewis and Milton Berle and to survey the litter we need only record Jack Benny, Red Buttons, Sid Caesar,

Imogene Coca, Jimmy Durante, Ed Wynn, Eddie Cantor, Abbott and Costello, Joe E. Brown, Martha Raye, Alan Young, Ben Blue, Phil Silvers, the Ritz Brothers, Pinky Lee (although Red Buttons has recently alleged that the present-day Cary Grant is really Pinky Lee in excellent make-up), Henny Youngman, Wayne & Shuster, Jerry Lester, Doodles Weaver, David King, Allan Sherman, Ransom Sherman, George Gobel, Danny Kaye, Garry Moore—well, the plains are covered with the skins of top bananas, second bananas, in bunches and stalks and warehouseful.

There has been more comedy on television in 20 years than the civilized world has seen since the first cave man took the first pratfall for the tribe. Quantity has supplanted quality and the incredible appetite of television has consumed funny men who might have reigned for 40 or 50 years before the tube started its restless, luminous scanning.

And drama? What of 20 years of television drama? George Schaefer's production of Loring Mandel's play, "Do Not Go Gentle into That Good Night," is the most recent original drama which television viewers have seen. Could it not have been written for Fred Coe's Philco Playhouse? In fact, as I watched it, I had the haunting vision that it had, indeed, been written for that show and Fred somehow couldn't get it on. Everyone has spoken so glowingly of the "Golden Age" of TV drama that Mr. Schaefer and Mr. Mandel took the whole sentimental yearning quite seriously and threw themselves into the task of turning the clock back. It went back and it somehow didn't look so great. Maybe it wasn't so great when it was around. There has been no artist who has ever gone back to beginnings who came up with any reassurance that a return to beginnings was worth the trouble. Thomas Wolfe's book title, "You Can't Go Home Again," sums it up, not only for Southern home cooking, but for television as well.

One trip back to the past has already injured our sentimental memories. A little earlier return to the past broke my heart. I refer to "Your Show of Shows" when Caesar reigned over a court of spectacular second bananas like Carl Reiner, Howard Morris and Imogene Coca in the early nineteen-fifties. Could they be brought back? As one of their manic fans, I put the question to Max Liebman, their producer. How about bringing back "Your

Show of Shows"? Mr. Liebman, a gentle man who has heard the question before, took me to a large storage room in his office in the Carnegie Hall building and showed me racks upon racks of video tapes. "There they all are. The quality of the kinescope is too poor to show today. And even if we could clear the rights and permissions with all those involved, there are sketches, songs, jokes which are too dated."

But the question must have been asked of Caesar, Morris, Reiner and Coca and they must have answered it for themselves, because they did return for a special a season ago. It was funny. It was wonderful and it was somehow all wrong. They looked older, they acted older, and we were older. That was where the magic had gone. Right into our own bones and our own livers and our own lives. Television buries its great moments in an electronic quicklime. Television is not only without conscience, it is without a memory.

The lack of memory might be a blessing. A nostalgic stroll down video lane is apt to produce heartburn and it may be that the pleasantest, and safest, way to return is to leaf through the picture pages of a lap-sized collection called "How Sweet It Was," edited by Arthur Shulman and Roger Youman. It is copyright 1966 and yet begins to have the look of being slightly antique. In television, this fall's shows may be winter memories and spring statistics and fodder for another book about the next 20 years.

The next 20 years? If the human race makes it, television will. What will it be like? If you read current signs, it is beginning to look as though it is all going to be double-feature night, seven evenings a week across the board. The growth of TV movie-viewing in the past 10 years has been enormous and the fairly recent decision of the major studios to sell off their backlogs of films for television exhibition has made the big difference in the quality and freshness of TV's movies. Now that the demand for new or newer movies on television is so great, N.B.C. has an arrangement with Universal to produce features solely for TV ("World Premiere Theater"); A.B.C. has launched an ambitious program in conjunction with its subsidiary, Selmur Productions; C.B.S., that perennial fat cat, which buys in the open market to keep "The Late Show" supplied seven nights a week, has established a new unit under the direction of Gordon Stulberg for the production of feature-length motion pictures which, presumably, will be reserved for its "powerhouse"—"Thursday Night at the Movies."

The reason for so many "nights at the movies" on television shows up in the ratings. The figures always tell the same story: movies are first choice over any regular television fare. There is no power on TV which seems to be able to hold its own against "good" motion pictures. "The Bridge on the River Kwai" (on A.B.C.) reduced the Cartwright Ponderosa to a parking lot, shattered C.B.S.'s ratings, stunned every sampletaker. Lesser pictures have done almost as well—provided they were of recent vintage. Knowledgeable television makers and shakers concede that movies are going to usurp television "prime time" and television networks are moving toward not merely acquiring movies, but the talent and real estate connected with their making.

But before movie times, and on local stations, other versions of Joe Pyne will be snarling at guests and audiences, "Ya creeps. Go back into the woodwork!" If they did go back into the woodwork, television would not be so close to becoming what radio has become. Radio is already in a two-stage affair—listeners are talking back to broadcasters. Well, why shouldn't viewers talk back to telecasters? I have, for some time, been talking back to the television screen and no one thinks it odd of me. C.B.S. or R.C.A. or I.T.&T. or some smock-frocked youngster at M.I.T. or Caltech is going to come up with a cheap home device whereby the viewer can talk back to the TV personalities and television will swallow us right into the tube, which is what it started out to do from the beginning.

The New Sound of Radio

by William H. Honan

RADIO STATION WEVD in New York City is looking for a Chinese disk jockey. Applicants should be acquainted with such personalities as Poon Sow Keng (the hottest rock 'n' roll singer today in Hong Kong), be able to report the time, news and temperature in easy-going Cantonese, and quote Confucius in the original. The resulting program may be of limited appeal—beneath the notice, one might guess, of a mass-media adman worth his double martini—and yet, it is chiefly this sort of specialization, or "fractionalization of the market," as they say in the trade, that accounts for the remarkable sonic boom reverberating from radio these days.

Right now, for example, there are more radios in the United States than people—262,700,000 at the last count. Forty-seven million sets were sold last year alone. Such profusion cannot be attributed merely to teen-agers buying transistor radios with which to annoy their parents—although that is a not inconsiderable factor. But parents are buying radios like hot cakes, too. They get them nowadays built into their tractors, hairdryers, Scotch bottles and even sunglasses. And the knobs on all these instruments are being clicked and twirled with astonishing frequency.

In fact—and this may be enough to make even Marshall Mc-
Luhan gulp with wonder—a recent Trendex survey conducted
for the National Broadcasting Company found that more Americans now listen to radio in the course of an average week than
watch TV. The audience for individual radio programs, of course,
cannot compare with that of the most popular TV shows, but on
a cumulative basis the figures indicate that 90.5 per cent of the
adult population tunes in a radio sometime during the week
as compared with 87 per cent who flick on television. That finding, the Trendex survey supervisor reported, "puts radio right
back in the league with the other major media in terms of total
audience dimensions."

The robustness of radio is also illustrated by the fact that
the giant advertisers, most notably such bellwethers as the soap
and automotive companies which shifted from radio to TV in
the early nineteen-fifties, have once again become substantial radio time buyers. Colgate-Palmolive, for example, which was not
even listed among the top 100 radio spot advertisers as recently
as 1964 was 23rd on the list last year. Ford, General Motors
and Chrysler were first, second and third, respectively, with a
total expenditure last year of $56 million—up 17 per cent over the
previous year and up 56 per cent over that of the year before.

The explanation for this renaissance of a medium which many
condemned to a lingering death as recently as 10 years ago lies,
to a great degree, with that sought-after Chinese disk jockey.
For, once radio broadcasters began to face up to the fact that
television had permanently taken their place as dispenser of general entertainment for the masses, they began experimenting with
new formats and discovered that, collectively, they could capture
their old audience piecemeal by directing strong appeals to specific fractions of the population.

This discovery led to the development of all manner of limited-
appeal programs, and the advancing trend is now doing away
with even these one-hour or half-hour shows, since the stations
themselves are beginning to take on the characteristics of a single, 24-hour program, narrowly addressed to a distinct slice of
the population. Such broadcast parochialism is now revolutioniz-
ing the industry, with several stations almost every month drop-

ping their old-style programing in preference for the new "continuous format."

Competition in a city like New York, where no fewer than 63 different AM and FM stations vie for attention, has naturally pushed specialization to an extreme, and some of the more popular formats appear to have been divided, subdivided and virtually pulled apart with tweezers in order that each station may find a niche (and presumably a distinct audience) it can call its own.

For example, WMCA, WABC, WJRZ, and WOR-FM are all what the casual listener might consider standard rock 'n' roll stations, but connoisseurs are aware that WMCA tries to add a local home-town flavor by using such disk jockeys as Joe O'Brien, who has a Yonkers accent; WABC seeks to impart an all-American tone to the proceedings with disk jockeys like Herb Oscar Anderson, who is from Minnesota and full of corn and good cheer; WJRZ restricts itself exclusively to that close relative of rock 'n' roll known as country-Western music; and WOR-FM lays stress on the subdivision known as folk rock, which may include such controversial ballads (which the other stations would never touch) as Phil Ochs's "I Ain't Marchin' Anymore" and Country Joe and the Fish's prickly L.B.J. put-on, "Super Bird."

Even in lesser cities than New York, however, format specialization has proceeded to a surprising degree. There are as many as 1,500 radio stations across the nation substantially if not exclusively devoted to country-Western music, according to the Country Music Association. And the all-talk or telephone-participation format is not only popular in New York City, where N.B.C.'s Brad Crandall and the insomniac Long John Nebel have large followings, but Philadelphians like to hear themselves gabbing over the telephone with Jack McKinney over WCAU, and nearly everybody in Salina, Kan. (pop. 43,202) listens at one time or another to Mike Cooper on KLSI to catch the latest chatter about the local school merger and to hear Cooper adding his laconic "uh-huh" to a phoned-in beef about how all the rain in June loused up the local wheat crop.

Typical of the trend is a middle-sized city like Peoria, Ill., which now has as many as six radio stations, each with its own distinctive format. WIRL, Peoria's leading outlet, is a "top-40" or predominantly rock 'n' roll station. WXCL, the local N.B.C. affiliate, is devoted to country-Western music, WMBD, the C.B.S. affiliate, is strong on conversation and plays "middle-of-the-road" music (Frank Sinatra, Peggy Lee, Vic Damone). WMBD-FM specializes in "potted-palm" fare (schmaltzy renditions of the Warsaw Concerto, and the themes from "Intermezzo" and "Gone with the Wind").

WIVC-FM has female disk jockeys—or "program hostesses," as they are known in Peoria—and plays "adult" pop, jazz and classical music. Finally, WPEO, the Mutual affiliate, having recently tried and then dropped "top-40" and "middle-of-the-road" formats, became a virtually "all-talk" station in January of this year and then in September raided WXCL's country-Western disk jockey—Cal Shrum, an old Gene Autry sidekick—and is now trying to blend the recorded yodeling of assorted farmhands-turned-vocalists with its decidedly right-leaning cast of talkers, whose ranks include Fulton Lewis 3rd, the Rev. Carl McIntire and the suave pitchmen of H. L. Hunt's "Life Lines."

Such quick shifting from one format to another as practiced by WPEO is possible because the process is remarkably cheap. There is no retooling to be done, and usually disk jockeys who can handle one type of music can handle another as well. Subscriptions to the various record library services required to keep a radio station jangling with the latest tunes of whatever genre it chooses rarely run more than $300 or $400 a year. Furthermore, stations like WPEO—far from spending revenue when shifting to the seemingly expensive all-talk format—actually coin money in doing so. For every Fulton Lewis or Bill Stern whose tapes the station has to pay for, WPEO broadcasts several "Life Lines" or "20th-Century Reformation Hours" which are actually advertisements for which the station is handsomely compensated.

With specialization paying off in radio, a rise might be expected in new small stations throughout the country. Actually few new stations are being formed. As of Aug. 31, there were 4,145 AM and 1,712 FM stations—and these figures have held fairly steady for the last few years. It costs a minimum of $35,000 to start a station in a city the size of Fort Worth, Tex.—and this figure does not include promotion expenses, which are likely to be enormous.

But even that cost is not what stops people from starting new stations. The F.C.C. controls the issuance of new licenses very closely, since the radio band is now almost saturated, and thus even if an entrepreneur had the $35,000 to $100,000 to spend, he would have a tough time convincing the F.C.C. that Fort Worth, say, really needs a new radio station.

So far has format specialization progressed among radio stations throughout the United States today that local affiliates of the national networks have been ignoring network programing in preference for their own locally originated material. In response to this trend, the A.B.C. radio network has recently announced that it plans to split up its piped fare into four separate subnetworks, each of which will cater to stations with distinctly different formats. There will be one subnetwork for stations with an all-talk or music-and-news format, another for "top-40" stations, one for those with more sophisticated FM formats and another for stations still using the old-style eclectic format. A.B.C.'s hope is that its subnetworks will be more congenial to highly specialized stations and will, in addition, make possible more than one A.B.C. affiliate in a given community.

There are, of course, other possible explanations besides specialization for the comeback of radio—among them the portability and convenience of the new transistor sets, the fact that car radios have become virtually standard rather than optional equipment, the development of sophisticated techniques of audience measurement to demonstrate to advertisers the large, new, out-of-home listenership, and so forth. But the basic reason for the boom is that people are listening to the radio again because it is offering them something they want to hear and cannot find elsewhere.

Of New York City's bewildering array of radio stations, three picked more or less at random—WINS, WHOM and WBAI-FM —illustrate the latest types of specialization and to whom those new formats appeal.

In April 1965 WINS, a Westinghouse station, dramatically gave away its rock 'n' roll record library to Fordham University, kissed its disk jockeys good-by, hired 27 radio newsmen and began broadcasting news for 24 hours a day. Skeptics had said that the WINS anchor men would grow hoarse by early afternoon of the first day, and that if no worse disaster overtook the station, the babbling brook of news would simply run dry, and, on the first really slow day, WINS would be begging to get its records back from Fordham.

Neither of these eventualities came to pass. WINS provided enough anchor men so they could spell one another in half-hour shifts. And far from running out of news, a veritable geyser of gab was churned up by the stations 21 "airmen" covering New York City, by the squad of rewrite men who had access to all the major wire services and by correspondents of the Westinghouse communications network who were sending in "voice cuts" from such far-flung places as Madrid and Saigon.

As time went by, the WINS team of broadcasters developed an original and often rather exciting manner of news presentation, in which the process of news gathering is exposed to the listener in an unfolding drama. In a major news break, for example, the presentation begins with a high-pitched BEEP-BEEP-BEEP-BEEP which, according to high Westinghouse policy, may even interrupt a commercial (but never has). The beeping fades and the voice of the anchor man rises over it with: "Late word has just been received at the WINS newsroom that President Johnson and Premier Kosygin will meet tomorrow in the college town of Glassboro, N. J. Stay tuned for further details as they are received in the WINS newsroom."

Whatever was cut into is then resumed, but pretty soon "Jim McGiffert at the editor's desk," who has been madly pawing through a stack of reference books dumped in front of him, whisks the anchor man a "sidebar" about Glassboro—where it is, its population, principal industry, etc. The next morning, Sid Davis tells about the President's helicopter chugging up off the White House lawn; there is a quick switch to Doug Edelson at the Soviet Mission in New York describing the departure of Kosygin's limousine; then reports from Rod MacLeish, Paul Parker and Jim Gordon in Glassboro shouldering their way through the crowds and finally telling of the arrival of the dignitaries the moment they appear.

So impressed by this dramaturgy was Angus McDermid, the B.B.C.'s U.N. correspondent, that he was moved to do a special feature about WINS for the B.B.C., in which he commented enthusiastically: "I found myself waiting for the next thrilling installment. It was better than many a fictional radio series I can think of."

More jaundiced listeners, however, may note that all too often the instant news in these "thrilling installments" winds up having to be retracted or modified. For example, during the emergency session of the United Nations in the wake of the six-day war in the Middle East, WINS reported that a Mohawk Airlines jet bound for Washington, D.C., had crashed near Blossburg, Pa., and that many of the 34 passengers aboard were U.N. delegates. It was a thrilling installment, all right, but it later turned out to be an example of what Elmo Ellis of WSB, Atlanta, a sharp critic of broadcasting, once characterized as "rip-snorting, inaccurate news reports." No U.N. delegates had been on the flight.

WINS spokesmen argue that the Mohawk Airlines story was an unusual case. They add with pride that WINS newsmen are not merely "rip-and-read" announcers who rip off the wire-service stories and blather them uncritically into the microphone, as do the "newsmen" at other stations they say they could name. The WINS newsmen, they say, have had analytical experience—four-fifths of them are former radio or TV station news directors—and normally they "don't jump." They did not jump on the air, for example, as did WQXR, with a rumor circulated by The Associated Press during the Newark rioting to the effect that Stokely Carmichael was leading a caravan of 33 cars into Newark. WINS newsmen were on their toes and knew Carmichael was in London at the time. And it was not a WINS man, they say, whom Newsweek pictured poking his stick microphone into the anguished face of a woman felled by a bullet on a Newark street; that, too, was "a man from another station we could name"—in this case, WMCA.

The all-news format for radio was originated not by WINS but by Gordon M. McLendon, the flamboyant Texas promoter who was also one of the first to use the "top-40" or "rock-around-the-clock" format. McLendon's station XTRA in Tijuana, Mexico, which broadcasts to Southern California, in 1961 became the first to go on an all-news bender, and was followed three years later by another McLendon property, WNUS in Chicago. (Philadelphia, Washington, Denver and St. Louis now have all-news stations, too.)

The original McLendon format, however, is substantially different from that of WINS. McLendon likens XTRA and WNUS to the weather- and time-dialing services of the telephone company, and believes that they will succeed to the degree that they strictly adhere to a "monotonous" recital of the headlines, eschewing all features and commentary. The ultimate disaster for an all-news station, McLendon once remarked, would be for its listeners to tune in expecting to hear the latest bulletins and get instead a book review.

Disagreement is voiced by Charles F. Payne, the stocky, natty-looking general manager who now presides over WINS at its chic, midtown Park Avenue headquarters. Also a Texan and, by coincidence, the manager of two McLendon stations before he joined Westinghouse, Payne explains: "It's true, of course, that we cycle the headlines every 15 minutes, do a time check every 5, weather every 7 and so forth, so when you tune in you're never far away from the bulletins. But in between we have special in-depth reports, a shopping feature, theater reviews, even editorials and sometimes a feature that continues in sections all day long—we call it a 'blitz'—on topics like the poor of New York, the overcrowded air corridors or the coming Broadway season. Furthermore, even the news bulletins are not 'monotonous.' They're changing all the time. Someone once said we're like a newspaper with 48 separate editions every day.

"The key to our format," Payne goes on, "is being informally informative. What we try to avoid is the old H. V. Kaltenborn pompousness. We want to create the image of the working newsman, the guy who's on the scene."

Although the sound of news would seem to have a universal appeal, WINS's most faithful listeners, according to a recent Politz survey, tend to be those New Yorkers with high incomes, college educations and relatively high-status jobs. Most listeners are between the ages of 25 and 64, teen-agers and senior citizens being conspicuously absent. When WINS first shifted to the all-news format, its audience, which had been accustomed to rock 'n' roll, fell off sharply. According to the latest surveys, however, the station has now more than doubled the size of its former audience—a success story which must have been read with interest across town at WCBS, which switched in August to an all-news format, too.

Another increasingly important specialization in contemporary radio is known as ethnic broadcasting, or, less euphemistically, as ghetto radio. There are now, for example, no fewer than three Negro stations broadcasting in New York City. WWRL, by far the most popular of these, anticipates that its annual revenue from advertising will rise above the $2-million mark this year, having practically quadrupled over the last four years.

WEVD, the formerly all-Yiddish station which now broadcasts in 13 different tongues, including Japanese and Norwegian, says that 1966 was "the best year ever" in its 40-year history. And *The Wall Street Journal* recently reported that because Pepsi-Cola was the first soft drink to advertise intensively on the local Spanish stations, Pepsi now outsells Coca-Cola two-to-one among New York's 1.5 million Spanish-speaking residents—a state of affairs that Coca-Cola is now trying to rectify by plugging away over "the Spanish Main," as the three stations between 1280 and 1480 kilocycles are known, with the jingle *"Todo va mejor con Coke"* ("Things go better with Coke").

Typical of the sound and format of ethnic broadcasting is that of WHOM, New York's foremost Spanish station, which is so hot-bloodedly Latin that it has, quite literally, blown its fuse. The program responsible for this occasional boiling over—called *"Debate Musical"* ("Musical Debate")—is the top-rated Spanish disk-jockey show in New York and is hosted by Juan Rodriguez Diaz, a deceptively placid-looking Puerto Rican. On the program, which is broadcast live every weekday afternoon at 4, Diaz spins a couple of Spanish pop records and then urges his listeners to call in and "vote" for whichever one they liked best. He can stimulate as many as a thousand calls on a good afternoon, working himself into a frenzy as the votes mount up and bawling into the microphone in Spanish:

"The vote is even! It's even! We don't want any sleepy-heads here! No, you have to be *awake* to listen to *this* show! Call in! My friends! Call in! Look, if you don't call in right away, I'll fall down and break 14 ribs. I'll smash my head against the wall! If I don't get 400 calls right now, I'll break 44 ribs!"

Suddenly, the lights on all the studio telephones begin to flicker, indicating a shower of incoming calls. When this happens, Diaz puts his hands to his temples, closes his eyes and shrieks with ecstasy: *"Esto es treMENNNDO!"* WHOM's engineers, not one of whom understands Spanish, have learned to watch their volume-units meter with a hawk's eye when El Tremendo, as they call Diaz, gets lathered up and they "ride gain" on him with their volume controls like a destroyer captain in a gale. Nevertheless, on two consecutive days last summer, when Diaz was unloosing his *"Esto es treMENNNDO!"* he overloaded the station's 5,000-watt transmitter and blew out a high-voltage fuse, temporarily putting WHOM off the air.

That is overdoing it, perhaps, but the Latin sound and volatile temperament is all that WHOM has to sell, and the management evidently would rather err with too much than too little. "Language is our most important product," explains Ralph Costantino, WHOM's affable program director, who is himself of Italian extraction but survived the station's changeover in 1957 from Italian to Spanish broadcasting by virtue of his fluent Spanish. The dialect spoken over WHOM, he says, is Caribbean Spanish, interspersed with plenty of *ay benditos* and *Ave Marias!,* which are characteristic of the Puerto Rican and Cuban idiom one hears on East 125th Street.

So important is the sound of the Spanish language to the station's identity, in Costantino's opinion, that he has a rule of long standing that popular music, which constitutes from 65 per cent to 75 per cent of the station's programing, must be vocal rather than instrumental. Moreover, with the current unusual exception of The Monkeys and The Turtles, vocalists who sing in English are strictly *prohibido.* WHOM even snubbed Frank Sinatra's last big hit, "Strangers in the Night," and played instead Andy Russell's Spanish rendition *"Estraños en la Noche,"* which had more tropical zing.

It is not only the disk jockeys and vocalists one hears over WHOM who radiate Latin excitement: newscasters do, too. Last summer, for example, one of WHOM's newsmen broke into a musical program almost hysterically shouting a news bulletin. Fortune Pope, the station's co-owner, who does not speak Spanish, happened to be listening and promptly called in to find out what in blazes was going on. "Has war been declared?" he asked. No, he was told, the news bulletin merely concerned a report that Che Guevara was then rumored to have been seen somewhere in Venezuela.

"Our announcers become emotionally involved in the news when they read it," says Costantino. "It isn't that they aren't professional. It's just the Latin way. You should have heard them reporting the rioting in El Barrio the last week in July. It was . . . well, pretty loud."

Baseball games and soap opera—the latter still a great favorite with Spanish-speaking audiences—round out WHOM's regular fare, and they, too, are as popular as they are tempestuous. One of the most avidly followed "soaps" carried on WHOM is called *"Collar de Lagrimas"* ("Necklace of Tears"), and seems to consist chiefly of organ music and the sound of a woman sobbing, punctuated now and then by gunfire and commercials. (It also has an enormous audience in Cuba, and Fidel Castro will not permit Havana stations to broadcast it while he is making a speech.) The soaps are gradually giving way on WHOM, however, to the jiving sound of the *boogaloo* and *la nueva ola* (rock 'n' roll with a Latin beat), since the younger generation, according to the surveys, is now the dominant group in Spanish Harlem and it would rather twist and wriggle than sniffle and sigh.

So firm is the grip of the ethnic stations on their audiences that a recent Pulse survey shows the Spanish-speaking population, for example, listening to radio for an average of four hours a day, which is almost twice as much time as other Americans devote to the medium. This audience, according to surveys, is profoundly influenced by what it hears, whether commercials, news or comment.

It is particularly regrettable, then, that WHOM has an intellectual content of zero, and offers little that might be considered of genuine public service. (A notable exception among ethnic broadcasters is WLIB, the Harlem Negro station that last year won a Peabody Award—the highest honor in broadcasting—for a telephone-participation program that was believed to have served as a sort of social safety valve by permitting the frank airing of Negro grievances.) The rationale for the low level of programing by WHOM, according to Costantino, is that "most Puerto Ricans who have intellectual capacity are bilingual and thus get their stimulation from English-language sources" (which is a dodge), and that the station did in fact "give free air time to Spanish-speaking deputies of Mayor Lindsay and Cardinal Spellman to appeal for restraint during the summer rioting" (which is true enough, but surely the minimum in terms of social responsibility). A strong case can be made that ethnic radio stations like WHOM, which exploit commercially the linguistic handicap of their listeners, actually serve to perpetuate that handicap, and therefore ought to be charged with providing special counterbalancing educational services.

Another highly specialized area of radio broadcasting is occupied by the 350-odd licensed noncommercial stations in the United States which are affiliated with schools, churches, municipalities and foundations. A good many of these have undergone as much format refinement as any all-news or rock-around-the-clock station on the dial. Perhaps the best known of them in New York is WNYC, the city-owned station.

Other local noncommercial stations specializing in fine music and thoughtful discussions and lectures include Columbia University's WKCR-FM, Fordham University's WFUV-FM, the Riverside Church's WRVR-FM and the Pacifica Foundation's listener-sponsored WBAI-FM, which is the left-leaning "free-speech" station that was put off the air for 52 hours in September when its transmitter was wrecked by vandals. An articulate spokesman for WBAI is Larry Josephson, the hip disk jockey. Josephson, a rather corpulent, bearded, 28-year-old computer-programer by day, has for the last year and a half been conducting a far-out breakfast club for the station, irreverently called "In the Beginning," which is—in marked contrast to the usual fare at that hour —refreshingly grumpy, lusty and alienated.

Noncommercial stations have specialized just as have the commercial broadcasters, Josephson believes, not only because of the pressures of competition, which naturally affect them less, but in response to "the great diversity of life styles today." Back in the thirties, he says, cultural unity gave rise to relatively undiversified styles in the communication media. But today, in an era of cultural splintering, a great many people find themselves "disfranchised by the mass media" and they begin to seek new styles of experience elsewhere.

WBAI is attractive to at least some of these seekers—no one knows how many since its call letters have never appeared in a general audience survey—because it offers, according to Josephson, programs attuned to the new life styles, programs which are, in his words, "no longer sequential, but random, associative and parallel." Josephson cites as an example of such programing the breakfast club he convenes every weekday morning at 7 A.M. or whenever he gets around to arriving at the station (he is frequently late and sometimes never shows at all), and on which he is likely to say anything that pops into his head—it may be something fairly salacious or he may just indulge in a long spate of moaning and groaning.

Josephson points with admiration to his WBAI colleague, Bob Fass, the station's after-midnight disk jockey, who has lately been achieving remarkable effects by playing two records simultaneously—for example, pairing speeches by Timothy Leary and Lyndon B. Johnson about their respective visions; playing the voices of soldiers in a United States Army basic-training course along with a dog-training record, and so forth. Similar effects, Josephson says, were to be found in the dramatization of Christopher Morley's "The Trojan Horse," which juxtaposed cynicism and romanticism, and which the station broadcast, under the direction of Baird Searles, in a four-and-a-half hour spree on Oct. 8 and 9.

WBAI, like its commercial counterparts, Josephson says, has its very own sound. "Some people say it is the sound of boredom," he begins, adding: "To some extent that's true. Some say it's aggression—a kind of postured hipness. That's true, too. Some say it's amateurishness. Some call it humaneness, or love, or naturalness. It's all of that. Naturalness, especially. For example, when we're running behind time, we say so. When we make a mistake, we admit it. We don't try to come up with our radio-broadcast *persona grata* intact. When we read news, we try to read it like human beings. I hate WINS. They read everything in the same excited monotone. It isn't human."

A few weeks ago, Josephson took over WBAI's regular book-review program for half an hour, and what he said as well as the manner in which his material was presented pretty well illustrates the WBAI "sound" he was trying to describe.

To begin with, the program, which was scheduled to follow a commentary by a spokesman for the Socialist Labor party at 7 P.M., did not start until about 7:07. Then the announcer, who introduced the program as "Books to Buy, Borrow or Burn," tripped over a word, and neglected to say who the reviewer was going to be or to give the titles of the books to be discussed. The next voice was that of a newscaster announcing the beginning of World War II on a scratchy old record.

When it was finished, an obviously "live" voice came on the air and explained that the recording was from a broadcast by Edward R. Murrow from London. The live voice went on to say in a very intimate and unradiolike tone that Murrow was "the best broadcaster ever produced by this country." Murrow had also been an intelligent and effective foe of McCarthy, the voice said, but he should not be mistaken for a true liberal because he had condoned the execution of Julius and Ethel Rosenberg.

In any case, the voice continued, Murrow was great because he came through on the human level and he made you stop and think. A collection of Murrow's broadcasts, the voice added, had been published by Alfred A. Knopf Inc., in a book called "In Search of Light," which might well be read along with "Due to Circumstances Beyond Our Control" by Fred Friendly, who, as everybody knows, resigned from C.B.S. after the network refused to permit him to drop a rerun of "I Love Lucy" in order to carry the testimony of George F. Kennan before the Senate Foreign Relations Committee. Taken together, the voice commented, the two books reveal what is good and what is bad about broadcasting in America. "This is Larry Josephson," said the voice, and stopped.

There was a long pause—a *very* long pause—and then an old recording of Murrow's voice came on again, this time saying that he had just been with the first wave of U.S. troops to arrive at a concentration camp in central Germany called Buchenwald. His voice trembled perceptibly as he said: "Now let me tell this in the first person." Murrow then described the terrible scene in short, clipped language, remarking at one point: "Men tried to lift me to their shoulders. They could not. They were too weak." And later: "When I came in, they applauded. It sounded like the handclapping of babies."

After describing several other such scenes, Murrow said fervently: "I *pray you* to believe what I have reported about Buchenwald!" He closed by adding: "If I have offended you by this rather mild account of Buchenwald, I am not sorry."

Then the first voice, that of the WBAI announcer, came on once more to say that "Books To Buy, Borrow or Burn" was over, and, tripping over a word again, he introduced the next program, which was in French.

Will the specialized formats such as those represented by WINS, WHOM and WBAI continue to proliferate? Most radio spokesmen say yes. In fact Timebuyer, the trade magazine, recently declared that "everyone from career girls to bird watchers to traveling salesmen could well be the special province of a particular station." Others have suggested that an important area of specialization in the future will be politics—with radio stations not only backing candidates, as did WMCA in 1960 (endorsing John F. Kennedy for President), but identifying themselves as, for example, "the National Review of the air."

These notions may not be as far-fetched as they sound, what with stations like WNCN-FM in New York broadcasting programs of special interest to physicians, to which the general public is discouraged from listening, and like KADS in Los Angeles—another Gordon McLendon creation—which has become the first radio station in the country devoted exclusively to classified advertising.

Just as radio is now going through a fractionalization previously experienced by the printed media, so television will follow, industry spokesmen agree, especially once the U.H.F. stations begin to catch on. The interesting upshot of all this specialization may then be that the mass media, only recently condemned as purveyors of a bland, regularized sameness, may be counted in the near future as a vigorous force working for cultural diversity.

The level or quality of that diversity, of course, is another question, and that remains to be seen—perhaps to be overseen.

Part 3

FILM AND STAGE

> *There aren't twelve hundred people in the world who understand pictures. The others pretend and don't care.*
> —Rudyard Kipling

> *The wild vicissitudes of taste.*
> —Samuel Johnson

SINCE 1945 the cinema has changed perhaps more than any other mass medium, for reasons discussed at some length in our Introduction. One major aspect of change can be discerned in the screen career of Elizabeth Taylor, the shy, innocent adolescent of *National Velvet* who became the neurotic, sexually obsessed harridan of *Who's Afraid of Virginia Woolf?,* and ascended a staircase in the nude in John Huston's *Reflections in a Golden Eye.*

So prevalent did simulations of sexual intercourse become in the movies of the 1960's that Hollywood finally had to adopt a classification system (G, M, R, X) to protect the "innocent" youngsters. Nudity and sexual openness became part of the Broadway scene in the same period, though, of course, the theater had previously used dialogue that would never have passed the Motion Picture Code of the forties or even the fifties. Revues such as *Hair* or *Oh, Calcutta!* raised a few eyebrows even on jaded, blasé Times

Square, but the public made the producers of these musicals quite rich. The underground films of Andy Warhol looked at the seamier side of sex so explicitly that one wondered where the exploiters of the film experience would turn next for sensationalism. Will Rogers may have given us the answer when he said, "Some say, what is the salvation of the Movies? I say, run 'em backwards. It can't hurt 'em and it's worth a trial."

Until the 1950's the motion picture in America was regarded essentially as a form of mass entertainment that seldom if ever challenged the viewer, aesthetically or intellectually. This has changed in the past twenty years, especially since film has become *the* medium of the young audience. Among this young audience (age seventeen to thirty) there appears today to be more interest in motion pictures as an art form than in the theater. Carl Foreman, himself a noted film writer (*High Noon, Champion*) and producer-director of the war-adventure film *par excellence, The Guns of Navarone,* is naturally a strong advocate of cinema as an art form. In the first two essays in this section, Foreman debates with Sir Tyrone Guthrie on the relative merits of film versus the theater.

Foreman and Guthrie are articulate and knowledgeable men, and their arguments are forcefully presented. Foreman makes a point that deserves to be underlined. He commends the vitality of the European and Far Eastern film centers, not only because of the intrinsic worth of their best films, but because such competition for the interest of the discerning, new young audience "serves as an inspiration to our own film makers." Sir Tyrone does not deny the attractiveness of movies as a mass art form, but he is less certain that film can achieve true rapport with an audience. As to whether the best acting is to be found on the screen or on the stage, here the two debaters disagree sharply.

Richard Schickel, one of the most perceptive American film critics, explains why the movies have moved in their present direction. Fifty per cent of the movie audience is under twenty-four, and 75 per cent under forty, and those who attend movies regularly (i.e., once a month or more) tend to be college students or graduates. The simplistic homilies of a *Quo Vadis* or *The Robe,* which might have sufficed for the 1950's, when Robert Taylor or

Victor Mature was surrounded by eight thousand extras, no longer works.

Although the dating crowd constitutes the largest segment of the audience for today's movies, it would be an error to disregard the forty to fifty million older people who have been going to films since Joan Crawford's earliest movies and who will always remember Gable's Rhett Butler with a nostalgic smile. True, a film like *The Graduate* quickly became a symbol of our times for the young audience, and had grossed nearly $75 million by the end of 1969. But another film of the mid-sixties, as old-fashioned and wholesome as Grandma's apple pie, has now broken all previous box-office records and may soon exceed $100 million. Joan Barthel analyzes the appeal of this musical and in so doing provides us with a valuable case study of mass-audience taste. By interviewing Richard Zanuck, Julie Andrews, Robert Wise, and others who were involved in this film, Miss Barthell provides an excellent view of the "old" Hollywood, rapidly diminishing but without a peer when it did its thing well as in this spectacularly successful movie.

In the final article of this section, the eminent film critic of the London *Observer*, C. A. LeJeune, discusses Shakespeare's adaptation to film. Primarily, LeJeune discusses Sir Laurence Olivier's productions of *Henry V* and *Hamlet*, probably the two most successful film versions of the Bard's works. Shakespeare has challenged film-makers throughout the medium's history, and most of the time nobody has won. One recalls Douglas Fairbanks and Mary Pickford in *Taming of the Shrew*, and a more recent Zeffirelli production with Richard Burton and Elizabeth Taylor. Norma Shearer and Leslie Howard were *Romeo and Juliet* in the thirties, and again Zeffirelli has given us a recent version. Hollywood's attempts, even with Max Reinhardt's *Midsummer Night's Dream*, or Marlon Brando as Mark Antony in *Julius Caesar*, have seldom caught the spirit of Shakespeare's plays, and LeJeune explains why.

Will the cinema become the most "fragmented" of the mass media during the next decade? The days when kids went to Saturday afternoon matinees for a dime, and 50 cents bought a seat for pictures like *Sergeant York* are long past. If cinema-goers are going to pay $2.50 to see a film in any large city's downtown theaters, the product has to do something more than merely entertain. Television can fill a couple of hours at much less cost: no transportation into the city, no baby-sitter fees—but no challenge for the audience most of the time, either.

For the Movies

by Carl Foreman

I AM WRITING this article in a New York hotel, en route to my home in London, and if I finish in time, I will have this evening to myself. I should like to go to the theatre, and I have already checked the entertainment section of this morning's Times in anticipation. However, on and off Broadway, I find nothing of more than routine interest, except for "A Man for All Seasons," "Ross," "A Passage to India," and "The Aspern Papers," all of which I have already seen in London and have no desire to see again.

On the other hand, the film section tells me that I can see Antonioni's "The Night," Fellini's "La Dolce Vita," Resnais' "Last Year at Marienbad," Clement's "Purple Noon," and Vadim's "Les Liaisons Dangereuses," all of which I should dearly love to see again, plus literally a dozen more first-class French, Italian, Japanese, Swedish and Russian films, an equal number of excellent American films and, as a bonus, a wonderful double-bill revival of "Night Must Fall" and the Marx Brothers in "The Big Store." So I'm going to the movies tonight. Entertainment? The world is my oyster. I have only one problem: there are so many I can see, and I have to make a choice.

In other words, if I want an exciting evening in the theatre these days, my best buy is a good movie, and there are a lot of them. For the fact is that there are many more good movies nowadays than there are good plays; the fact is that the movies have grown more in the last fifty years than the theatre has in the last five hundred; the fact is that the so-called living theatre remains a limited and primitive form of entertainment that has not kept pace with its audience; the fact is that if the function of art is to hold a mirror up to life, the screen is far more capable of performing that function today than the stage.

I can hear the outrage of the culture snobs, the people who react to the word "Hollywood" as mindlessly as less polished Philistines react to the sound of "Brooklyn." What? Canned theatre better than living theatre? Never! And already we are speaking in the language of cliché.

Well, I know that I am attacking the great sacred cow of our times but, nevertheless, let me tell you as simply and honestly as I can why I feel that the movies (and I mean theatrical movies, not television) are more rewarding and fulfilling today than plays.

(1) The movies can take us anywhere in time or space, in terms of either fantasy or realism, and make us believe it. Thanks to the camera, here is a magic carpet that really flies. The stage, on the other hand—once it moves out of an interior set—is pathetically earthbound. And, of course, when it comes to production design or scenic effects, there is no comparison. The effort of will and imagination needed to pretend that stage settings are more than canvas and papier-mâché necessary a millennium ago, should not be required of the audiences of today. To make a virtue of the physical limitations of the stage is as silly as to say that good coffee tastes even better in a paper cup.

(2) The level of content in the movies, at home (despite censorship and pressure groups) and overseas, is constantly rising, and richer and more serious themes are being explored. In contrast, if one accepts that dirty words do not necessarily make for adult entertainment, then one must admit that the Broadway seasons of the last five years have not been particularly inspiring or edifying to the adult mind. Why has this come about? Because the insane economics of the theatre makes it even more ruthlessly commercial-minded than Hollywood ever was supposed to be. In New York, experimental or, if you like, *nouvelle vague* theatre can be found only off-Broadway where, unfortunately, the level

of both production and acting is, let's face it, wretchedly low.

(3) The general standard of acting in the movies is infinitely better than that provided by the stage. Why? Because a movie serves its audiences the best acting an actor is capable of, meticulously and painstakingly selected by the director. And that best performance captured on film is preserved forever.

Theatregoing, however, is a lottery. The more successful a play is and the longer it runs, the more the likelihood of lazy, slip-shod performance, dulled by familiarity and monotony. There is, and always has been, a great deal of nonsense talked about acting in the "flesh," but flesh is notoriously weak, and fortunate is the playgoer who attends on a night when the star is not tired, or hasn't a headache, or hasn't had a quarrel at home, or too many Martinis at lunch, or isn't just bored with the whole thing.

True, the theatre may be more fun for the actor, and particularly for the actor who needs a large audience, but surely the satisfaction of the audience, not the actor, is what we are discussing here.

So, how many theatrical companies are consistently up to the mark throughout a run? How many directors stay with a play throughout a run to keep its level high? And why should an audience have to gamble on what it is going to get for its money? And to make matters worse, most so-called "national" companies are a disgrace, carelessly and cynically thrown together.

Incidentally, when was the last time you were so moved in the theatre that you wept, openly and unashamedly?

(4) Practically any seat in a movie theatre is a good seat; I know that the moviemaker will have gone to every possible length to make sure that, no matter where I sit, I will see and hear and be given the chance to receive and react to everything the film has to offer. Visually and acoustically, I am treated with respect.

Moreover, the wonderful fluidity of the camera and the miracle of editing transport me into the center of the action. I see the faces, the very eyes of the players, and I become one with them. I hear the slightest whisper, the faintest sigh. Music stimulates and enhances my emotions and my thoughts, allowing me a full and uninhibited appreciation of the events taking place before my eyes.

In the theatre, however, the price I pay for my seat must determine both my empathy with the players and the amount of pleasure I derive from the performance. But if I am too close, I can see the make-up, and the illusion is destroyed by the painted faces. And if I am too far away, I cannot, usually, hear what is going on way down there, a city block away. And yet there are so many, many scenes that cannot, and should not, be played loudly enough to be heard in the balcony.

(5) The movies are the great mass art of our times, the people's art, the international theatre of this century, and theatre that knows no boundaries. When we go to the movies, we can see the works of the great foreign film-makers of our time exactly as they created them, not domestic imitations of the original vintage wines.

What is more, the continuing vitality of the European and Far Eastern film communities not only indicates an increasing flow of exciting and stimulating films in the future, but serves as a challenge and inspiration to our own film-makers. And the majority of the overseas film-makers are dedicated to the exploration of the problems and issues of our times. Most foreign playwrights, on the other hand, seem, like our own, to be trimming their sails to conform with the prevailing commercial winds.

(6) In this country, a new generation of film-makers whose first and only love is the movies, a generation steeped and schooled in the grammar of films, is taking command. The old factory system of production is breaking up. The writer is moving into the pivotal position he has long been denied and, as director or producer, he is more and more dominating the creative process. And the independent producer is bringing a new sweep and daring to bear on the Hollywood scene.

(7) The movies, being basically a visual art form, give the audience more work to do, and consequently more scope for the imagination. The theatre, since it must rely almost solely on dialogue, subjects the audience to a constant and unnatural flow of words, words, words. If people talked as much in real life as they do on the stage, we would all go out of our minds.

(8) The theatre is far too expensive. One can take an entire (reasonably sized) family to the movies for the price of one

Broadway theatre ticket, and at the same time be treated with considerably more courtesy and consideration. The cost of theatre-going is high because of the ridiculous economics of the stage business, and because of the get-rich-quick philosophy of the theatre industry. But why should the audience be forced to pay ransom to a business that does not know how to manage itself?

(9) The theatre is so horribly old-fashioned, so rigid. Why must we be forced out of our seats twice during the course of the evening? And those cumbersome scene changes, breaking the mood. All those antiquated conventions, indicating only a hardening of the arteries.

(10) Lastly, what of our children? At least the movies make an attempt to provide for children, and there are generally enough films suitable for children to keep them occupied and happy on weekends throughout the year. But the stage, with its high admission prices, has no concern for youthful audiences.

For all these, and other, reasons movie-going is more satisfactory than play-going today, and it will continue to be so. Time does not reverse itself, and the machines cannot be broken. And a film like "Last Year at Marienbad" shows us that the full potential of the cinema as an art form has yet to be explored, but the explorers are already on the quayside, and there are more and more of them every day.

I do not, of course, say that there are not good, indeed excellent, plays being written today. I say that the writers of these good plays would be better served by the movies. I do not say that the so-called living theatre is dead. I say that it is both senile and corrupt. I do not say that it has nothing to offer. I say that its great days are gone forever. I do not say that it should be treated with contempt. I say that it should be viewed from a proper perspective, as it really is and not as it once was. I do not say that it should disappear from our cultural life. I say I should like to see it at least make an attempt to keep up with the twentieth century.

And I should like to see it preserved, if for no other reasons than to provide training for young actors and directors and writers, and to keep alive the works of the great playwrights of the past. In other words, despite its manifest limitations, I should still like to see it live up to its responsibilities as an art form, however primitive. However, it will not do so until and unless its practitioners and entrepreneurs treat the audience with the respect it deserves.

And that is why, together with millions of other lovers of the drama throughout the world, I will be going to the movies tonight.

For the Theatre

by Tyrone Guthrie

I HOPE TO establish that live drama has certain superiorities over its canned rivals, movie and television drama, so important that they outweigh various admitted inferiorities and will ensure its survival, not as the most popular form of dramatic expression—it has ceased to be that for at least forty years—but as the most significant.

I need hardly enlarge upon the commercial advantages of canned drama. A television play can command in a single performance an audience that would fill the theatre eight times a week for ten years. This means that enormously more money is available, not only for the production of canned drama but for its advertisement. By huge outlays for promotion, a demand can be created for a product which would otherwise be of negligible interest, even commercially.

But larger budgets are not the only advantage of canned drama. There are also certain important technical advantages. To me, the most important of these is the ability of camera and, to a much lesser extent, microphone to change their focus. At one moment, we can command an immense panorama—a triumph, say, in Imperial Rome. Then—cut—and, in literally the twinkling of an eye, we come into closeup, see the expression on a single face, hear a whispered message passed from one spy to another, watch a hand close surreptitiously upon a bribe.

From the *New York Times Magazine,* April 29, 1962, copyright © 1962 by The New York Times Company.

The canned drama will always tend to outdo the live in realistic plays, partly because of this flexibility; partly because the background can be so much more "real"—if the scene is supposed to be Mount Everest, you can take a camera there and photograph the actors scrambling about the real thing; and partly—this is the subtlest advantage of all—because there need be no discrepancy between a real actor and his supposedly real background. In a realistic play on the stage, the real, live actors perform in front of a background which pretends to be real, but is, instead, a highly artificial contrivance. The movies in this respect are consistent: the background and the characters alike are photographs of the real thing.

But there, precisely, is the rub.

They are only photographs; and, as Puck says, "the best in this kind are but shadows."

Mind you, I do not offer the argument that a live actor must be, without qualification, better than the shadow of an actor on a screen. I do believe that, other things being equal, a real live creature, breathing and feeling and thinking his part right then and there before you, is apt to be more vivid than a photograph reproducing, perhaps for the thousandth time, movements made, maybe, years before and on another continent. But then other things hardly ever are equal.

The casts of canned entertainments are, on the average, more expensive than any the stage can muster. This does not mean that they are invariably better. But cost does bear some relation to quality and I confess that I would rather see the shadow of a good actor than the substance of a bad one.

Further, live acting is only vivid for those within easy distance for seeing and hearing. This in a large theatre applies only to a minority of those present. When there was no better alternative, the public was prepared to buy seats where the best that could be expected was a dim and distant relation with the stage. But as soon as it was found that in the movies everyone could see and hear fully, then very naturally the theatres began to feel a terrible drought.

Nevertheless, while in the movies one can see and hear fully, what one sees and hears is inevitably greatly distorted. Even the best soundtracks signally lack the nuance and variety of which the human voice is capable, when they have been enlarged to the degree needful to make them audible all over a large house. And even in television, where the sound always seems to me far more satisfactory than the picture, there is, for instance, scarcely any difference in volume between the enormously magnified mutter, in which closeups are acted, and the loudest roars and screams. Also, while it is pleasant to see clearly, don't you agree that, in the movies, especially since wide screens came in, we tend to get too much of an eyeful?

I was at a spectacular movie recently with masses of people de-Milleing about in gigantic sets. It was distinctly impressive, but only administratively and financially. Dramatically, these block-busting, supercolossal scenes were frightfully tedious. And then— SNAP—the wide screen was filled with nothing but the jumbo-sized features of a handsome young man, each of whose splendid, regular, white teeth was larger than a postcard. And when, like two gargantuan meat curtains, the lips parted and revealed dozens more postcards . . . well, it was only the frank, boyish grin of a peach-fed California Ham, but I had to be led away, sweating and trembling, to be revived by a draught of strong waters and by resolutely thinking beautiful thoughts about children and flowers—very small flowers.

The fact, however, remains that it is better to see, even distorted, overwhelmingly large visions and to hear clearly the tiny, simplified voices of the loudspeaker than to suffer the frustration of neither seeing nor hearing enough. Indeed, the theatre will not survive unless the fact is faced—and that right soon— that live acting is not indefinitely expansible. It is my belief that anything subtle or intimate cannot be projected much beyond fifteen rows.

Theatre management, however, is still conducted on the assumption that a play must be a "success"; and, since success can only be objectively measured by numbers of tickets sold, quality gets confounded with quantity, value with popularity.

The confusion is the greater because, owing to the insane pressure of competition on Broadway, currently the only stronghold of professional live theatre on the American continent, everything needed for a production—from the rent of a theatre to the wages of sceneshifters—has become exorbitantly expensive. This compels managers to pursue the sort of success which will keep them solvent.

Confusion is worse confounded because, just now and again, about once in ten or twelve times, the golden goose lays a stunning 18-carat gold egg, like "My Fair Lady," and the backers make such mouth-watering profits that the field of theatrical finance becomes thronged with greedy and ignorant speculators. I reckon that the money lost by speculators every season on Broadway—and lost for the most part in backing the most ephemeral trash—would exceed tenfold the endowment of a sumptuous national theatre.

It is not on this account implied that theatrical speculation ought to be forbidden, or that only government-endowed and government approved theatres should be permitted. Far from it. I merely suggest that our theatre is still operating in a financial and administrative framework based on its being the principal, indeed the only, form of theatrical entertainment; as if, in short, its business were to supply the mass market.

The mass market is being taken care of by the movies and television, which are administratively and financially set up for that very purpose—and no other. The theatre must turn its attention to a smaller and therefore less materially rewarding market. But it is perhaps more truly rewarding to try to please a less massive, but possibly more important, public which has some considered standards of value, which will not therefore be bamboozled by the childish ballyhoo of the mass salesmen, and which will regard its entertainment as being something affecting its physical and spiritual welfare at least as much as, and in just the same way as, its food and drink and the company it keeps.

Movies and television frankly, and even proudly, proclaim themselves to be not arts but industries. Their aim is to create a mass market, and to sell their products in the most profitable way. This, I suggest, leaves not only room but need for a theatre which consciously aims at a less numerous, but ultimately more influential, public of more than average intelligence and sensibility.

Further, because the film or television play has to be regarded principally as an investment, people who have money at stake, but no taste at all, feel entitled to tell an author what he may, and especially what he may not, say, and how and why. It would not be true to say that the live theatre is entirely free of such interference. In the production of big musicals especially, because of the size of the investment and because the aim of the operation is nearly always commercial, there has to be a good deal of pandering to the wishes of people whose only claim to attention is their dough.

But the theatre need not so operate. It is possible to operate on a budget which enables the directors to be chosen because their artistic judgment is thought to be sound rather than because they are shrewd money-men. Such a theatre might operate at a loss. No one expects research laboratories, museums, hospitals, churches, universities, art galleries or symphony orchestras to be commercially profitable. The idea that a theatre should be so is simply a hangover from a period when the theatre was the sole provider of dramatic fare.

The point is that a well-run theatre can still, though not in New York, present a first-class performance of a first-class program, not necessarily at a profit, but at a loss so moderate that a few hundred backers could make up the deficit without any pain. This is because the budget, even without any skimping, is, compared to the budgets of movies or TV, chicken feed.

Third, the role of the audience at a canned drama is a passive one. Its reaction cannot affect the product. In the live theatre, on the other hand, the audience's role is creative. Every audience evokes from the actors the performance which it deserves. Acting is more, much more, than a mere recapitulation of a planned routine. Within the framework of a precisely executed routine, a good actor "feels" his audience.

Like a good rider in charge of a horse, he knows when to leave matters in the spectators' hands, when gently to encourage them, when their attention and energy have to be commanded, even against their will, even with whip and spur. And he knows, as a good horseman should, that an audience wants above all else to surrender itself with trust and affection to the guidance of a skillful and confident master.

I think it is true that the value we place upon an object is proportionate to our association with it. We value the cheap little watch, which Father gave us on our twelfth birthday, more highly than the grand, gold repeater bequeathed by unloved Uncle Silas; we value the nasturtiums we ourselves grew on the back porch more highly than the splendiferous exotics which "they" grew in the Botanical Gardens. It is the same with experience. We value a performance to which we ourselves have contributed blood, sweat and tears more highly than a possibly more expert and elaborate performance, which owes nothing whatever to our participation, at which our "assistance" was perforce and solely passive.

I have admitted that in realistic plays the canned drama is at an advantage. But there are other, and perhaps more important, kinds of plays. The theatre has an advantage in that it commands the repertory of dramatic classics. A classic is so because leaders of opinion agree for several generations that it has exceptional merit.

Classics of the theatre are, of course, constantly "adapted" for screen and television. But such adaptations can hardly fail to be damaging reductions of the originals. It is scarcely reasonable to suppose that the work of adapting Shakespeare, Molière or Ibsen will be done by persons of comparable genius, or in a fine frenzy of creative energy. It will be done by dispirited hacks to pay their bills.

Also, it is a fact that few, if any, great classic works are realistic in a way that movies and TV can cope with; they tend to be concerned with large thoughts and feelings expressed with eloquence by beings of greater than average stature.

Now camera and microphone are ill-suited to reproduce large eloquence. They are better suited by a kind of acting so small that it doesn't seem to be acting at all. It is true that certain actors can, even without the aid of eloquence, project on the screen an importance which is commensurate with classic stature. Jannings did so; Charles Laughton and Lillian Gish have done so many times; Pauline Frederick, for all that she appeared in meretricious trash, had the dignity and power of a tragedienne.

But on the screen these people have to make their effects with limited means, on a miniature scale. They cannot pull out all the stops and stun an audience, as great acting should, battering it like a typhoon.

Likewise, the writers of canned drama start with an almost insuperable handicap in that they must eschew the big speech, the *"scéne à faire,"* the great theatrical effects, corny when inefficiently attempted but which, in the hands of a master, make drama uniquely thrilling and memorable.

Finally, movies and television will continue to be forced to change their dramatic techniques to keep abreast of technological developments. Just as the makers of silent movies were, after about thirty years, beginning to get some mastery over the job, along came talkies and revolutionized the whole business. Long before the technical and artistic problems of talking pictures had been solved, color photography added a whole new complication. Now it is wide screen. Soon it will be stereoscopy.

In television, the technological changes are even more bewilderingly rapid. And—this is the point—while such changes doubtless make for fuller and more realistic reproduction of factual images, the goal is achieved by ever-increasing technical complexity and expense. That means that the media are being dominated more and more by engineers and financiers, taken more and more out of the hands of artists.

The theatre, on the other hand, tends, possibly in reaction, to get more simple in technique. For example, simplified, composite sets are more and more used, where formerly a series of pseudo-realistic pictures would have been demanded, with desperate and costly devices to hasten the cumbersome changes from one to another.

All this encourages, maybe even compels, an extravagance in the canned media and imposes an economy on the live theatre, which I regard as importantly in favor of the latter. The discipline of strict artistic economy in story-telling is valuable to authors. A like economy in production is valuable to directors. It forces them and it forces their audience to use the one essential tool of the theatrical trade—imagination.

To sum up: canned drama has commercial and technical advantages, but I have never seen a talking picture or TV play which succeeded in rising above the rank of journalism—sometimes very witty, wise or provocative journalism, but not important enough to stand a chance of impressing a discriminating taste once it has ceased to be topical.

This is not just because the administrative and financial structures of the canning "industry" are so inimical to creative work of a high order. It is because of limitations inherent in camera and microphone. They are marvelous mechanisms for reproducing facts—visual and aural facts. It is when drama leaves matters of fact and concerns itself with ideas and personages which transcend the facts of everyday experience that photograph and soundtrack convey only a feeble, just because matter-of-fact, impression.

But it is with just such ideas and personages that classic drama is predominantly concerned. They are the concern, too, of such modern dramatists as may eventually attain a classic status.

Eventually, the creative person who has something important to say will find that both the administrative and technical limitations of the canned drama stand between him and his expression. The need to express himself, to what he believes to be the best of his ability, will prove to be more important than the wealth and the kind of celebrity which canned drama can offer and which are its sole, though extremely attractive, lure to the artist.

If you doubt this, why did Paddy Chayefsky quit the worlds of cinema and television at the very moment when he had reached the top of the heap? Are not the best movie scripts of Tennessee Williams, Arthur Miller or Lillian Hellman painfully inferior to the best of their work for the stage? Have Arthur Penn and a dozen other of the best directorial talents, here and in Britain, nurtured in TV, forsaken their good, kind nurse for that tricky, painted, ill-provided whore, the stage?

Talking of Paddy Chayefsky, two customers recently stormed out of a performance of "Gideon" purple with rage. "Why must they?" one said to the other. "Will you *please* tell me, why?"

Suspecting that he was referring to the performance which they had just left, and feeling that the man's question was addressed to the cosmos as well as to his companion, I decided to eavesdrop. "Gideon, for God's sake!" he shouted. "And GOD, for God's sake! Who wants them? Why can't they write about ordinary Americans?"

If you want dramatic journalism, and on the whole lively, capable journalism, about ordinary Americans, ordinary Russians, ordinary Chinese doing ordinary things in an ordinary way, then it's telly and the movies for you. But, if you want something larger, louder, wilder, more high-colored and—yes—nobler than ordinary life, I can give you her address. She's tricky, ill-provided and she's been at it for more than two thousand years. But go up and see her sometime. There's life in the old girl yet.

The Movies Are Now High Art

by Richard Schickel

CULTURAL CLICHÉ: "Movies are the central art of our time." Or the most relevant of the arts. Or the one that most efficiently reveals ourselves to ourselves. Or, more simply, the one we like best.

All rise . . .

Be seated.

This Sunday's sermon attempts to analyze this particular tidbit of the conventional wisdom, and it begins, as all good sermons should, with a *mea culpa*. Like everyone who makes his living around movies, I have indulged in this particular form of ego-centricity; we all like to feel that we're operating at the red-hot center of things. Indeed, together with the New Leader's John Simon, I recently edited a little symposium in which a dozen film critics addressed themselves to the question of film's centrality to modern experience and, not surprisingly, the majority of us more or less unquestioningly agreed that film was The Thing. To be sure, Newsweek's Joseph Morgenstern suggested that it would probably continue to take second place to "the mother art of weaponry." And the redoubtable Andrew Sarris of The Village Voice raised some good caveats, pointing out the pot scene was better reflected in pop music than in pop movies, that a cinematic equivalent of "Pale Fire" is an impossibility, that TV has taken over many of the social functions the movies used to perform. But most of us went along with the proposition, and it is probably right that we did. It would be a poor lot of critics who believed the art with which they perforce live is an insignificant or meaningless thing. Only the masochist—or a Dwight Mac-Donald—engages himself critically and regularly with an art for which he has no fundamental affection or at least respect.

Still, we are obviously prejudiced witnesses, and I am beginning to wonder if this prejudice—necessary to us if we are to maintain our sanity as we trudge from one screening room to another in midtown Manhattan—is necessary or sensible or desirable for the audience. I am beginning to think that the movies now bear a heavier weight of cultural ambition—and anxiety—than they were intended to bear. The very notion that they are as important to us as the centrality doctrine implies raises our expectations as we approach each film, to heights unprecedented even a decade ago, which means that the letdown, when the film fails to live up to those expectations—as inevitably most will—is all the greater.

Why, one wonders, have movies—humble, once-despised movies—become so important to us? The beginning of the answer lies, I think, in carefully defining that little word, "us." Who are we, those of us who care so much about the movies? Well, a recent survey taken at the behest of the Motion Picture Association of America discovered that some 50 per cent of the movie audience is under 24 and that 75 per cent of it is under 40. The moguls also discovered that the regulars, the people who go to the movies once a month or more, tend to be college students and college graduates. And it is reasonable to guess that, had they pressed their inquiry a little further, they would have found that among high school kids it is the ones who plan to go on to college who most regularly flick out.

Now, of course, from the vantage point of a writer for this magazine, or one of its readers, that means that everybody who is anybody is going to the movies—our friends, our co-workers, our kids. But really it only seems that way. The fact is that for the majority of Americans movie-going is not even a peripheral, let alone a central, concern. Back before that great watershed date in our cultural history, 1948 (when television networking began), that was probably not the case. In that year some 3.4 billion admissions to the movies were sold. Since 1963 the number of tickets sold annually has stabilized around 1.1 billion—and this in a period of population growth. The industry's prosperity, thanks to increased ticket prices and the sale and production of films for TV, is now booming, but the fact is that it sells only 21 million tickets a week, meaning that all the movies on view in such a period attract an audience no greater than that of the weekly episode of a television show that is close to the peril point in the ratings.

So it turns out that Mr. Nixon's army of silent citizens—the factory worker and the farmer, the aged and the middle-aged, the people whose incomes range from poor to middle-middle class—besides grousing about taxes, worrying about law and order and flirting with the Wallace fantasy complete their misery by generally shunning such solace as the movies might provide them. Typically, however, John Q. Silent takes a dim view of what he hears is going on these days down at the old Bijou, which a few years ago was renamed The Art—about the time they ripped out the popcorn counter and replaced it with an espresso bar. Sex and Violence, sex and violence, that is what is going on down there. And they call it culture.

O.K. Movies aren't movies any more. They are the playthings of The New Class, those who are custodians (or, perhaps, prisoners) of the technostructure. This is, I think, no small point, for it means there has been a fundamental reordering of film's place and function in our society. In the beginning, in the days of the nickelodeon, movies—because of their brevity, their cheapness and their silence—were truly an art of the masses and, as experience if not art, truly central to the lives of many people. They imposed no language barrier, no intellectual hurdles not easily surmountable by the illiterate (or the merely uncultivated), whether he was child, immigrant or rube. Even the addition of sound did not fundamentally change that basic relationship between film and audience.

As we have seen, it required television—free, damnably convenient, even less challenging than the typical pre-1948 film—to break up the longstanding love affair between the movie medium and its traditional audience. To put it simply, the new medium freed the older one from its thrall to the 12- or 13-year-old mentality for which, in the past, the moguls cheerfully admitted they aimed. Though it seems, on the face of it, preposterous to regard any form of art or entertainment that attracts over a billion customers a year as anything less than a mass medium, that is precisely what movies have become: Something Less than a Mass Medium. Indeed, it seems to me that everything that is not television is, given that medium's potency, Something Less than a Mass Medium today.

What, then, are the movies? Is there some positive definition of them? I think they are best defined in terms of a process rather than in a single word or phrase. Film is a form that is now about halfway toward creating a conscious definition of itself as an art. It has yet to sever completely its ties to its folkish past. It has yet to fasten firmly to its future, which is, alas, as a high art, a thing to be savored more or less exclusively by what will pass as an élite—a new class—in the quite radically different society we are, willy-nilly and without malice aforethought, building in this country.

Now, two quick explanations must be appended to the foregoing. First, there is nothing unique about the development of movies in the direction I have outlined. All the arts—poetry, prose fiction, the graphic arts, music, the dance—had popular roots and developed, finally, into élite affairs over fairly long historical spans. The only difference between them and the movies is that the latter are an industrial art born in an age of rapidly accelerating industrial change, which means that they are going to complete this evolution much more quickly than the other arts did. It has taken them only a little more than a half-century to reach the mid-point in this development; it should take them no more than another 25 years to complete it.

Second, the élite to which films will soon be more or less exclusively directed will, obviously, be much larger, much less homogeneous, than any previous cultural élite the world has ever known. It will be an élite less sure of itself, less intensely educated, more panicky about its status than any we have ever known. But an élite it will be, for as journalist William A. Mc-

Whirter has put it, "The world is not so much divided between classes, races and religions as it is between those who know and those who don't; between Them and Us."

That little word again. For "us" the movies are, comparatively speaking, an easy art to appreciate. Even the very greatest films require only a couple of hours to consume, to get yourself in a position where you can claim to have "seen" them. The great novels, in contrast, demand far greater commitments of time in order merely to claim that one has "read" them. They also demand, as do the other traditional arts, a heavy investment in effortful study, not only of the texts themselves but of the vast body of critical literature that surrounds them. Filmic literacy is much more easily and pleasurably acquired; indeed, a fairly good grasp of film techniques is to be obtained more easily than is a good technical understanding of music, dance or even painting. In short, movies are an almost ideal medium for half-baked intellectuals and, the population and educational explosions being what they are, we are very shortly going to have more of them than any other class of people. If the notion that the film is the central art of our time has any validity, it lies simply in the fact that this New Class is the most significant socioeconomic group of our time. They are the great consumers, not only of culture but of all the other doodads of affluence—notably such items as foreign food, foreign cars, foreign travel.

And foreign movies. In this, they recapitulate the special kind of provincialism of the wives and daughters of the industrial statesmen (or robber barons, as we used to know them) who established the institutions of our formal culture in the late 19th and early 20th centuries and who would not buy a painting or go to a concert unless the artist were European, or at least, European-trained. The value of the Continental cachet has largely disappeared in the traditional arts, but, for the moment, it is very potent in film.

There is no question that much of the interest in foreign films is esthetically justifiable. Those that have been released here have generally been more interesting, more liberated and liberating, than the best American products. It should, however, be remembered that we have seen only the crest of sundry new waves; we are rarely allowed to sport in the troughs, except, of course, when it comes to exploitable sex films, which are to our time what French postcards were to other epochs.

On the other hand, one observes a lack of critical spirit in our approach to many of these films, a certain faddishness—even cultishness—in the enthusiasm for them. Moreover, there is a great lack of historical perspective in our appreciation of the European film. The directors who created the French New Wave and the young Czech directors who have lately so excited us have been quite careful to note their debt to the great American directors whose work has profoundly influenced them; but, excepting the *auteur* critics, who hold that the director is the author of a film, few in this country have responded by taking a serious interest in these men or in the younger American directors who might, in time, achieve a comparable status in world cinema. In fact, it generally remains for the critics associated with the Parisian magazine, Cahiers du Cinéma, to point out to us the merits of people like Nicholas Ray, Don Siegel and Sam Peckinpah, which does not seem to help them get work.

Of course, these three, along with many other equally underrated American directors, are more or less committed to genre films, and Hollywood, though it continues to turn out Westerns and crime films and musicals, no longer has its heart in these matters. The New Yorker's Pauline Kael recently and rightly observed that since blacklisting and the breakup of the big studios (whose B pictures were the training ground for young directors) we have lost several generations of young moviemaking talent, men who were not perhaps destined for greatness, but for the kind of professional competence that is the bedrock on which a vital film industry is built. Unable or unwilling to tell good from bad among the European directors, afraid of entrusting large investments to young American directors, the industry has turned to what Miss Kael calls "the mediocrities and the bunglers of England"—a nation whose culture has always seemed very classy to us, but whose filmmakers (although they may not quite be "the sad joke" she says they have always been) are certainly joyless, imitative squares and have been (with a few great exceptions) since the earliest days of the movies. To hire these people to superintend the production of films on classic *American* themes is preposterous on the face of it, especially when someone like Peckinpah has not made a theatrical film in almost four years.

Miss Kael attributes this state of affairs to the "classic acumen" of our producers and that is certainly a factor. But there is, I think, more to it than that. The people now in charge in Hollywood are, like their basic audience, members of the New Class. As such, they are bright, bright, bright in their shallow little ways. They sense that they—that we—have lost something, some set of commonly held, virtually unconscious beliefs that helped the individual to define himself, that prevented the society from flying apart at the seams.

That something was recently defined by psychoanalyst Rollo May as "the myth of the mythless society." Like all the nations of the Western world since the 18th century, the United States has been energized by a belief in progress, both personal and social, through rationalism and individualism. However, as May is by no means the first to observe, both of these beliefs are, today, in a state of crisis, and nowhere is that crisis more deeply felt than among the New Class, which, of course, prides itself on getting news of this kind first. As a result all of our culture is in a state of anxiety that borders on the frantic. There is a legitimate feeling that none of the traditional cultural forms—including the traditional film genres—truly reflects the unpleasant day-to-day psychological reality that all of us experience. It is for this reason that we have turned, rather desperately, to Warhol and McLuhan, to "Futz" and "Hair," to Happenings and light shows. Never in history—at least in American history—has each sneeze, cough and burp of the avant-garde been so earnestly and intensively studied by so many for (*a*) clues to cultural salvation and (*b*) portents of a happier future and (*c*) escape. It is for this reason that we are presently putting such heavy pressure on the movies to grow up, to get serious, to be art.

But, as social critic David T. Bazelon pointed out some years ago, serious moviegoing has always involved a conflict "between one's desire to dream and one's desire to have a firmer relationship with high culture." In other words, there is a part of us that remains a child before the larger-than-life figures on the screen, figures that, in the darkness, inevitably have a magical, mythical quality about them. There is also a part of us that resents this reversion, that sternly calls us back to duty, "to relevance."

Now, back in the days when we really believed in the myth of the mythless society, there actually were, according to Dr. May, two integrating myths that had a peculiar hold on us—the one which dealt with the frontiersman and the one which dealt with the Horatio Alger figure. They were, if you will, a country myth and a city myth, and each figure, in his way, embodied those qualities of individualism and rationalism in which all of us held an implicit, unspoken faith. Much has been written, of course, about the movie Westerner and the movie gangster (who was merely Alger's boy grown up and grown rancid because no one else believed, as he still did, in really free enterprise). When these two characters were very well done, as they so often (indeed, routinely) were in the films of the nineteen-thirties and forties, conflict between the desire to dream and the desire for relevance was elegantly resolved by the simple expedient of satisfying both. These were "the good old-fashioned *movie* movies" that sentimental critics are always mourning for these days (and which, thank God, they still occasionally find). These were, as Bazelon said, "the heart of movies as cultural events [and] as release of dreams."

And now, I think, the heart has gone out of them—and out of our comedies and musicals which also revolved around familiar archetypes. Some producers try desperately to revivify the old forms, mostly by adding strong doses of very explicit sex and violence to them. (I am convinced that the outcry against S-and-V is an expression of cultural shock, not genuine moral outrage, by people who just don't expect to find such material in genre films where, not long ago, even a discreet kiss between cowpoke and schoolmarm was frowned upon and where death, when it came, was a bloodless "drilling.") Occasionally, we get an attempt at self-conscious purification of these forms, the sort of arty reactionaryism that made "Shane" and "High Noon" middle-brow bywords in the postwar years, when, in fact, anybody who really cares about the Western could name a half-dozen films (including, currently, "The Stalking Moon") that were considerably more interesting variations on the standard themes. Most often these days, one sees campy parodies of all the genres because, very simply, most of us simply can't believe in them anymore or, at the very least, don't want to be caught seeming to believe in them.

The desperation of movie people confronted by this cultural phenomenon is beautifully exemplified by the new Kirk Douglas gangster film, "The Brotherhood," which the star caused to be produced under the direction of the heavy-handed Martin Ritt. Its ineptitude would do credit to perfidious Albion, but there is a special kind of moral blindness about it that I found intriguing. Douglas plays an old-style Mafia hood, running an assortment of labor and, one assumes, vice and protection rackets in the crude, small-timey way of his forefathers. He is still content to have his gunmen take care of stool pigeons in the old, vulgar fashion—they are seen taking one for a ride to the city dump and, when he is bumped off, stuffing the corpse's mouth with a symbolic canary. "No, no, no, Kirk," cry the leaders of his gangland family, "you don't understand. Times have changed. We're going into electronics, defense contracts, the big time." He turns out to be stubborn, unable to shift with the times and, ultimately, he must receive, from his own brother, the kiss of death.

Clearly, there is little to choose morally between the old-style and the new-style mobster. But the movie does choose. It actually gets very sentimental, almost lyrical, about the type Douglas portrays. In effect, it is a last hurrah for the *little* Caesars of our movie past, nostalgia for the small-scale, free-enterprise crook of our movie childhoods now invoked (simple-mindedly, to be sure) to divert us from his true nature, a diversion that no maker of the much more humble progenitors of "The Brotherhood" would have thought necessary or wise.

What it comes to is this: we have run out of myths. In the early forties, Albert Camus wrote: "The whole effort of Western art is to provide our imagination with types. . . . In desperation, it has invented the movie hero." But now the movies are full of antiheroes, and the institution of movie stardom, which was based on a system of heroic typology, is in total decline. Dr. May tells us, as many have, that the preferred life-style of our new age emphasizes cooperation, subjectivity and collectivism, and who can doubt that he is right. And who is genius enough to make a satisfactory mythical hero out of a cooperative, subjective central figure whose aim is a harmonious collective society? Perhaps it can be done, and surely there will continue to be an atavistic place for the old stories and characters in television, which is aimed at those primitive souls who still think that we live in a highly competitive, individualistic and more or less rational society, poor dears.

There are, of course, citizens of our world who might make very suitable mythic heroes for movies—revolutionary leaders, for example, foreign and domestic, black and white, young and old, though it is possible that they represent threats to the *status quo* too potent for comfortable assimilation into fiction. In any case, it is certain—as films like Jules Dassin's "Up-Tight" prove—that there is very little intelligent understanding of the type among professional filmmakers and thus small hope of their soon becoming the source of a new mythic richness in film. It is also possible that over a longish period of time an interaction between the underground and the aboveground moviemakers will produce a style of filmmaking so radically different from any we have known up to now that none of what we have been discussing will be germane. That, however, seems unlikely. The avant-garde produces a very abstract form of film, a thing of lovely surfaces, and stylistically exciting, but with none of the psychological resonance of either truly great art or, oddly, of the best popular movies.

For the moment, one imagines, the balance in our films will remain tipped in favor of our yearning for a firmer relation with high culture, away from the desire to dream—although Bazelon argues persuasively that the desire to dream at the movies remains very much alive. The audience that snobbishly refuses to attend American movies but goes religiously "to every lousy French film" is, he says, also looking for a dream—"It's just that you're not dreaming about this country." The implication— that we can no longer live psychologically in the United States— is interesting and more than a little frightening, and although this makes it very difficult for an excellent movie like the recent "Pretty Poison" to find its audience here, I do think that over the long run this, too, shall pass.

Meantime, if the new, more or less restricted film audience has yet to achieve the connection with high culture that they want and seem to need on a more than intermittent basis, there nevertheless has been one substantial gain in the content of our movies.

They are, finally, beginning to examine, with an unprecedented degree of truthfulness, with a fine eye for accuracy of detail in setting and decor, a fine ear for language, some of the common issues of middle-class life. This year "Pretty Poison," "Petulia," "Rachel, Rachel" and, most notable of all, John Cassavetes's "Faces," have all, one way and another, plunged exploratory scalpels into the quivering flesh of the very culture that now supports the movies. All are about bourgeois yearnings—for love, for existential meaning—in the midst of affluence. All deal with various attempts to trick shallow life into making some sort of satisfying sense.

It seems to me, too, that since postindustrial societies are so much alike, we are not always escaping America when we go to see a foreign film. "Blow-Up," for instance, was a profound metaphorical examination of how technology as art fails us when we confront the timeless, universal mysteries of existence. Ingmar Bergman, whose stubborn insistence on making very difficult movies has rendered him unfashionable with the in-crowd lately, deals brilliantly in his latest films with the silencing effect of modern life on the humanistically oriented artist. Godard keeps probing in his infuriating, fascinating way at the half-formed revolutionary spirit of middle-class youth the world over.

In short, though we may have lost something quite valuable since movies became the "central art" of the "central people" of our time, we have also gained something. Or, more properly, we have gained a potential (still too often unrealized) for a greater, more direct understanding of the quality of our inner lives and of the external world of both things and ideas which we inhabit.

That is—to re-emphasize my basic point—some of us have made a gain. There is a part of me that dislikes and distrusts this business of taking over what was once an art (or was it, then, merely a medium?) that belonged to everyone and making it into a semiprivate preserve. To put it very simply, the movies have their historical roots in the mass, and anything that is cut off from its roots is in danger. The experience of such a detachment may be exhilarating, but the risks should not be minimized.

To take just one example, whole generations learned to love movies in their preteen years, when they represented a very special kind of escape, when they were among the first, and the few, experiences one was allowed to engage in alone, free of parental supervision. In those days, when all movies were allegedly made for that conventionalized 12-year-old mentality, that was perfectly feasible. Now, people find it impossible to allow their young children such freedom, and the kids are condemned to the generally wretched films made expressly for them and to a handful of more expensive—but generally no better—pictures that are advertised for family consumption. Worse, the movies have now formalized this style of censorship and, under the new classification system, theater managers will become moral cops, barring kids under 17 from "X" category films. It is hard to see how, under these ground rules, a new generation will regard films as a "central" experience; absence may make the heart grow fonder, but one must first experience the presence for that cliché really to work.

What it all comes to is this: the first art (or quasi-art or presumptive art or whatever it is) that was entirely the creation of modern industrial society, the only art in living memory that operated, however crudely, on the basis of a kind of participatory democracy (with tickets the equivalent of ballots) is in the process of exchanging its broad-based democratic status for a more prestigious social and intellectual status, and one must measure the obvious gains that are accruing to it against the less obvious but no less real losses implicit in its new role. No one who believed, however fleetingly, however warily, in the movies' potential as a genuine art of the masses, one which appealed to all classes, one which could serve an invaluable function as a kind of social cement, can be anything but saddened by the alienation that very large numbers of people now feel about the movies, an alienation that is imperfectly expressed by the protests against sex and violence now so common. This shrinkage in the audience, this slippage in the general interest in movies, the indignant, hurt and puzzled tone that pervades the letters any critic with a large audience receives, are all cause for alarm.

One is tempted to fear for the future of theatrical film, especially with cable television, pay TV and the possibility of home film libraries which can be played through a television set now technologically feasible and therefore inevitable. Movies truly will not be movies anymore if we do not share them in public, in large groups before a large screen in theaters. We do not need more socially fragmenting experiences; we do need more integrative ones.

And yet the fear is controllable. There is—at least for a sizable number of people—something mysteriously fascinating and basically resistant to analysis about the attraction of film. Andrew Sarris put it very nicely in that symposium of ours: "I happen to derive more pleasure from film than from any other art, but that is *my* sensibility speaking, not necessarily modern sensibility. I enjoyed movies before they were intellectually fashionable, and I shall enjoy them long after they have gone out of fashion. I can no more renounce movies than literary men can renounce books."

Precisely. As he says, there is no way of knowing how history will regard the role of films in the shaping of our century's culture. All one knows, finally, is that for some of us, no matter what our general views about the broad trends in film and filmmaking, the movies are the only game in town; and if all they were showing in the theaters was Warhol's "Sleep," we would probably drag ourselves to see it, mourning the while for the good old days and wondering whatever became of Randolph Scott. I suspect—no, I am absolutely certain—that there will always be a few million of us around. Enough to form some kind of audience for some kind of movies. For us, they will always be the central art of our time.

Biggest Money-Making Movie of All Time— How Come?

by Joan Barthel

HOLLYWOOD

"IT DEALS WITH good, wholesome subject matter—kids, nuns—and it entertains in a charming, romantic way."

"There's nothing in it to offend or upset anybody."

"A pit of sticky-sweet whipped cream, not of the first freshness."

"It's irresistible if you like people and children."

"A fantasy about a world which no longer exists, where everything comes out right in the end."

"I kept thinking of Red China . . ."

"It's cheaper than therapy."

"It makes me feel good."

"The sugar-coated lie."

You pay your money—perhaps $2.50 for a midweek matinee, $3.75 on Saturday night—and you take your choice of these comments about "The Sound of Music." They belong, in the order given, to Richard Zanuck, vice president in charge of pro-

From the *New York Times Magazine,* November 20, 1966, copyright © 1966 by The New York Times Company.

duction at 20th Century-Fox; the publicity man for Robert Wise, producer-director; The New Yorker; Richard Rodgers, who wrote two new songs for the movie; Ernest Lehman, who wrote the screenplay; a newspaperman; a California psychiatrist; Elizabeth Pick, a 38-year-old Los Angeles typist who has seen it more than 100 times (spending more than $300 in the process); and Pauline Kael, who was fired as movie critic for McCall's shortly after the women of America read that in her column.

The film is the three-hour, spectacular adaptation, in Todd-AO and DeLuxe Color, of Rodgers and Hammerstein's Broadway musical about the Trapp Family Singers. Its plot, if anyone still doesn't know, centers on Maria, a postulant from a Salzburg convent sent as governess to the seven children of a naval captain who is wealthy, widowed and severe to the point that he does not allow them to sing or frolic. She promptly teaches them the title song and a couple of others, eventually winning over the captain ("You've brought music back into the house"), who marries her, and the nine of them—by now accomplished enough to sing in public—flee across the mountains to freedom when the Nazis take over.

In Egypt the movie is called "Love and Tenderness"; in Portugal, where nobody under 12 may see it, "Music in the Heart"; in Italy, "All Together with Passion"; in Thailand, where the King played "Do Re Mi" on the clarinet at its premiere, "Charms of the Heaven-Sound"; in Spain, "Smiles and Tears"; in Argentina, "The Rebellious Novice" (but it's doing well anyway); in Germany, where it bombed, "My Song, My Dream"; in Hong Kong, "Fairy Music Blow Fragrant Place Place Hear." It has been dubbed in five foreign languages, including Parsi (for the Iranian market), and—to indulge in irresistible cliché—in any language, in any of the 29 countries where it has broken all previous box-office records, it's the crisply gratifying sound of money.

Since its premiere 20 months ago, it has brought the screenwriter more than $1,000 a day. The director expects to make at least $8-million. It has been to the 20th Century-Fox Film Corporation what a Mae West is to a man overboard; the company, which showed a $39.8-million loss in 1962, chalked up a pretax profit of $20.2-million for the year ending last June. Although the movie is still playing on a reserved-seat basis—in industry jargon, on "roadshow" or "hard-ticket"—it is on the verge of overtaking the six-times-rereleased, 27-year-old "Gone with the Wind" in domestic earnings, and the surface has barely been scratched, since it has generally been shown in only one theatre to a city or, to be precise, in 3,164—only 275 in this country—theaters out of a possible 35,000 worldwide. Still ahead are the neighborhood houses and drive-ins, when it goes into multiple release, and the prospect of rerelease until the last vestige of recorded time. In about six months, Fox officials project, it will pass "Ben Hur" as the top overseas grosser. In short, it is well on its way toward earning more money than any picture has ever earned, any time, anywhere.

How come?

"If we knew the answer to that, we'd know the answer to a lot of things," says Zanuck. But if answers are in short supply, opinions abound, now that "The Sound of Music" has become the talk of this talkative town: happy talk, wary talk, I-couldn't-care-less talk, sometimes frank and amused talk.

"We've played the 'let's-analyze-"The-Sound-of-Music" ' game many times," says Leslie Bricusse, the breezy young Britisher imported by Fox to write the music, lyrics and screenplay for "Dr. Doolittle," a $14-million bauble being gift-wrapped for Christmas of next year. "The first act was good, but the second act might have been written by different people—say, Irving Hammerstein and Fred Rodgers. Or it could have been Romberg, couldn't it? 'The Student Nun.'

"It has everything: children, religion, high society, royalty, Nazi Germany and Julie Andrews as the fairy on top of the Christmas tree. It's helped our film, because I can't believe that any studio that didn't have 'The Sound of Music' behind it would get involved with such a brave, expensive project." But the suggestion that he might therefore be tempted to copy some of its sure-fire elements is met succinctly: "Oh, God, no."

George Cukor, whose "My Fair Lady" has most certainly *not* been helped by the competitor, talks genially of the picture's "true innocence. In spite of its naiveté, you find yourself caught up; there's a tug at the heart. My principal emotion is jealousy." By and by, the geniality lessens: "No, I don't wish I'd done it. That's an academic question anyway. And I don't know whether we can expect to see copies of it. That's the kind of question I don't speculate about, darling. May I say it's a question that doesn't interest me?"

The role of Max Detweiler, the roguish impresario who maneuvers the Trapp family onstage, is played by Richard Haydn. "Everything in it is nice and homey and bread-and-butter and simple," he says. "I think the people who go back to see it time and again are going back for another dose of this reassurance. It's wholesome, that's what it is. And that brings me to Julie. She's incredibly wholesome; she's everybody's wife, mother, daughter. It wouldn't have been the same picture with, say, Susan Hayward."

Nobody seems to think so. For, while there are a few differences—Zanuck gives substantial credit to the beautiful scenery, while Lehman says, "Nobody goes to see a picture because they love the Alps so much"—there is eventual consensus that the secret of its stunning success is people.

The people who put it together.

The people who acted in it, which boils down to Julie Andrews.

And the people out front. Not only the extremists like Miss Pick, or the woman in Wales who sees it every day, or the man in Oregon who saw it so often he sent the studio a copy of the script written from memory, but the average, garden-variety movie-goer who has seen it once, twice, perhaps three times, and has spread the word. Like the people in Moorhead, Minn., where the picture ran for more than a year in the town's only movie house and sparked a protest demonstration by students of the local college who, under the name POOIE (People's Organization of Intelligent Educatees), picketed—"49 Weeks of Schmaltz is Enough"; "Don't Get Caught in the von Trapp"—for a change of bill. Or the people in Manila, who got so unruly in their demand for holiday tickets that police emergency squads had to be dispatched to cope. Or the people in Salt Lake City, where the theater showing it recorded an attendance of 509,516 as of last month, although the city's population was only about 190,000 in the last census. Or the people in Syracuse, or Colorado Springs, or Orlando, or Cedar Rapids, or Atlanta or any other of the two dozen or so cities where attendance has exceeded the population and thus earned them Fox's "Outstanding Achievement Award," suitable for framing, in red, off-white and blue. (The demand for appropriate publicity items to keep pace with the picture has heavily taxed the ingenuity of Fox staffers and theater managers, who have come up, so far, with anniversary cakes, "favorite scene" contests, on-stage quiz shows and Gargantuan postcards addressed to Miss Andrews.)

Because the picture's success is pegged to people, the story behind the success turns out to be as rambling, as gossipy, as digressive and contradictory—and ultimately as intriguing—as people tend to be. ("I said, 'As far as I'm concerned, there's only one person who can play this role: Julie Andrews' "—Ernest Lehman. "I mentioned Julie Andrews"—Richard Zanuck. "I gave it up [but] I think I made a contribution by casting Julie Andrews"—William Wyler.)

The story would, "logically," begin with Wise, who, as producer-director, can take either the credit or the rap, depending on the point of view, for the finished product. But there is a lengthy prologue involving William Wyler, who started out to direct the film, but didn't; Lehman, who was asked to write the screenplay, and did; and Zanuck, who started the project moving.

Richard Zanuck looks so young—he is 31—that the effect of his slight figure behind an imposing desk in his beige-carpeted office on the Fox lot could be a scene from "Andy Hardy Runs a Studio." But his talk is intent and serious.

"It was a gamble for us," he says, "because $8.2-million, which is what it cost to make, is a lot of money; it was not the most distinguished show Rodgers and Hammerstein had ever done, and our cast was relatively unknown. Julie Andrews' 'Mary Poppins' and 'The Americanization of Emily' had not yet been released.

"A crucial decision for us was taking it on location in Salzburg. We could have approached it à la 'My Fair Lady,' where it was all done in the studio, but I think a lot of the value would have gone down the drain. Outside of the terrible weather in Salzburg, which took us a million dollars over budget, everything went very smoothly.

"We previewed it in Minneapolis, because we wanted a totally fresh audience. The weather was miserable, and we thought nobody would show up. But the theater was full, and at intermission the whole audience stood up and applauded for five minutes. They did it again at the end—and these were people who had paid to see the preview. Bobby Wise and I looked at each other, shell-shocked. Right then we knew we had an audience-winner, but we had no idea it was going to be the biggest picture of all time.

"Then we opened in New York and got a couple of lousy reviews from Bosley Crowther and Judith Crist. I called up Bobby early in the morning at his hotel and his wife said he was out walking in the park. I said, 'I know he's there; put him on.' He came on and said, 'How could they do this to us?' I was very depressed, too. A lot of kind of intellectuals attacked us for being too saccharine. We'd taken a lot of that out of the original show, but it still didn't appeal to some of the reviewers and some of the snobs. The public has answered them in a big way, though, all over the world.

"If it had been a catastrophe, I doubt if we would have three musicals on our schedule. 'Dr. Doolittle' will be the most expensive musical we've ever made. We think it can stand on its own, but naturally, when it's proved that millions of people love certain ingredients, that gives us reassurance. And 'Doolittle' has some of those ingredients: charming music, adventure, and it appeals to a broad-based audience.

"There have been attempts to copy us—I think the clearest was 'The Singing Nun'—but I think people are still making musicals with caution, unless you have a big, blockbuster kind of thing, like we're going to have in 'Hello, Dolly,' which Ernest Lehman is doing for us, and 'The Star,' with Julie Andrews, which Bobby is doing—so all the major elements are here."

Zanuck got his job as studio boss when his father, Darryl Zanuck, won control of the company in the summer of 1962, the year that the $39.8-million was lost and Spyros Skouras was floated out of the president's office on a not terribly seaworthy $31-million barge named "Cleopatra." "The Sound of Music" had been bought for $1,250,000 in January of that year, but had been shelved while the play wound up its three-and-a-half-year Broadway run and Fox rode out the storm over the Nile.

When the Zanucks moved in, the company was shut down and its employes, except for some maintenance men, laid off. On the TV side, the company was down to its last few episodes of

"Dobie Gillis" (today it is waxing fat on nearly a dozen series, including "Peyton Place" and "Batman"). Then, one day, Zanuck got in touch with Ernest Lehman.

"I'll tell you how shut down they were," the writer recalled. "When we were talking about the project, I said, 'Where will my office be?' and he said, 'Where would you like it to be?' It was like calling a theater and asking, 'What time does the movie go on?' and they say, 'What time would you like it to go on?'"

Lehman is a wry, wistful-looking man with mournful blue eyes and an impressive reputation based on such earlier pictures as "Sweet Smell of Success," "Executive Suite," "The King and I" and "West Side Story," and, since "Music," "Who's Afraid of Virginia Woolf?" He sat in the plush bar at the Bel Air Hotel and told what had happened:

"What I'm going to tell you is the really wild secret of my life. It was too fantastic. I had been approached to become the head of 20th Century-Fox. I went walking on Malibu Beach with Peter Levathes—he was the head of the studio and was being mentioned to replace Spyros Skouras as president—and we discussed it.

"Well, not only did the negotiations come to nought, but Mr. Levathes came to nought, Mr. Skouras came to nought, Darryl Zanuck won control and Richard Zanuck was put in charge. But still, the plant was shut down.

"I know this sounds boastful, but, hell, this is the way it was. The announcement that I had been signed to write the screenplay was front-page news in the trade papers, because it meant that 20th Century-Fox was back in business.

"I went to New York to see the play again; I'd seen it just after it opened and I'd thought, 'This will make a wonderful movie someday.' I saw Dick Rodgers. He said, 'I suppose you people are going to use Doris Day in the picture.' I said, 'Why do you think that?' He said, 'It figures.' I said, 'As far as I'm concerned there is only one person who can play this role: Julie Andrews.' And he just looked at me with those rich, melodic, steely eyes of his and said, 'So what else is new?'

"Then I met with Darryl and Dick Zanuck and we talked about possible directors. I honestly don't remember whose idea it was, but we said, 'Willie Wyler.' So Willie flew to New York and I went to the show with him. There had been cast changes, and the show wasn't so good at this point. When the curtain fell, Wyler said, 'Ernie, I just hated it, but please don't stop trying to change my mind.'

"We went back to the Coast and I was put in charge of twisting Willie Wyler's arm. One night we were invited to a party at Glenn Ford's house, and there was a demonstration of ESP. Afterwards, the expert said he'd be available for private consultation in the bedroom. Willie Wyler went in for a seance with this mentalist and said, 'Tell me if I should do "The Sound of Music."' The mentalist said, 'Let me hold the screenplay in my hands.' Wyler said, 'There is no screenplay.' And I said, 'Why didn't he hold *me* in his hands?'

"Finally he agreed to do it, but in a rather uncertain way. He came to my office when I'd finished the first draft of the screenplay and said he liked it, but didn't have any concrete ideas to give me. Then he went off to play gin rummy with David Lean and Sam Spiegel. And I said to myself, 'No ideas? Then he's never going to do the picture.'

"Not long after that, his agent went to Dick Zanuck and asked for a leave of absence so Wyler could do 'The Sandpiper' first. Dick said, 'Not a day.' So Wyler withdrew, and Bobby Wise agreed to do it, provided that Saul Chaplin could come along as associate producer."

Wyler did not do "The Sandpiper," but "The Collector," for which, ironically, he received an Academy Award nomination that pitted him against Wise and "Music." Wyler lost, but still sounds determinedly cheerful. "I'm delighted that 'The Sound of Music' is doing so well. Of course, it's an infallible piece of material. Even when second- and third-rate road companies were doing the play, they did enormous business. It looked like 'The Sound of Music' would even surpass 'Ben Hur,' and I thought it would be unfair for me to have done both. I thought I'd leave something for somebody else." A pause. "That's a quip."

Why, *really,* did he withdraw? "Oh, you know. You get hot and cold on things, and it's not my style of film, exactly."

Zanuck says Wyler felt it was "too schmaltzy," and Lehman confirms that there was, indeed, a "sugary curse" on the property.

"I remember 'The Sound of Music' had a certain—well, stink is not quite the right word—about it. I saw Burt Lancaster, who was doing 'The Leopard,' in the cafeteria one day, and he looked at me and said, 'Jesus, you must need the money.'

"It wasn't as sickly sweet as it might have been, though there are those who will disagree with that. But the very things we were on guard against are the things that appeal to so many people. In a world which has changed enormously in the last few years, the movie is a kind of fantasy about a world which no longer exists, where everything comes out right, the Nazis aren't *really* Nazis, and it's happy-ending time. Our astronauts have succeeded in getting out of this world, but those who haven't go to see 'The Sound of Music' one more time.

"We didn't know at the beginning it would be such a phenomenon. We'd gotten some crippling notices. Then suddenly the figures began looking a little crazy, jumping instead of trailing off. I hadn't read the reviews, because I have a theory that if you never read it in print the brain traces aren't grooved and you don't remember it, even if someone tells you what Judith Crist wrote.

"The subject matter is vital to its success, of course; after that there are pluses and minuses. For instance, I could have played Maria and it wouldn't have stood a chance.

"But we had no formula. When you think of a picture's success you have to think of the world market, and there's no formula for that. I was surprised it was so successful in Tokyo, but what do I know of the Japanese, huh? Maybe they want to escape, too; maybe they're tired of making transistor radios.

"Then there's the parent-child thing, which is a kind of universal language. Maybe people like to think they were closer to their parents than they really were. This interpretation covers that emotional tug at the moment the captain hears his children singing —even though that wasn't too marvelously done, ever. And maybe this atavistic, parent-child thing is more important than the 'escape' interpretation, because that implies that people's lives are lousy and the world is lousy."

It is precisely that "emotional tug" that Miss Kael, in her fateful column, deplored, calling it a manipulated response. "Whom could it offend?" Only those of us who, *despite* the fact that we may respond . . . are aware of how self-indulgent and cheap and ready-made are the responses we are made to feel," she wrote.

"The best of all possible worlds, that's what 'The Sound of Music' pretends we live in . . . it's the sugar-coated lie that people seem to want to eat . . . and this is the attitude that makes a critic feel that maybe it's all hopeless. Why not just send the director, Robert Wise, a wire: 'You win, I give up'?"

Mr. Wise sat in the executive suite at Fox's New York headquarters and smiled a gentlemanly smile. "I was not trying to take an easy line to it, but to get the proper response, the one which was right for our project. I studied my responses in the emotional area; I had seen the father singing with his children in the stage play and I was on the edge of embarrassment. At one point I planned to shoot the scene without having the father join in the singing, but it seemed to work the other way.

"You have to judge what its intentions are, what it was meant to be. It was never planned as a documentary of the Trapp family, and for that reason I didn't read the book or see the German films that had been made earlier. The large bones of it are true, but the way it was put on are renditions of the truth." The smile flickered. "Let her come see my new film, 'The Sand Pebbles,' where people get sliced to pieces with bayonets."

(Ironically, "Pebbles" will displace "Music" at the Fox-Wilshire here and at the Rivoli in New York in mid-December, not because "Music" is fading at the box office, but in order for "Pebbles" to qualify for this year's Academy Awards. The manager at the Fox-Wilshire is not anxious to see "Music" go. "There's a crying need for this kind of picture," he says. "Last week we had four busloads of senior citizens from Santa Monica and Long Beach, and we're having full houses for our Saturday morning youth shows for Cub Scouts, Campfire Girls and little Brownies. This is the first picture, in my experience, of such wide appeal. I just wonder how the critics who condemned it so much feel now!" * At a press conference in New York announcing the coming of "Pebbles" to the Rivoli, a vice president of the company that owns the theater confined himself to pleased comments about the Rivoli's happy association with Fox on both

---

* Not all critics felt hostile. "We took 100 journalists from major roadshow markets to Salzburg when we were filming," says a Fox executive. "As a result, they were great friends of the picture."

films, and did not discuss the lawsuit filed by his company against Fox for giving it "an inferior attraction" in "Cleopatra.")

Wise came to the project trailing clouds of glory for "West Side Story," which won 10 Academy Awards, including two for him as producer and co-director. ("Music" won five, including one for him, one for "best picture," others for best achievement in sound, best film editing and best scoring adaptation or treatment.) He started out as an odd-job man at the old R.K.O. studio in 1933, and became a director after editing Orson Welles's "Citizen Kane" and "The Magnificent Ambersons" (even though Welles commented publicly that the latter film "must have been cut by the studio gardener"). He is gray-haired, soft-spoken and, when asked how he rated "Music" in comparison with "West Side Story," exceptionally candid.

"I like the business of 'The Sound of Music' and the film of 'West Side Story,' which was new, exciting and cinematically more advanced and daring.

"But I think that, by and large, in 'Music' we came close to the mark. To our mark. The play was very, very saccharine, and obviously we haven't eliminated that for all people. But we tried to tone it down. We didn't go in for too-cute costumes or turreted castles, and we were careful not to overdo colors.

"For me, one of the crucial decisions was casting Christopher Plummer. I wanted the character of the captain to have bite, incisiveness and real dimension. I felt we must go on the basis of the story, and not bastardize it with just big names—say, Bing Crosby and Kate Smith."

The decision led to complications, though, when Plummer was told his singing would be dubbed. Reports vary on his reaction. Lehman says Plummer said he would feel castrated, and walked off the picture. "They called me back from Palm Springs to talk him into returning to work." Leslie Bricusse recalls that Plummer, a friend of his, "was so fed up that he began calling it 'The Sound of Mucus.' "

Wise and Chaplin say Plummer did not walk out, but that he had indeed wanted to do his own singing. As it turned out, he did the singing throughout the shooting, and his singing was dubbed in later by Bill Lee, who also does chewing-gum commercials. (The other performer who did not sing for herself was Peggy Wood, playing the Mother Abbess. When she approves, in song, of Maria's marrying, the voice is that of Marni Nixon. Miss Nixon, who has been heard through the mouths of some of Hollywood's most leading ladies, also appears briefly on camera. So does the real Maria von Trapp, now a resident of Vermont, who happened by Salzburg during the filming and was used in one scene as an extra.)

"I wasn't trying to say a damn thing in 'Music,' " Wise concluded. "No message. That's as good a face as I can put on it. People just feel good when they see it; there's a sense of warmth, of well-being, of happiness and joy. And then, perhaps, it's come out at a time when people around the world want to get away from their problems."

The theme is echoed, finally, by the figure at the heart of the matter, Julie Andrews. "It's very joyous. It's refreshing and not too complicated. A love story, with children and music. And I think, from the enormous amount of mail I get, that word 'joyous' has an awful lot to do with it."

Thus, in the last roundup, although other factors are mentioned—some Fox officials feel the success of the movie abroad is related to the rewriting of the song lyrics in French, German, Italian and Spanish—the "escape" theory remains the most popular. Chaplin recalled hearing a woman say, as she left the theater, "If only life were like that." Wise's press agent, Mike Kaplan, who wears a tie clasp with a gold treble cleff and the title, says, "It's a homespun fairy tale, and people still like fairy tales." (Indeed, the souvenir program sold in theaters has a text beginning: "Once upon a time. . . .")

And, as in any self-respecting fairy tale, there is that brimming pot of gold at the rainbow's end. Worldwide box-office receipts are more than $125-million. Fox's current share is $67.5-million, meaning that its profit, after the cost of the movie and advertising, distribution and publicity, already stands at more than $45-million.

Ten per cent of the profits go to Wise and his Argyle Enterprises, Inc., in which Chaplin has a share. A handful of people involved with the stage show, including Richard Rodgers and the estate of Oscar Hammerstein, get 10 per cent of the gross, after exhibitors' costs and profits.

Lehman was reluctant to specify his piece of the action, but, according to Zanuck, he gets "a token 2 per cent" of the profits or, at this point, more than $900,000. "I guess I feel a little guilty about it," says Lehman. "Why should some idiot movie star make 10 times as much as the President of the United States?" (He was not referring to Julie Andrews. She was paid a flat fee of $225,000, and neither she nor anyone else in the cast has a share in the profits.)

Even the citizens of Salzburg, who issued a special postage stamp, but didn't like the movie ("Really rather nasty of them," murmured the star), came in for some of the gold. The film company spent about $900,000 in its three months there, and a "See the Locations of 'The Sound of Music' " tour is doing, according to Kaplan, "fantastic business" at $20 a head.

And the end is nowhere in sight. Fox has collected more than £4-million from Britain alone, where the picture has grossed £6-million, more than twice as much as any other film has ever taken in there, even though the play is still running—in its sixth year—in London. Zanuck projects an eventual worldwide gross to Fox of $85-million, then says he thinks that's conservative. So do other knowledgeable sources, who talk of $100-million, maybe more.

But is it Art?

"I think I'm satisfied with it," says Wise.

"I'm delighted with it—who wouldn't be?" says Rodgers.

"It's beautifully made," says Zanuck.

Ernest Lehman, in the Bel Air bar, answers slowly. "Dick Zanuck and I were walking back from the commissary one day and he said, 'It's a great picture, isn't it?' I said, 'I just don't make a habit of getting too enthusiastic about pictures.' He said, 'I want to hear you say it. Say it's a great picture.' So I said, 'Yes, Dick. It's a great picture.' "

"The Bard" Competes
with "The Body"

by C. A. LeJeune

LONDON

AND NOW WE come, ladies and gentlemen, to today's question. What celebrated Englishman stated, in a published interview, "I don't really like Shakespeare on the screen at all: the shot is too big for the camera"? No, sir, not George Bernard Shaw (although he is alleged to have said of "Henry V," "Fifteen minutes of cinema and the rest just Shakespeare"). No, madam, not Noel Coward, and no again, madam, not Mr. J. Arthur Rank, although he must have had his moments of temptation. Sir Laurence Olivier, in the days before he had a handle to his name.

There is something rather piquant, not to say sinister, in recalling this candid avowal from the man who, above all others, has been responsible for the current screen vogue in Shakespeare. Make no mistake about it, it is the star's share in the production of "Henry V" and "Hamlet," not the Bard's, that has caught the public's volatile imagination. Producers have been making films out of Shakespeare's plays for upward of thirty years, and until the darling of the Old Vic, and the idol of London's West End, came along to sponsor the job, only the people who wanted another stick to beat the movies with stopped to bother about it.

From the *New York Times Magazine,* December 12, 1948, copyright © 1948 by The New York Times Company.

A useful script writer, Will Shakespeare was one of the earliest scenario boys on the screen. In the days when motion pictures took a day to shoot, and production was done on an open lot with ball games for a break, they were already grinding out movie versions of "Romeo and Juliet" and "Hamlet," "The Merchant of Venice" and "Henry VIII." Long before the first World War, a British studio offered a super-Hamlet in twenty-two scenes; each scene built inside the next like a nest of Chinese boxes, to save shooting time; a primitive example, one might also say, of Alfred Hitchcock's "wild walls" and his celebrated nine-minute take.

The only piece of casting done in advance was Hamlet, for whom it was thought expedient to use an actor who had at some time read the role. The rest of the cast turned up casually as a result of postcards, announcing an audition at 8:30 A.M., and those who wanted more than $2 a day need not apply. The producer picked a tall man for the Ghost, and then, passing his pencil down the list until he came to the name "Ophelia," asked hopefully, "Can any lady swim?" The finished film took fifteen minutes to show, and there is no record of riot at the box office by infuriated pundits.

Even when the talkies came in, and Mr. and Mrs. Fairbanks offered their version of "The Taming of the Shrew," "with additional dialogue by William Shakespeare," the public maintained an imperturbable calm, only suggesting diffidently that an Italian shrew was possibly not the World's Sweetheart's line of country. The Warner Brothers' "A Midsummer Night's Dream," with Mickey Rooney as a Warwickshire fairy, caused an academic grunt or two, but our Mr. Basil Dean, who stood for the classic English theatre at that time, had only just got around to sending telegrams to the press—"Shakespeare was an Englishman"—when Elisabeth Bergner came along, with "As You Like It," to suggest that he was an Austrian, and Norma Shearer turned up in "Romeo and Juliet" to hint that he was a Canadian, with high Hollywood priority.

None of these films, however, did more than idly entertain the public—"As You Like It," I think I am correct in saying, was one of the biggest box-office flops on record—and provide a passing topic for the newspaper correspondents. It was not until

Laurence Olivier came along with his "Henry V" project that anybody bothered his head very seriously over the suitability of Shakespeare for the screen.

Mr. Olivier was a different proposition from any other producer who had tried to feed the public Shakespeare. Mr. Olivier was, and is, the god of the British theatre. The Old Vic was his temple: worship of him among the younger set was already mounting to fanaticism. Young men and women who had stood, not once but scores of times, all night and day on the sidewalk, to get a glimpse of Mr. Olivier striding from his car to the stage door, and swooned at the sound of his voice across the footlights, were not likely to pass up his star appearance in his own movie version of Shakespeare.

To add to "Henry V's" chances, the actor had just won himself a big picture following with his work in "Wuthering Heights" and "Pride and Prejudice." To see such a romantic actor in a big heroic role and in Technicolor, even if it meant sitting through a lot of dreary talk about nothing, was a chance that young England found it hard to miss.

"Henry V" made a fine, rousing film, gathered critical awards wherever it was shown, and won over most of the diehards who had hitherto opposed the filming of Shakespeare, even though it did not make especially big news at the box office. Nevertheless, it did well enough to justify Mr. Rank in allowing Olivier to have a second try, and "Hamlet" came to London last summer to find West End audiences already on their toes.

It proved to be a maturer work than "Henry V"; more certain in its touch, infinitely more ambitious in technique and conception, but also less exciting. "Henry V," when all is said and done, is not major Shakespeare, but it has all the pictorial qualities of pageantry and showmanship that unite it to the screen. "Hamlet" is a close psychological study of a man's mind, and a man's mind, however ardently the producers may try to experiment with it, is not photogenic. When the film is over, the real essence of "Hamlet" remains untouched, untranslated and untranslatable.

Nobody can possibly tell, until the books are finally balanced, what the evidence of "Hamlet" will do for the case against screen Shakespeare. The film has had no general release yet in this country. It played to packed houses, with particularly heavy advance booking, on its first run at the Odeon, Leicester Square, and the customers never wholly neglected it during an extended season. There is nervous speculation, however, as to what may happen at the box office as a result of "draining the suburbs," and the view has been advanced that the distributors have hung on to the film a mite too long to catch the top of the market.

The critics, as a whole, were less cordial to "Hamlet" than they were to "Henry," and various aspects of the production—the Ghost, the cut and transposed speeches, the startling blond hair-do that secured for Sir Laurence Olivier the effect of playing in a permanent spotlight—have come in for comment somewhat less than kind.

Taking it by and large, the film has been best liked by people who admit to an indifference to Shakespeare in the theatre; in the main these are literate folk who find the stage medium for which Shakespeare wrote confined and archaic, but who like to curl up in a corner with a copy of the Bard. To these people, the argument of the play means more than the swell of its music, and for them Sir Laurence Olivier has a peculiar gift, a special knack of simplification and clarity.

In reducing "Hamlet" to manageable length, and casting it in a form readily understandable to large mixed audiences, he was faced with much the same problem as Charles and Mary Lamb when they collected their tidy little "Tales from Shakespeare." The play runs four and one-half hours in its original form: Olivier had to reduce it to two hours and three-quarters. In order to do this, he was forced to take great liberties with the text, cutting whole passages of dialogue and even some of the more famous soliloquies, transposing the speakers' lines, changing the order of events, and eliminating several characters altogether. That he has managed to do so without making nonsense of the text is a fine achievement, but produces a "Hamlet" that gives the sense of being organically unsound.

Rosencrantz and Guildenstern, for example, are not mere supernumeraries in the play, although one might be pardoned for thinking so from the way the roles are customarily performed in the theatre. They are part of Hamlet's student world, as much an aspect of his youth as Horatio, and they help to fill in the picture of a social order and a generation. Fortinbras has much more than a political significance in the chronicles of the time; he gives the end of the play its balance, and suggests the healing and unifying force that provides Hamlet's death with its justification. A soliloquy such as "Oh what a rogue and peasant slave am I" is not a slab of beautifully empty words, designed to fill a gap in the action; it is an integral part of the development, and in its matter lies the key to a man's whole character.

Shakespeare knew very well what he was doing when he wrote "Hamlet" as he wrote it: furthermore, he wrote it for popular audiences just as simple and uninstructed as the modern movie audience. Allowing for the changes in diction, Shakespeare's text is just as quick and lively today as Sir Laurence Olivier's and cannot be violated without loss.

It is periodically argued by the highbrowed and hopeful that a Shakespeare play filmed in its entirety would command as eager an audience as a Shakespeare play performed in the theatre; to which the immediate answer is, of course, that $4,000,000 movie productions do not get their money back from an audience that's eager. Nor has it been financially established that any play screened in extenso, even the best, is utterly satisfactory entertainment; for howsoever closely the two forms coincide, the play remains primarily something to listen to and the movie something to look at.

The great snag that every producer who tries to screen Shakespeare strikes sooner or later is the soliloquies, without which there is no play and with which there is apt to be no picture. The device employed by Olivier when he records his soliloquies as thoughts on the soundtrack, while the camera moves right along and frequently in a close-up with the silent speaker, has not really solved the problem effectively.

Shakespeare had the knack of cramming a world of action as well as argument into his big speeches, and a medium as free of time and space as the movies is only disputably justified in telling the customers what it could just as readily show.

One clear gain in translating Shakespeare for the cinema on the scale and with the quality that Sir Laurence Olivier brings to his productions is the opportunity it gives to out-of-town customers to see the best work of the best actors and technicians in comfortable seats at reasonable prices. Not one moviegoer in a million has a chance ordinarily to watch players of the caliber of Olivier, Eileen Herlie, Basil Sydney and the others in a major work conceived with care and displayed to perfection. Films like "Hamlet" and "Henry V" are comparable to the best phonograph disks of the greatest artists and as such they merit their place in the culture of the day.

There has been no hint, yet, either from Mr. Rank or Sir Laurence Olivier, that the Shakespearean series is likely to continue, and although Hollywood, panicked with the fear that somebody else may sign up a rising author, has several times threatened to give us the major masterpieces, only Orson Welles' "Macbeth" has so far materialized. There has been, or at least I have heard, no public outcry for more Shakespeare in the cinemas, as there is a periodic outcry for more "good" music, more French pictures, more films about the English countryside, and more Garbo. It seems likely that saturation point has been reached, and that fresh audiences will have to be conscripted if Shakespeare is to become a profitable business on the screen.

It would be nice to think that there were large numbers of potential customers waiting with ill-concealed impatience for some film producer to offer them the Complete Works of Shakespeare, but I'm afraid that neither the Shakespeare fans nor the movie fans really fall into this category. It is not possible to deny, after the brilliant experiment with "Henry V," that a certain number of the plays have the color, the pageantry, the swift and marked vigor of action that make them not wholly inappropriate to the film medium.

But broadly speaking, Shakespeare can do very well without the movies, and the movies can get along nicely without Shakespeare. Those of us who already love the plays may accept the spectacle in some cases as an added, though not necessary, diversion; those who do not love Shakespeare will enjoy the action sequences and spectacle, and frequent changes of scene, and fidget unhappily through the rest of the piece.

There are two forces that militate against the general acceptance of Shakespeare on the screen: the plots and the diction. It is generally conceded that the dialogue of the plays is tough for audiences trained to the literary standard of lyrics by You-Know-Who, but I don't think the critics have really got around to studying the toughness of the plots. The majority of Shakespeare's stories are mere Elizabethan novelettes, and nothing dates like your novelette, especially when it is a really full-blooded sample of the type.

The sort of work the family cook would slide into the bureau drawer of a Victorian kitchen would arouse hoots of mirth from the bobby-soxers of today. It is not really sensible to expect the modern generation to sit enthralled by the story of a college student who can't make up his mind to run a rapier through his uncle, or of a lady attorney who contemplates carving a meat ration off her client. That the plays are all costume plays is bad enough, but that the people in them act kinda crazy, and are all plain cases for a psychiatrist, is even worse.

When you add to the problem of an archaic plot the extra problem of archaic dialogue, you begin to understand the circuits' sales resistance to Shakespeare. The blunt truth is that it is impossible in these days for a person without some literary training to make sense of, let alone appreciate, the most human playwright in our language. Obsolete words, or words charged with a different modern meaning; unfamiliar constructions; esoteric simile; all these combined, and spoken with an accent that is not common to all of us, through the medium of an often ill-used sound-track, may make the play unintelligible to a movie-goer who does not know what Shakespeare would be up to.

But the difficulty goes deeper than the problem of archaic language; the average moviegoer does not care for poetry in its proper sense at all, for the simple reason that he never reads or hears any.

The people who appreciate Shakespeare today have for the most part acquired their affection in the first place through the medium of print. It is true, as Sir Arthur Quiller-Couch has pointed out somewhere, that Shakespeare is written to be acted, not to be read (though he does not deny us the additional pleasure of reading). But I submit that the initial affection for Shakespeare is born of familiarity with the printed word, and that the people who enjoy him best today are the people who studied him at school.

It is a pleasant dream to suppose that, deep down in the hearts of all English-speaking people, there is an instinctive passion for the playwright that only demands his plays should be enacted before them to be warmly embraced. But the fact remains that the ordinary modern customer in the loges is far less concerned with The Bard than he is with The Body or The Voice, and there seems little point in trying to adapt Shakespeare to the people, until the people can be adapted to Shakespeare.

Part 4

MUSIC

FEW, IF any, popular artists have equaled the Beatles in making an impact on a generation. Without demeaning the inventiveness and sheer musical virtuosity of this celebrated quartet of Liverpudlians, one questions whether they would have achieved their living deification by the Young Audience had it not been for the elaborate apparatus of publicity know-how and the exploitive powers of the mass media. The generation that grew up to the sounds of Glenn Miller and Benny Goodman's big bands, the lyrics of Cole Porter, Jerome Kern, and Jimmy McHugh, seems light years removed from the music their kids listen to incessantly via records, radio, and whenever possible in "live" concerts.

It is probably no exaggeration to suggest that the alleged death of any world figure (including Pope Paul) would have meant far less to college kids in the autumn of 1969 than Paul McCartney's. A superb example of the psychology of rumor which flourishes in anxious times, whether McCartney was in truth dead or not became the greatest topic of conversation on campuses throughout the country since the assassination of John F. Kennedy. Even when a front-cover picture of McCartney with his wife and babies appeared in *Life* magazine with a lead story, collegians were still skeptical. A couple of ingenious students at MIT matched voice prints of early Beatles records with their latest and verified an 80 to 90 per cent similarity in the albums.

Rock, which was almost exclusively the listening province of the Young Audience in the 1960's, began finally to sound less raucous to middle-aged parents, perhaps won over by sheer exposure to the sounds from their kids' bedrooms. As we enter the 1970's, radio ratings indicate that people in their forties or fifties are tuning more and more to the FM rock stations. The final note that rock had achieved respectability came when Wiley Housewright, president of the Music Educators' National Conference (representing 58,000 music teachers) asked President Nixon to sponsor a rock festival on the White House lawn. The President was noncommittal about the proposal.

In the first essay in this section, Thomas Meehan analyzes the impact of Bob Dylan on the Young Audience. An informal survey at three Ivy League universities indicates that the favorite contemporary writer of English majors was Bob Dylan. Meehan shows why Dylan's lyrics are memorized, studied, idolized by millions of young people. To the 100,000 pilgrims who came to the Isle of Wight in early September 1969 to hear Dylan in his first public concert since 1966, it would seem quite natural to hear him compared with Homer. Didn't poetry begin with Homer wandering about reading his verses to anyone who would listen to them, a pro-Dylan critic asks?

David Dempsey's article examines the reasons why girls scream, weep, and approach hysteria when they attend a concert by the Beatles. Turning to scholars in both anthropology and psychology, Dempsey cites the work of the late social psychologist T. W. Adorno, who viewed modern youth's leisure patterns with considerable misgivings. Adorno recalled that the Bacchantes literally tore Orpheus limb from limb when his playing of the flute drove them into a frenzied state. Actually, teen-age girls have been flipping and screaming since the early days of Frank Sinatra, undoubtedly spurred on by a publicity man's claque in the audience.

Benjamin DeMott discusses the concept of the new pop music as a real religious force in the lives of the Young Audience. Although this may seem far out on first consideration, DeMott cites evidence that rock is being taken seriously by such groups as the United Presbyterian Church, which engaged a rock group known as the Astrakhan Sleeve to produce religious records in 1968. In both DeMott's insightful essay and the article on rock music by Karen Murphy and Ronald Gross, it becomes apparent that rock lyrics are in closer touch with contemporary life than pop music used to be. But rock contains contradictions as well. The youth who have made rock their salvation might well say, as did Walt Whitman, "Do I contradict myself? Very well, I contradict myself; I contain multitudes."

Public Writer No. 1?

by Thomas Meehan

FOR THE PAST three and a half years, since the death of William Faulkner, on July 6, 1962, American literary critics have been nervously scanning the horizon in search of a novelist or poet who can be definitely called the nation's Public Writer No. 1, in the way that Faulkner and, before him, Hemingway, answered to this title. Not surprisingly, the critics, gazing out the windows of The Partisan Review, etc., have been keeping a close eye on who is being read by the country's college undergraduates, who are, after all, today's more selective readers as well as tomorrow's writers, professors of English and even critics for The Partisan Review. Thus, in intellectual circles from Berkeley to Philip Rahv's apartment, where all the talk has been of writers like Robert Lowell, Saul Bellow and Norman Mailer, a number of jaws dropped noticeably a couple of weeks ago when an informal survey of students majoring in English at three prominent Ivy League colleges revealed that their favorite contemporary American writer is a 24-year-old folk-song writer, composer and singer named Bob Dylan.

Unlike Lowell, Bellow, Mailer or any of the dozen or so other writers esteemed by the quarterlies, explained the students, Dylan, whose songs are mainly of social and personal protest, is writing about things they care about.

From the *New York Times Magazine,* December 12, 1965, copyright © 1965 by The New York Times Company.

"We don't give a damn about Moses Herzog's *angst* or Norman Mailer's private fantasies," one earnest Brown University senior noted. "We're concerned with things like the threat of nuclear war, the civil-rights movement and the spreading blight of dishonesty, conformism and hypocrisy in the United States, especially in Washington, and Bob Dylan is the only American writer dealing with these subjects in a way that makes any sense to us. And, at the same time, as modern poetry, we feel that his songs have a high literary quality. As far as we're concerned, in fact, any one of his songs, like 'A Hard Rain's Gonna Fall,' is more interesting to us, both in a literary and a social sense, than an entire volume of Pulitzer Prize verse by someone like Robert Lowell."

(The undergraduate vote was not, of course, unanimous. One Harvard unbeliever, for example, asserted that it was "absurd" to take Dylan's writing seriously.)

If Bob Dylan is, indeed, an emerging major literary figure, he will then have things going for him three ways, for he is already a leading figure in the American folk-singing world and, at the same time, a teen-age popular-music idol whose recordings of so-called folk-rock songs, a hybrid form of his own recent invention, like "Positively 4th Street" and "Like a Rolling Stone," have in the past few months frequently been nestled next to Beatles' numbers near the top of WABC's All-American Super-Hit survey. Folk rock, by the way, is nothing more than a folk song sung to a rock 'n' roll big-beat background, but when Dylan introduced this new form at the Newport Folk Festival and at an outdoor concert at Forest Hills last summer, singing for the first time to the electronic accompaniment of a blaring rock 'n' roll combo, he was roundly booed by folk-song purists, who considered this innovation the worst sort of heresy. "It's all music," drawled Dylan in reply, "no more, no less."

For those who are not familiar with him, Dylan is, in appearance, the Ultimate Beatnik; cowboy boots, jeans, wrinkled work shirts and dark glasses, plus frizzy, unkempt hair and a lean, pale and haggard face. He somehow curiously resembles a combination of Harpo Marx, Carol Burnett and the young Beethoven. Most often accompanying himself on a guitar—between verses he plays a harmonica attached to a contraption slung around his neck—Dylan tends to snarl his songs rather than sing them, spitting out the iconoclastic lyrics in a whiny, high-pitched hillbilly wail.

If and when Dylan makes it into the pages of "Twentieth Century Authors," the entry will show that he was born in Duluth, Minn., on May 24, 1941, the son of a pharmacist, and was raised in Hibbing, Minn., a small mining town near the Canadian border, where he lived off and on until he was 18. "Hibbing's a good ol' town," wrote Dylan not long ago. "I ran away from it when I was 10, 12, 13, 15, 15½, 17 an' 18. I been caught and brought back all but once." Dylan's real name was Bob Zimmerman. He changed it because of admiration for poet Dylan Thomas.

His first excursion from Hibbing was to Chicago, where, at the age of 10, he bought his first guitar and taught himself to play it. By the age of 15 he had further taught himself to play the piano, the autoharp and the harmonica, had become hooked on singing folk songs—and, indeed, had written his first folk song, a love ballad he dedicated to Brigitte Bardot.

After graduating from Hibbing high school and spending six desultory months at the University of Minnesota, Dylan struck out on a hitch-hiking career as an itinerant folk singer, roaming about from places like Gallup, N.M., to Cheyenne, Wyo., to Sioux Falls, S. D., for more than three years before finally heading East in the late fall of 1960 to pay a call on Woody Guthrie, the famed folk singer of the thirties who had a profound influence on Dylan as a writer, a performer and a thinker, and who was then lying seriously ill in a New Jersey hospital.

In early 1961, Dylan made his New York performing debut at Gerde's Folk City on West Fourth Street in Greenwich Village, the La Scala of the American folk-singing scene, and at once he took the place by storm, bowling over everyone from Pete Seeger to Joan Baez with verses like this one from his "Talkin' New York," a comic, Guthrie-like talking blues:

> *Winter time in New York town,*
> *The wind blowin', snow around*
> *Walk around with nowhere to go*

Somebody could freeze right to the bone.
I froze right to the bone.[1]

From talking blues, Dylan quickly progressed to more serious work, including a series of anti-war songs ("Masters of War," "God Is on Our Side," etc.) and a series of songs protesting social injustices ("The Lonesome Death of Hattie Carroll," "The Ballad of Hollis Brown," "Who Killed Davey Moore?", etc.). In 1962, Dylan wrote "Blowin' in the Wind," which became the rallying song of the civil-rights movement and which made Dylan nationally famous.

Earlier, in the fall of 1961, he had made his first record album, for Columbia Records, called simply enough, "Bob Dylan," and the album had been at once an enormous success. And he has made five subsequent albums, all of which have been equally successful. Meanwhile, he has sung to overflow audiences at colleges and in concert halls over the country and, in New York, has given several standing-room-only one-man concerts at Town Hall, Carnegie Hall and Lincoln Center.

His songs, sung either by himself or by such other folk and folk-rock interpreters as Joan Baez, Odetta, Judy Collins, Pete Seeger, Peter, Paul and Mary, Sonny and Cher, the Byrds and the Turtles, have in the past couple of years virtually revolution-ized American popular music. "Until Bob Dylan came along, all of the hit songs were lachrymose teen-age laments about unhappy high school love affairs," a New York recording executive commented the other day. "But now, to an amazing degree, the hits are about things like war, foreign policy and poverty. Dylan started it all with 'Masters of War' and 'Blowin' in the Wind,' and his imitators are now making it big with folk-rock songs like 'Eve of Destruction,' 'Home of the Brave' and 'We Gotta Get Out of This Place.'

"All in all, Dylan has had a great deal of responsibility for the surprising interest the younger generation has today in serious questions like civil rights and Vietnam. In fact, he's probably had more direct influence on what's going on with young people in America today—protest marches, picketing and so forth—than almost any other one person in the country."

1. Copyright 1962 by Duchess Music Corporation. Used by permission.

Most of Dylan's reputation rests on his talents as a performer and a writer of lyrics rather than as a composer, for his melodies are fairly ordinary and decidedly derivative—although perhaps unique in that they mix for the first time the sounds of Negro blues with the twang of Nashville country music. "Dylan breaks all the rules of song writing," folk music critic Robert Shelton has written, "except that of having something to say and saying it stunningly."

As a literary stylist, he seems something of an anachronism, for many of his songs are written in a manner reminiscent of the protest, "Waiting for Lefty" pseudo-poetry of the thirties. For example, in 1937, Odets—or Maxwell Anderson—might well have written these lines from "Masters of War":

> *You fasten the triggers*
> *For the others to fire*
> *Then you set back and watch*
> *When the death count gets higher*
> *You hide in your mansion*
> *As young people's blood*
> *Flows out of their bodies*
> *And is buried in the mud* [2]

On the other hand, future Ph.D. candidates in English, writing their theses on Dylan, will not find him that easy to pigeonhole, for he tends to write in a number of styles, among them an extraordinarily lyrical and traditional folk-song style. "Blowin' in the Wind," for example, is very much a traditional folk song:

> *How many years can a mountain exist*
> *Before it's washed to the sea?*
> *Yes, 'n' how many times can some people exist*
> *Before they're allowed to be free?*
> *Yes, 'n' how many times can a man turn his head*
> *Pretending he just doesn't see?*
>
> *The answer, my friend, is blowin' in the wind,*
> *The answer is blowin' in the wind.* [3]

2. Copyright 1963 by M. Witmark & Sons. Used by permission.
3. Copyright 1962 by M. Witmark & Sons. Used by permission.

And then there are Dylan songs like "Girl of the North Country," which could have been composed in the back hills of Kentucky in 1824, with verses like this one:

So if you're travelin' in the north country fair,
Where the winds hit heavy on the borderline,
Remember me to one who lives there,
She once was a true love of mine.[4]

At the same time, oddly enough, mixing a traditional folk-song style with the techniques of modern poetry, Dylan can at times be extremely obscure. His "A Hard Rain's a Gonna Fall," for instance, is scarcely any "On Top of Old Smoky," as this verse may suggest:

Oh, what'll you do now, my blue-eyed son?
Oh, what'll you do now, my darling young one?

I'm a goin' back out 'fore the rain starts a fallin',
I'll walk to the depth of the deepest black forest,
Where the people are many and their hands are all empty,
Where the pellets of poison are flooding their waters,
Where the home in the valley meets the damp dirty prison,
Where the executioner's face is always well hidden,
Where hunger is ugly, where souls are forgotten,
Where black is the color, where none is the number,
And I'll tell it and think it and speak it and breathe it,
And reflect it from the mountain so all souls can see it,
Then I'll stand on the ocean until I start sinkin'.[5]

Those conditioned by the likes of "Red River Valley" to think of folk songs as simple and uncomplicated are inevitably confused by Dylan's songs. Dylan, however, claims that folk songs have always been difficult to comprehend. "Folk music is the only music where it isn't simple," Dylan told an interviewer recently. "It's never been simple. It's weird, man, full of legend, myth, Bible and ghosts. And, yeah, chaos—watermelons, clocks, everything."

The use of slang like "man" is typical of Dylan, for he is very much the motorcycle-riding hipster, but this surface pose masks an extraordinarily intelligent, sensitive, concerned and surprisingly well-read young man. For example, he is familiar with most of the classic and modern poets and at times his verses sound like those of a hillbilly W. H. Auden—specifically the earlier Auden of such poems as "September 1, 1939," as these lines from Dylan's "It's Alright Ma (I'm Only Bleeding)" might suggest:

> *Disillusioned words like bullets bark*
> *As human Gods aim for their mark*
> *Made everything from toy guns that spark*
> *To flesh colored Christs that glow in the dark* [6]

Perhaps Dylan's principal appeal to the young (and to an increasing number of the not-so-young) is his rude defiance of all authority and scorn for the Establishment, which he puts down with unrelenting and unforgiving bitterness, as in "Masters of War," which begins with this verse:

> *Come you masters of war*
> *You that build all the guns*
> *You that build the death planes*
> *You that build the big bombs*
> *You that hide behind walls*
> *You that hide behind desks*
> *I just want you to know*
> *I can see through your masks*

And ends with this one:

> *And I hope that you die*
> *And your death'll come soon*
> *I will follow your casket*
> *On a pale afternoon*
> *And I'll watch while you're lowered*
> *Down to your death bed*

6. Copyright 1965 by M. Witmark & Sons. Used by permission.

> *And I'll stand o'er your grave*
> *Till I'm sure that you're dead* [7]

But Dylan doesn't viciously put away only the death-plane builders; he also goes after those guilty of the most ordinary day-to-day hypocrisies, as in "Positively 4th Street," a savage little number that was near the top of the WABC survey just a few weeks ago:

> *You got a lotta nerve*
> *To say you are my friend*
> *When I was down*
> *You just stood there grinning*
>
> *You got a lotta nerve*
> *To say you gotta helping hand to lend*
> *You just want to be on*
> *The side that's winning . . .*
>
> *You see me on the street*
> *You always act surprised*
> *You say "how are you?", "good luck"*
> *But you don't mean it*
>
> *When you know as well as me*
> *You'd rather see me paralyzed*
> *Why don't you just come out once*
> *And scream it . . .*
>
> *I wish that for just one time*
> *You could stand inside my shoes*
> *And just for that one moment*
> *I could be you*
>
> *Yes I wish that for just one time*
> *You could stand inside my shoes*
> *You'd know what a drag it is*
> *To see you* [8]

7. Copyright 1963 by M. Witmark & Sons. Used by permission.
8. Copyright 1965 by M. Witmark & Sons. Used by permission.

Dylan himself refers to his compositions as "stories" rather than as songs, and most have a kind of narrative line to them, a straight narrative, as in "The Lonesome Death of Hattie Carroll," which concerns itself with the killing of a Negro maid by a wealthy young white man (based on an actual incident), or a nightmare-fantasy narrative, as in "Bob Dylan's 115th Dream" which is a satiric retelling of the story of the discovery of America:

> *I think I'll call it America*
> *I said as we hit land*
> *I took a deep breath*
> *I fell down, I could not stand*
> *Captain Arab he started*
> *Writing up some deeds*
> *He said, let's set up a fort*
> *And start buying the place with beads*
> *Just then this cop comes down the street*
> *Crazy as a loon*
> *He throws us all in jail*
> *For carryin' harpoons.*
>
> *Ah me I busted out*
> *Don't even ask me how*
> *I went to get some help*
> *I walked by a guernsey cow*
> *Who directed me down*
> *To the Bowery slums*
> *Where people carried signs around*
> *Sayin', ban the bums*
> *I jumped right into line*
> *Sayin', I hope that I'm not late*
> *When I realized I hadn't eaten*
> *For five days straight. . . .*
>
> *Well I rapped upon a house*
> *With the U.S. flag upon display*
> *I said, could you help me out*

I got some friends down the way
The man says, get out of here
I'll tear you limb from limb
I said, you know they refused Jesus too
He said, you're not him
Get out of here before I break your bones
I ain't your pop
I decided to have him arrested
And I went lookin' for a cop. . . .

Well, the last I heard of Arab
He was stuck on a whale
That was married to the deputy
Sheriff of the jail
But the funniest thing was
When I was leavin' the bay
I saw three ships a sailin'
They were all heading my way
I asked the captain what his name was
And how come he didn't drive a truck
He said his name was Columbus
I just said, good luck [9]

Those students who claim that Dylan is the best writer in America today point not only to his lyrics but also, curiously enough, to the copy Dylan writes for his record liners. This is usually a hundred lines or so of free verse, like these characteristic, somewhat Brechtian (with punctuation by Cummings) excerpts from the liner of the recent album "Bringing It All Back Home":

i'm standing there watching the parade
feeling combination of sleepy john estes, jayne mansfield,
humphrey bogart
mortimer snurd, murph the surf and so forth

9. Copyright 1965 by M. Witmark & Sons. Used by permission.

> *erotic hitchhiker wearing japanese blanket.*
> *gets my attention by asking didn't*
> *he see me at this hootenanny down in puerto vallarta, mexico*
> *i say no you must be mistaken.*
> *i happen to be one of the Supremes*
> *then he rips off his blanket*
> *an suddenly becomes a middle-aged druggist,*
> *up for district attorney.*
> *he starts screaming at me you're the one.*
> *you're the one that's been causing all them riots over in*
> * vietnam.*
> *immediately turn to a bunch of people and says if elected,*
> *he'll have me electrocuted*
> *publicly on the next fourth of july* [10]

Surprisingly, a number of leading American literary critics profess never even to have heard of Bob Dylan, while, among those who are acquainted with his work, the critical opinion is sharply divided between those who don't take him in the least seriously and those who agree with the students that Dylan may well be an important new figure in American letters.

"I don't see Dylan as a writer of any consequence—he's simply a pop-culture figure," says one of the anti-Dylan critics. "Granted, he has an interesting imagination, but his ideas and his techniques are dated and banal—we've been through all this before in the thirties. Like most pop-culture heroes, Dylan will soon be forgotten—he'll quickly become last year's vogue writer."

On the other hand, a pro-Dylan critic argued this way recently: "Dylan is taking poetry away from the academicians, Poetry, and the Y.M.H.A., and giving it back to the masses, which seems to me an extremely healthy development. Moreover, he is an interesting poet, even if he is a teen-age idol. After all, poetry began with Homer, wandering about reciting his verses to anyone who'd listen to them and, in a sense, stretching matters a bit, Dylan is a kind of 20th-century Homer, if, however, 'Motorpsycho Nightmare' and the rest are scarcely 'The Iliad.' "

Dylan's fellow poets tend also to be somewhat divided in their assessment of him, as in the opinions of:

Stanley Kunitz—"I listen with pleasure to Bob Dylan, but I would term him a popular artist, a writer of verse rather than of poetry. All in all, though, I think the interest taken in him is a healthy sign, for there is no reason why popular art and a more selective, esoteric art can't cheerfully coexist. And popular art is the foundation on which fine art rests. Thus, the higher the level of taste there is in the popular arts, the more promising is the hope for the evolution of great fine art."

Louis Simpson—"I don't think Bob Dylan is a poet at all; he is an entertainer—the word poet is used these days to describe practically anybody. I am not surprised, though, that American college students consider him their favorite poet—they don't know anything about poetry."

W. H. Auden—"I am afraid I don't know his work at all. But that doesn't mean much—one has so frightfully much to read anyway."

Among those who tend to agree with the pro-Dylan critics is Dylan himself, who has nothing but scorn for the American literary Establishment and who not long ago had this to say to an interviewer: "The only thing where it's happening is on the radio and records. That's where people hang out. It's not in book form, it's not on the stage. All this art they been talking about, it just remains on the shelf."

And, finally, those writers and critics who refuse to take Dylan seriously might give some thought to the second verse of Dylan's "The Times They Are A-Changin'," a song that enjoys immense popularity with the current college generation and has, in fact, become the somewhat subversive secret theme song of that generation:

Come writers and critics
Who prophecies with your pen
And keep your eyes wide
And don't speak too soon
For the wheel's still in spin

And there's no tellin' who
That it's namin'
For the loser now
Will be later to win
FOR THE TIMES THEY ARE A-CHANGIN' [11]

Rock As Salvation

by Benjamin DeMott

ALL AT ONCE "they"—the opinion makers, taste makers, types who Know and Know—were hailing rock music as a high road to cultural and even spiritual salvation. Should sane folk buy that jazz?

They are not likely to tomorrow, certainly. For most people pop music is one thing, intellectual or spiritual transformation is another; closing the gap between the two means rearranging a whole cluster of assumptions about art, order and values. And while such rearrangements have occurred in the past, just at the moment some barriers exist.

The most obvious barrier to grown-up, middle-class receptivity to rock is the disquieting life style of rock groups and audiences— the hair, the costumes, the volume, scarifying hints of sexual liberation, etc. But there are others. One is the tendency of a number of preachers of rock as Revelation to shock rather than argue or explain—witness Allen Ginsberg's comparison of the Fugs with Jesus Christ ("The Bible says that when Christ comes back, 'every eye shall see.' . . . When the Fugs break thru . . . every eye shall see"). Another is that rock lyrics are often, speaking mildly, hard to fathom—witness the Lemon Pipers' "Jelly Jungle (of Orange Marmalade)":

> *In the jelly jungle of orange marmalade*
> *There are tangerine dreams waiting for you in orange*
> *marmalade*
> *In the jelly jungle of orange marmalade.*[1]

Still another problem: Rock seems at moments only a footnote to the pot or drug experience, not an independent meditative engagement in its own right. William Kloman recently reported, in this newspaper, on the marked increase in rock records designed for use as background music for pot parties—"intricate harmonies, gently orchestrated melodies, and abrupt shifts in tempo which would strike the normal listener as pointless and distracting."

Beyond all this—a further obstacle to acceptance of rock as a vision—stands the seeming faddishness of the phenomenon, the belief that rock is "merely" a fashion—part of the Now culture that is bound to age and may already be passing away. How can serious thought and feeling flourish amid such ephemerality? So runs the inevitable squarish question.

That the idea of the new pop music as a religious force is so far credible only to With-Its does not signify, however, that it will never gain credibility for others. Rock is already being taken seriously in many quarters usually thought to be proof against chichi or frivolity—the upper echelons of the United Presbyterian Church, for one (the leadership of this institution recently retained a rock group called the Astrakhan Sleeve to produce religious records; a spokesman explained that rock is a "forum for serious messages far removed from the moon-June variety").

And there are signs that secular organs of opinion which, in the past, have exerted powerful, if trickle-down, influence on majority thought, are moving in a comparable direction. On the appearance of the Beatles' last LP, Partisan Review carried a long tribute by Prof. Richard Poirier, chairman of the English Department at Rutgers and a P.R. editor—an essay that invoked Shakespeare and T. S. Eliot in characterizing the Beatles' gifts, saw a likeness between their "knowledge" and that of contemporary writers like Beckett and Borges, and, at its climax, argued

1. Copyright Kama Sutra Music.

that the Beatles speak with an intensity of philosophical-esthetic insight matched only by titans of the past:

" 'And the time will come,' it is promised in one of [the Beatles'] songs, 'when you will see we're all one, and life flows on within you and without you.' As an apprehension of artistic, and perhaps of any other kind of placement within living endeavor, this idea is allowable only to the very great."

The Beatles are by no means the only group that has inspired writing at this pitch of awe. The third issue of New American Review carried a discussion of rock music by Prof. Albert Goldman of Columbia in which a rock composition was compared to "King Lear," and the group called The Doors was said to "achieve their purpose as gurus, which is to confront their audience with the most basic unbearable truths." In the course of this essay Professor Goldman laid down numerous other claims for rock music:

"[Rock] has cleared a channel from the lowest and most archaic to the highest and most recent, and through that conduit is now flowing a revitalizing current of energy and of ideas. The result has been the elevation of rock to the summit of popular culture and the accelerating expansion of its interests and resources.

"By pushing toward higher levels of imaginative excellence, rock has begun to realize one of the most cherished dreams of mass culture: to cultivate from the vigorous but crude growth of the popular arts a new serious art that would combine the strength of native roots with the beauty flowering from the highest art. . . .

"No other cultural force in modern times has possessed [rock's] power of synthesis."

Claims are just that, needless to say—claims. Some eyes confronting the ones just quoted may find vexing resemblances between them and youth-cult paroxysms on the same subject—effusions like those of Mr. Gene Youngblood of The Los Angeles Free Press: "There is only one word for [Jimi] Hendrix: inspiring. He's an electric religion. . . . After he hurled his guitar at the screen in a cataclysmic-volcanic-orgasmic finale we fell back limp in our seats, stunned and numbed."

But a resemblance of any sort between low-cult and high-cult accounts of the rock experience demands to be taken as evidence in itself that that experience is indeed no negligible "cultural force." The questions arising are: Why is rock making it, in the homely phrase, so big? What specific qualities of this musical experience explain its attractiveness to rude youth, thoughtful youth, literary intellectuals, "cultivated minds"? Finally: Whom, among the mass of listeners, can rock truly "save"—or truly harm —and how?

As may or may not go without saying, rock fans hold that the success of the movement is best understood in musical, not metaphysical, terms. That argument is not wholly absurd on its face. The movement has produced several inventions in the field of singing style (Ray Charles is the most gifted of the inventors). The performers in the "mainstream soul" division—in particular, Aretha Franklin and the late Otis Redding—are not much inferior in freedom, exuberance, range of color and individuality of phrasing to the best singers in jazz and blues history. A dozen Beatle songs can be played with delight by any amateur musician who relishes tunes with surprising changes, structural inventiveness and melodic lines of uncommon length and sweetness. There are passages of genuine musical excitement—who is unaware of this?—throughout "Rubber Soul," "Revolver" and "Magical Mystery Tour" (the entrance into "Blue Jay Way" is especially lovely). A fine fragment of music drama—the poised, ironical stiff-arm called "Lady Jane"—turns up in a Rolling Stones album. (The Beatles best the stony Stones when the latter imitate them, but not invariably otherwise; no third group can compete with either—even after so many years.) Several groups possess able instrumentalists (slightly overrated by rock fans)—the guitarists Mike Bloomfield and Eric Clapton, for two examples. And, viewed as a disaster epic, a Hendrix concert is only a shade less terrorizing—though there are no dancers and much less blackness—than the much-praised Merce Cunningham–La Monte Young "Winterbranch."

Moreover—still in the area of musical accomplishment—there are some feats of assimilation in the development of rock that have few parallels in the history of pop music. Over the past two decades, a long list of performers contributed directly and indirectly to the development in question. (Rock "began" in a sense, with a Cleveland disc jockey's decision, in 1954, to feature some obscure rhythm-and-blues records made by Negro record companies in the South.) Some names on the list are still familiar, either because the performers were superstars in their time or ours, or because they remain active now—Elvis Presley, Chuck Berry, Ray Charles, the Beatles, Bob Dylan. Others, who were in their way not less important, have not quite become household words —Frankie Lymon, for instance, Bo Diddley, Little Richard, B. B. King and several more.

But the roster of names testifies that rock came to its eminence by mixing into the basic rhythm-and-blues texture other musical elements and traditions—materials that hitherto had separate publics of their own. The audience for rhythm-and-blues (R.&B.) records of the early nineteen-fifties lay mainly in the black ghettos of the North. But new vocal sounds that were added in the mid-fifties—the gospel sound (Little Richard), country and Western (Presley), an unprecedented crossing of gospel and blues (Charles)—widened the audience geographically and socially.

And there were comparable developments in instrumental sound and in rock lyrics. B. B. King, the guitarist, moved the rock band on from the scrappy, haphazard sound of R. & B., and other major contributions came from the eclectic Beatles, from the inventors of the supergorgeous Mantovanian Motown Sound, and from the pioneers of progressive or art rock.

As for rock lyrics: California surf and drag rock superimposed the "contexted" experience of middle-class white youths upon the original blues-based shouts; Bob Dylan and the school of folk rock complicated the blend with political and social commentary; the work of the Stones and the Fugs steadily sharpened the ironical edge or fury of that commentary. As Professor Goldman puts it:

"The Rock Age has assimilated everything in sight, commencing with the whole of American music: urban and country blues, gospel, hillbilly, Western 'goodtime' (the ricky-tick of the twenties), and Tin Pan Alley. It has reached across the oceans for the sounds and rhythms of Africa, the Middle East and India. It has reached back in time for the baroque trumpet, the madrigal and the Gregorian chant; and forward into the future for electronic music and the noise collages of *musique concrète.*"

But while all this is true, the musical possibility supposed to have been created by rock's assimilating power—the possibility of a "new serious art that would combine the strength of native roots with the beauty flowering from the highest art"—still looks frail and remote.[2] Market pressures touch rock no less directly than they have touched every other kind of music in the American pop past. As there were crashing, mindless set pieces in the Swing Era to excite the "Go-go-go! Saints! Saints!" big-tipper mob ("One O'clock Jump," "Sing Sing Sing"), so there are a hundred versions of Jimi Hendrix's "Wild Thing" and "Purple Haze" now (wilder and louder, naturally, than in olden times). As the dance bands of the late nineteen-thirties "advanced" toward fancy charts, with cathedral voicings of reed sections (Glenn Miller) and few opportunities for individual musical creativity, so the Motown rock rises to a comparable glossiness at a comparable musical cost and commercial profit.

Again and again, in truth, the listener to rock records is haunted by echoes of the kitsch sounds of the thirties—not to mention echoes of the old anxieties about integrity vs. sellout. Martha and the Vandellas singing "My Baby Loves Me"—the background here is pure Big Sky music, appropriate for Joel McCrea's Arizona, or for a DeMille epic, or even (at a pinch) for backing some footage of the Olivier-Oberon "Wuthering Heights." Diana Ross, that wispy lead singer heard on The Supremes' "Stop in the Name of Love"—her timbre (or no-timbre) is straight out of "Oh Johnny"-ville, is it not? And where, oh where, in *schlock* rock like Tommy James and the Shondells, is there even so much as a memory of the authentic gritty joyousness of Otis Redding singing:

> *On a cold, rainy, windy night*
> *She shut all the doors*
> *She cut off all the lights*
> *She holds me and squeezes me tight*
> *She tells me Big O everything's all right . . .*

2. Some jazz lovers claim that, for esthetic reasons, it will ever be thus. But several rock groups—Cream, Jefferson Airplane—have lately taken tentative steps toward meeting the flatly dismissive objections of the jazz buff. The objections are that the high volume and blocky, pounding, monotonous 4/4 beat rule out rhythmic intricacy and pliancy, as well as subtlety in dynamics, and that, while there is a jazz and blues foundation to the music, improvisation has never become a prime feature of the form.

Come on now
Bring my breakfast to the table
When I go to work she knows I'm able
Do my job I come back in
You oughta see my baby's face
She just grins, grins, grins.[3]

The progressive or art-rock school does, to be sure, continue to experiment, and newish groups like The Doors are more venturesome in pattern and theme than most of their American competitors. And there are the Beatles and the Stones. The Beatles, though, are in full flight from rock to a kind of show music—and it must be said, furthermore, that their smoothie, nice-lad manner never much engaged lovers of mainstream soul. As for art rockers like Van Dyke Parks, they don't sell. And while The Doors do, their trade appears to depend not upon musical freshness, but upon exploitation of the sexiness of the singer Jim Morrison. (On one recent occasion Mr. Morrison began a public performance by recounting his latest sexual adventure: it had taken place five minutes before curtain time.)

The point of this glance at economics is that the subject has important bearing on the matter of the nature of the rock triumph. If the rock world were conscious of the junk, kitsch and exploitative sexuality that litters the present scene, if alertness to differences of musical quality in rock material were the rule, the argument that the success of rock is essentially musical would be less implausible. As it is, the suspicion lingers that the rock experience is as impure, by musical criteria, as most of the pop experiences that have preceded it.

The jazz intelligentsia of the thirties tended to embrace the entire jazz enterprise, excluding little that called itself jazz, regardless of how pretentious and incompetent the stuff might be. And the rock intelligentsia of the present day behaves similarly. Three decades ago, such refusals of judgment signified that the experience of listening to jazz was less musical than political in nature—an occasion on which a longed-for relationship (one of solidarity) between self and underdog or underadvantaged could

3. "Happy Song (Dum, Dum)." Copyright 1968, East Publications.

be achieved. Nowadays, the refusals signify that the experience of listening to rock is less musical than. . . .

Well, than what? What exactly is the rock audience hankering after? We are back, if not at the theme of rock as salvation, then at a restatement of the truth that the key to the success of rock music appears to lie elsewhere than in the music itself—perhaps in an adjustment or harmony between certain extramusical features of the rock experience and certain extramusical needs or desires characteristic of the rock audience. But the question remains: What needs, what desires, what precise means of gratification?

One need, undoubtedly, is that of the young to call the bluff of their elders—to *occasion* scorn, to stimulate the hypocrite (real or supposed) to display his nature. "Turn it down!" Good Folk cry, furious at disturbance, in love with their own complacency, hideously lacking in the imagination of disaster.

But the chief need, perhaps, and there is no sense, incidentally, in pretending that only rock types share it, is relief from significant life quandaries and guilt. And chief among the quandaries is one that comes down roughly to this: I, an educated man (or adolescent), thoughtful, concerned, liberal, informed, have a fair and rational grasp of the realities of my age—domestic and international problems, public injustices, inward strains that give birth to acts of human meanness. But although I know the problems, and even perhaps the "correct" solutions, I also know that this knowledge of mine lacks potency. My stored head, this kingdom—my pride, my liberalism, my feeling for human complexity —none of this alters the world; it only exhausts me with constant naggings about powerlessness. What can I do?

Pop tunes that begin "I'll build a stairway to the stars" [4] don't help much with that problem—which is to say, the thirties' pop lyrics didn't link up very directly with "reality." Rock lyrics, on the other hand, do link up—many of them. The world of the rock lyric encompasses war protest (The Fugs: "Kill for Peace"), overdue social justice (Bob Dylan: "Blowin' in the Wind"), black hippies' fury (Jimi Hendrix: "If 6 Was 9").

That world includes, in addition, intricate human relationships

4. Used by permission of Robbins Music Corporation, copyright proprietor.

in which people press themselves to define their feelings precisely (The Beatles: "She Said She Said"). And it blinks neither at sexual hypocrisies (The Rolling Stones: "Back Street Girl"), nor at depressing or disgusting visual details of urban scenes (John Hartford: "Shiny Rails of Steel"). Boosters of one or another rock lyric, true enough, often lose their cool.

" 'Learn to forget,' " a writer says in Crawdaddy, the rock magazine, quoting a snippet of a rock tune. "What power that phrase has! It's possible to get stoned for days by listening to this song. For a while it will seem the one truth available to us . . . a catalyst with more potential for generating truth . . . than anything since middle Faulkner."

But learn to forget boosters: Rock lyrics *are* in closer touch with contemporary life than pop used to be. And it is plain that contemporary minds and rock "groove" together partly because many rock songs take cognizance of the ills that exacerbate such minds. Partly—but not wholly. The complex case is that, if one phase of the rock experience is confirmation of what a man knows, the other phase, equally telling, is escape from the knowledge. "Bring along your views," says the rock invitation. "Your liberal opinions. Your knowledge of atrocities committed by numberless power structures of the past. Your analyst's ideas about today's Oedipal hangup. Your own manipulative, categorizing, classifying, S.A.T. braininess. You can not only cross the rock threshold bearing this paraphernalia, you can retreat to it, consult it, any time you want—by tuning back into the lyrics. No obligation, in this pop world, to mindlessness. . . .

"But now if you'd like something *else*—if you want your freedom, if you'd care to blow your mind, shed those opinions, plunge into selflessness, into a liberating perception of the uselessness, the unavailingness, the futility of the very notion of opinionated personhood, well, it so happens there's something, dig, real helpful here. . . ."

What is being said is that the rock invitation offers the audience a momentary chance to have it both ways: If I accept the invitation, I can simultaneously be political and beyond politics, intellectual and beyond intellectuality, independent and beyond personal independence.

I can be these contrary things because the rock experience at its most intense is an intimation of engulfment and merger, a route to a flowing, ego-transcending oneness. As fans and enemies alike know, rock sound overwhelms separateness, the mental operations that discern and define here and there, me and not-me. (Many of the lyrics work symbolically or subliminally toward the same end.) Pounded by volume, riddled by light, the listener slides free from the restraining self and from the pretenses of a private, "unique" rationality. Preparation for the descent is of various sorts. One man may have given house room in his head to a desire for connection with the unconscious roots of life—D. H. Lawrence's blood being. Another, unbookish, has experienced frustration in the public world of objective laws, ethnic or money interests—learned his impatience with the procedural and the discrete outdoors, as it were. Another despises the tyranny of his "family self" or his student role. All are alike, though, in their relish for a thunderous, enveloping, self-shattering moment wherein the capacity for evaluating an otherness is itself rocked and shaken, and the mob of the senses cries out: "What we feel, we are!"

That this half-real, half-metaphorical self-shattering lies at the tumultuous center of the rock experience is an observation made verbally (the music itself makes it to anyone who listens) over and over, by low-cult and high-cult critics alike. Paul Williams in Crawdaddy remarks that "the direct appeal to the mind made by 'folk' (straight-forward words, guitar, voice) cannot compare . . . to the abilities of rock to move people's goddam muscles, bodies, caught up and swaying and moving so that a phrase . . . can actually become your whole body, can sink into your soul on a more-than-cognitive level. Rock, because of the number of senses it can get to (on a dance floor, eyes, ears, nose, mouth and tactile) and the extent to which it can pervade those senses, is really the most advanced art form we have." Professor Goldman comments that, "like the effect of LSD, that of rock . . . is to spotlight [things] in a field of high concentration and merge them with the spectator in a union that is almost mystical."

And, as indicated, the rock lyricist is himself hip to the phenomenon of the "mystical union." The truth "allowable only to the very great" which Professor Poirier heard in a Beatles song is an explicit assertion of the arbitrariness of ego separations and of the desirability of soaring free from the mind-ridden world of subjects and objects. "I am within you and without you," these sirens call. "I am he as you are he as you are me and we are all together. . . ." The kitsch version of this "truth"—it emerges as an endorsement of a kind of universal group gropeism—appears in a hundred lesser songs:

> *I think it's so groovy now*
> *That people are finally getting together*
> *I think it's so wonderful—and how!—that people are finally*
> *   getting together*
> *Reach out of the darkness*
> *Reach out of the darkness, etc.*[5]

And its mate is a crude symbolic vision of the non-human world —the hard-edged manifold of objects, landscapes, nameable locations—as capable of losing its own still substance and flowing into a dislocating unassemblable gooeyness:

> *Mac Arthur Park is melting in the dark,*
> *All the sweet, green icing flowing down.*
> *Someone left the cake out in the rain,*
> *And I don't think that I can take it,*
> *'Cause it took so long to bake it.*
> *And I'll never have the recipe again,*
> *Oh no.*[6]

Admittedly, the point of substance here is itself slippery—hard to keep in sight. Speak in expository prose about a mind-blowing moment and you tame the sensations—the obliterating seizures of sound at a Hendrix concert or at the Electric Circus or any multimedia discothèque—by turning them into "evidence." Speak the rock writer's flaky, half-literate idiom and you either overheat the ineffable or identify the rock experience too directly with the drug experience, obscuring the specific features of both that

rockers value most. (" 'The End' [a Doors composition] is great
to listen to when you're high . . . but 'Soul Kitchen' will get you
high, which is obviously much . . . more important": Crawdaddy.)

The point is tricky, but it isn't trivial. That rock is a mixed
experience, appealing at once to my sense of my sophistication
and my sense of the unavailingness of sophistication; that rock
lifts from me the burden of knowing the good and yet believing
my knowledge to be useless; that rock permits me to be part of
others, not a mere resentful conscious self, not a perceiver har-
ried on every side by multitudes of other conscious selves pressing their analyzable differences—their values, opinions, interests,
greeds—forward into my space and notice: All these truths matter considerably. They establish that rock can possess quasire-
ligious force. It leads me past my self, beyond my separateness
and difference into a world of continuous blinding sameness—
and, for a bit, it stoneth me out of my mind.

Judging that trip, like judging any vision, is not work for a
journalist. But certain strengths and weaknesses stand forth in
plain sight. Grown men of mind can benefit from access to an
experience that shakes the grip of mentalism, allows the being
to sense the world again, restores a feeling of continuity with
"out there." Through it, they can preserve an idea of human
solidarity, as well as some consciousness of intellectual limits and
a seemly general humility.

For youngsters, too, it may be added, there is value in an
escape from the narrow worlds of schoolhouse or family dining
room into a sense of power, physicality, roughness, openness. (The
prepubescent middle-class kid who sings mimetically along with
Hendrix or Percy Sledge as he listens to a record is behaving
much like Penrod imitating Rube in Tarkington's wonderful
story. Such behavior recovers potentialities of being that are too
rigidly excluded by "nice" families in the name of an arid
politesse.)

At pubescent and postpubescent levels, though, over-indul-
gence in mystical I-am-you-you-are-the-tree-the-tree-is-me self-transcendence isn't all plus signs and roses. The schooling of a ma-
turing mind is often at its most intense, most interesting and most
life-enhancing when its business is to toughen the concept of
difference, or when it is occupied with hierarchies of aesthetic,

political, moral experience, or when the classroom or library effort is that of refining the imaginative power to comprehend a difficult otherness. And aptness for such studies can be weakened.

Once upon a time it was weakened by what was called class prejudice—or by inherited or inculcated religious or political self-righteousness. The WASP or the Mormon or the Catholic or the St. Grottlesex boy could not break out of himself, could not enter the "other point of view." So it was that teachers then complained about their pupils' inflexibility, their incapacity to stand one place while imaginatively penetrating another. So it was that 20 years ago the great teacher and historian of science Herbert Butterfield was writing about troubles dealing with people who were so convinced that one or another historical position or figure—Oliver Cromwell, say—was "right" that they could not stir themselves to fathom the innerness of King Charles's head:

"[Someone] who is so much the prisoner of his ideas that he [is] forever unable to summon the imaginative sympathy to enter into the mentality of men who are not like-minded with himself—is the very antithesis of what is required in history. He is no more a historian than that man is an actor who cannot play Othello as well as King Lear—in fact, he is only like that bogus kind of actor who . . . is always the same, always only himself."

The problem for the future, perhaps, will be the appearance of a generation so rich in experience of merger and self-transcendence that to its mind Cromwell and Charles and early-21st-century Harvard sophomores will seem all one, why so much fuss, man? A generation of characters whose problem won't be that they're always the same but that they're never the same. Because the self, like, man, the self is, like, an individuality, dependent on consciousness—and, like, consciousness, man, that's the trap we jumped. That was a nightmare. . . . Consciousness. Like, *ugh*.

Futuremongering and solemnity are handmaids. It is proper to shoo them off and turn on the phonograph again—Paul singing "Here There and Everywhere"—to temper the profundum about salvation as unconsciousness, and charm the mind back to pleasure and ease and ambiguity. You think as you listen: Perhaps in a way rock's too good a stuff to be wasted on youth. Or: Ridiculous, the idea that speaking a warm word for such attractive lyric inventiveness could ever corrupt a youth. . . . Then you think: Have to turn the volume controls all the way up for an hour before a person could even begin to approximate the whirly amiable slow-up available from two or three back-to-back joints of pot.

And then you think: Sound judgment is quite impossible anyway, for it must wait until we know what's to come of us, what the next human beings will be like, what qualities will be saved and lost, what "our" future is to be. A long wait.

But if that is the best final word, a further word is implicit in it—viz., people who like the tunes but reject the salvation—moldy figs who play the music at the old sound levels and hunt for the old musical pleasures and go on making the traditional musical discriminations and persist in thinking that chaps are dotty who claim they am I and I am they—these senior types, never blowing their minds, may still preserve a civilized value now beleaguered on many fronts.

What value, exactly?

Just conceivably, nothing less than that of the self itself.

"All You Need Is Love. Love Is All You Need."

by Karen Murphy and Ronald Gross

Poets are the unacknowledged legislators of the world.— SHELLEY.

*We have to keep new sorts of music away from us as a danger to society.—*PLATO.

Something is happening here but you don't know what it is, do you, Mr. Jones? [1]—BOB DYLAN

SHELLEY WASN'T TALKING about the books on the library shelf marked "Poetry." Rather, he meant language used at its most potent, to create and disseminate the notions of which kind of life is most worth living and which is most to be despised. And Plato knew that men were basically not what they knew, but how they felt their own existence. Today's young people find that the things they care about, and despise, and take delight in, are reflected and distilled most powerfully in the words and music of rock 'n' roll.

Two books of poetry were best sellers in America last year: the "Selected Poems" of Leonard Cohen and "Lonesome Cities" by Rod McKuen, the first a popular and respected rock song-

From the *New York Times Magazine,* April 13, 1969, copyright © 1969 by The New York Times Company.

1. Copyright 1965 by M. Witmark & Sons. Used by permission.

writer and singer, the latter a popular *schlock* songwriter and singer. And the critics and purveyors of the fine arts have dutifully decided that if rock lyrics have meaning and importance to young people they must then be something more than just lowly entertainment. In recent months, scholarly symposia on rock lyrics have been held in New York at The New School for Social Research (as part of a course called "Expanded Poetry") and at Columbia University. Joshua Brackett, the nation's first "media ecologist," is writing a Ph.D. dissertation at N.Y.U. composed entirely of exegeses of rock lyrics. The literary magazines are falling over one another to take rock lyrics seriously; a Partisan Review writer recently compared the Beatles' lyrics to Shakespeare. Leonard Bernstein says of rock: "Many of the lyrics, in their oblique allusions and wayout metaphors, are beginning to sound like real poems."

Despite Cohen's and McKuen's books, and the fact that publishers are issuing histories of rock and anthologies of rock lyrics, it really isn't a very good idea to abstract rock lyrics from the accompanying music for isolated scrutiny. Rock is essentially an appeal to the gut sense of rhythm, intensely energy-releasing and sexual. In this respect rock magnifies a condition of all poetry. Even so cerebral a poet as T. S. Eliot said that meaning in a poem is like the piece of sirloin that the burglar slips the watchdog as he burglarizes the house: It keeps the reader busy while the poet does his work through the poem's rhythmic and sensuous qualities. Since Eliot, poetry has stressed this aspect more and more. The Beat movement was very much an insistence on the rhythmic and spoken basis of poetry, and more recent experimentation goes even further in stressing the sensory basis of poetic experience.

But rock lyrics are notably more than a nod to Sweeney's realization that "I've gotta use words when I talk to you." In fact, they are a quite remarkable departure from anything that has ever appeared before in American popular music.

Years ago, when he was just a semanticist instead of a beleaguered San Francisco college president, S. I. Hayakawa studied the lyrics of Tin Pan Alley songs and concluded that they gave listeners an idealized picture of love and marriage which was exactly congruent with the stereotypes of the advertising culture and severely discordant with reality. They were full of "wishful thinking, dreamy and ineffectual nostalgia, unrealistic fantasy, self-pity and sentimental clichés, masquerading as emotion." Here is a typical lyric quoted by Hayakawa:

In a bungalow all covered with roses,
I will settle down I vow,
I'm looking at the world thru rose-colored glasses,
And everything is rosy now.[2]

If young people took such lyrics seriously, he warned, they would be headed for trouble when they projected them onto the tangle of real relations between men and women.

Today's rock lyrics are something else, though in the beginning (circa 1954) they were bad enough to make Tin Pan Alley look like a stronghold of realism and sophistication. The lyrics of the first rock superhit, Bill Haley's "Rock Around the Clock," went as follows: "One, two, three o'clock, four o'clock rock!/Five, six, seven o'clock, eight o'clock, rock!/Nine, ten, eleven o'clock, twelve o'clock rock!/We're going to rock around the clock tonight." [3] "Rock Around the Clock" however became a theme song of defiance; behind the idiotic lyrics kids heard: "We're going to rock around the clock—WHETHER YOU WANT US TO OR NOT."

The moronic metaphors that were common in early rock were transformed in the kids' minds, usually into a potent sexual code. For example, the nonsensical lines, "She's the one that walks around the store./She's the one that yells more, more, more!" [4] in "Be-Bop-A-Lula" somehow suggested that the song's heroine was an earth goddess of awesome erotic capabilities. And far-fetched metaphors could suggest worldly rebellion. When Carl Perkins sang, "Don't you/Step on my blue suede shoes," [5] he

2. Copyright 1926. Copyright renewed. Reprinted by permission of the publishers, Pickwick Music Corporation and Venus Music Corporation.
3. Copyright 1953 Myers Music Inc.
4. Copyright 1956 Lowery Music Co., Inc. Vincent and Davis.
5. Copyright 1956 by Hi Lo Music, public performance right in the United States of America and Canada controlled by Hi Lo Music—Hill & Range Songs Inc. All other rights for the world controlled by Hill & Range Songs Inc., N. Y., N. Y. Used by permission.

meant, or was understood to mean, a lot more than blue suede shoes.

These days, no topic of interest to young people is considered inappropriate for a rock 'n' roll lyric. Going beyond the spoon-moon-June of pre-rock pop, and the kiss-me-honey and parents-are-no-good of early rock, today's lyricists deal with politics (these are perhaps the least successful of the new rock songs), militarism, illegitimacy (there has recently been a tremendous boom in illegitimacy songs), miscegenation, prostitution, compulsive infidelity, the dangers and pleasure of drugs, the difficulties of rising above a slum background—the list could go on forever.

Here, for example, is "Substitute," written by Peter Townshend, of The Who. The song arouses in the listener not only the cynicism that is explicit in the lyrics but also, ironically, a nostalgia for a love, and life, where "the simple things" are not "all complicated," a nostalgia enforced by the simple, throbbing hard-rock music:

You think we look pretty good together.
You think my shoes are made of leather.
But I'm a substitute for another guy.
I look pretty tall but my heels are high.
The simple things you see are all complicated.
I look pretty young but I'm just backdated.
Yeah!

It's a substitute lies for fact.
I can see right through your plastic mac.
I look all white but my dad was black.
My fine-looking suit is really made out of sack.

I was born with a plastic spoon in my mouth.
Northside of my town faces East and the Eastside faces
    South.
And now you dare to look me in the eye.
But crocodile tears are what you cry.
If it's a genuine problem you won't try
To work it out at all, just pass it by.
Pass it by!

It's a substitute.
Me for him like Coke for gin.
You for my mum.
At least I get my washing done.[6]

Rock lyrics tend, in other words, as one rock writer puts it, to "look at the rose through world-colored glasses."

A great deal of *schlock* pop is still written and makes up the bulk of the programing on AM-radio rock stations. One recent Top 40 favorite featured the memorable refrain: "Yummy, yummy, yummy/I've got love in my tummy." [7]

Even the most stereotyped good-guy stations, however, have begun to program such songs as the haunting "White Room" by the recently disbanded group called Cream, which conveys in its music as well as its lyrics an elusive but terrifyingly real sense of alienation and emptiness:

In the white room with black curtains near the stations.
Black roof country no gold pavements tired starlings.
Silver horses rundown moonbeams in your dark eyes
Dawn light smiles on your leaving my contentment.
I'll wait in this place where the sun never shines
Wait in this place where the shadows run from themselves.[8]

The most fashionable heavy topic for rock at the moment is revolution. The Rolling Stones brought revolution-rock (which had been sung for years by the Fugs, who are more revolution-aries than rock singers) into Top 40 stations with their "Street Fighting Man." The lines, "Summer's here and the time is right/ For fighting in the street," [9] in "Street Fighting Man" are a switch on the lines, "Summer's here and the time is right/For dancing

6. Copyright 1966 Fabulous Music Ltd., London, England. All publication rights controlled by Tro-Devon Music, Inc., New York, N. Y., for the U.S.A. and Canada. Used by permission.

7. Copyright TM Music, Inc.

8. Copyright 1968 Dratleaf Ltd.

9. Copyright 1968. Publisher Gideon Music, Inc. Writers M. Jagger and Kieth Richards. All rights reserved. Used by permission. International copyright secured.

in the street," [10] from an old song by Martha and the Vandellas, a black Detroit group whose recent song, "I Can't Dance to That Music," is about the difficulties of the new rock. At the moment, the leading advocates of revolution-rock sing of political and sexual revolution as one and the same thing, as the MC5 do in their song "Kick Out the Jams." This lump-it-all-together approach was first popularized by the Doors: "We want the world and we want it now." [11]

It is perilous to make qualitative judgments about something as personal and subjective as rock 'n' roll. But certainly some, if not all, of the best current rock lyrics are not about specific weighty subjects but attempts to convey the *feel* of today's world, or at least the part of it that affects young people. Two masters of this art are John Lennon and Bob Dylan. The Beatles and Dylan are idolized by kids today primarily because, without losing their ability to be specific, they seem to understand the essence, the totality, of a fragmented world, or, as the kids say, "where it's at."

The latest trend in rock lyrics seems to be an attempt to deal with complexity instead of merely capturing it. The first great song of this genre was the Beatles' "All You Need Is Love":

> *Love love love*
> *Love love love*
> *Love love love . . .*
> *There's nothing you can make that can't be made.*
> *Nothing you can save that can't be saved*
> *Nothing you can do but you can learn how to be you*
> *in time.*
> *It's easy.*
> *All you need is love.*
> *All you need is love.*
> *All you need is love.*
> *Love is all you need.*[12]

This simple song (deceptively simple? simple-minded?) marked a return to basics in rock lyrics. The Beatles' first big hit in this country, "I Want to Hold Your Hand," had been a simple-minded, not very hard-hitting number that did not become very popular until the Beatles had been given a massive dose of that pop publicity now called hype. However, unlike many groups which have floundered in too much money and hype, the Beatles lived up to publicity that was, on the evidence, at the beginning greatly exaggerated.

Not that they really changed; their early songs were deliberate attempts to reach a mass audience; once they had the audience, they played them like sitars. They could do this because they reflected changes in their audience as much as they caused them; perhaps it would be most accurate to say that they brought to the surface and rendered conscious and explicit ideas, trends and feelings that would have emerged anyhow, but in less vivid and self-confident forms.

The Beatles have offered social commentary ("Nowhere Man" and "Eleanor Rigby"), social satire ("Paperback Writer"), dreamy, druggy fantasy ("Strawberry Fields Forever") and surrealism ("Penny Lane" and "I Am the Walrus"). "I Am the Walrus" has perhaps the most bizarre and culture-critic-tempting lyrics of any rock song ever written:

> *I am he as you are he,*
> *As you are me and we are all together—*
> *See how they run like pigs from a gun*
> *See how they fly*
> *I'm crying.*
> *Sitting on a cornflake, waiting for the van to come—*
> *Corporation T shirt, stupid bloody Tuesday*
> *Man—you been a naughty boy,*
> *You let your face grow long.*
> *I am the eggman*
> *Oh, they are the eggmen*
> *Oh, I am the walrus*
> *Goo goo g'joob . . .*
> *Yellow matter custard, dripping from a dead dog's eye—*
> *Crabalocker fishwife, pornographic priestess*

Boy—you been a naughty girl,
You let your knickers down.
I am the eggman
Oh, they are the eggmen
Oh, I am the walrus
Goo goo g'joob . . .
Semolina pilchards, climbing up the Eiffel Tower—
Element'ry penguin, singing Hare Krishna
Man—you should have seen them
Kicking Edgar Allan Poe.
I am the eggman
Oh, they are the eggmen
Oh, I am the walrus
Goo goo g'goo g'goo goo g'joob joob.[13]

At the end of the last verse, amid a lot of chaotic noise, there is some conversation that is actually 17 lines from "King Lear."

What does it all mean? In "Glass Onion," a song from the Beatles' latest album, Lennon writes, "I told you about the walrus and me—man/You know we're as close as can be—man/Well, here's another clue for you all/The walrus was Paul." [14] And in a recent interview in Rolling Stone magazine he adds: "The whole first verse was written without any knowledge."

The wild images in the song are not, in fact, connected in any logical way. There is no narrative meaning, no sirloin for the watchdog. But there is a larger, more important meaning: The quick flashing of disjointed phenomena reproduces the chaos of sensations in our world of information overload.

The high point of the Beatles' attempt to capture complexity, and the high point of the baroque period of rock in general, came with the release in June, 1967, of "Sergeant Pepper." Typical of the songs on the record is "Lucy in the Sky with Diamonds." When it was pointed out to Lennon that the initials of his title were "LSD," he denied any reference to drugs and said that his young son, Julian, had brought home a drawing from school that he said was called "Lucy in the Sky with Diamonds." In any case, "Lucy" came to symbolize a time of drugs, flower children, *art nouveau* and a dreamy, psychedelic escape from the real world:

> *Picture yourself in a boat on a river,*
> *With tangerine trees and marmalade skies.*
> *Somebody calls you, you answer quite slowly,*
> *A girl with kaleidoscope eyes.*
> *Cellophane flowers of yellow and green*
> *Towering over your head*
> *Look for the girl with the sun in her eyes*
> *And she's gone.*
> *Lucy in the sky with diamonds.*
> *Lucy in the sky with diamonds.*
> *Lucy in the sky with diamonds. . . .*[15]

Then, while the critics analyzed Beatles' songs in terms of Franz Kafka and Marshall McLuhan (though, as pop critic Richard Goldstein has remarked, "Is Ernest Hemingway responsible for Pete Hamill?"), the Beatles themselves moved on to a style called "The New Simplicity." In practice, it means a return either to basic nineteen-fifties hard-rock or to country music, but often with the simple lyrics parodied and the music complicated by elaborate electronic effects.

For example, the complete lyrics to one song in the latest Beatles' album are: "Why don't we do it in the road?/No one will be watching us/Why don't we do it in the road?"[16] To initiates, however, these lyrics represent (1) a take-off on the far-fetched euphemisms rock lyricists resort to evade radio censors, (2) an affectionate parody of gut-basic Rolling Stones songs like "Satisfaction" and "Let's Spend the Night Together," (3) a terrific sexy image in their own right.

While the Beatles write songs like "Revolution," which discourages violent Maoist rebellion, Bob Dylan is living what Lennon calls "his cozy little life." As the Beatles seem to be involved, just by their natures, in every trend or fad that affects young people, Bob Dylan is, by his nature, uninvolved, a very private person. It was not always so: In his old prerock days Dylan wrote songs with explicit social messages, like "Blowing in the Wind," "The Times They are A-Changing" and "Masters of War." But in his song "My Back Pages" Dylan renounces protest: "Ah, but I was so much older then/I'm younger than that now." [17]

Although he is socially aloof, Dylan is musically very much of his time. He was one of the first folk singers to go electric, to see the power of rock as a creative and persuasive medium. Like the Beatles, Dylan, too, had a baroque rock phase, typified by his "Subterranean Homesick Blues," a song that is similar to the Beatles' "Walrus" in that its disjointed, disparate images evoked a disjointed, disparate, rapidly changing world. But whereas in "The Walrus" shadowy benevolent God/father figures wait in the background (the eggman, the walrus, the element'ry penguin), the background figures in "Subterranean Homesick Blues" are brutal or bureaucratic: a plainclothesman, a fireman, a frontiersman, a district attorney, a weatherman. All threaten the innocent and confused young person. Dylan's message: "Look out, kid/Don't matter what you did/Walk on your tiptoes/Don't try 'No Doz.' " [18]

Dylan's childishly compulsive rhymes suggest a closer affinity with amphetamines than with French verse forms, but "Subterranean Homesick Blues" must be counted poetry in that it reproduces, in articulate and structured form, a nightmare vision young people hold of the world.

On his latest album, "John Wesley Harding," a return to the basic country style that is now so fashionable, Dylan writes and sings of simple but dreamlike and often elusively allegorical individual relationships. One of the most compelling songs on the album, "I Dreamed I Saw St. Augustine," conveys the chief message of "Subterranean Homesick Blues," and one of Dylan's main themes—"Don't follow leaders." In the song, St. Augustine returns to earth in a state of anguish looking for lost souls. "No martyr is among ye now/Whom you can call your own," he says,

"But go on your way, accordingly,/But know you're not alone." [19]
Yet the innocent youth of "Subterranean Homesick Blues" has
changed. Now the narrator accuses himself of being one of those
who has martyred the saint. A similar idea is expressed in a recent
Rolling Stones song, "Sympathy for the Devil": "Who killed the
Kennedys?/Well, after all, it was you and me." [20]

To the familiar question, "Do you think of yourself primarily
as a singer or a poet?" Dylan gave an answer of sorts in a West
Coast press conference a little over a year ago: "Oh, I think of
myself more as a song and dance man, y'know." Despite this
modesty (or false modesty), in a broad sense Dylan must be
called a poet because, like the Beatles, he speaks of, and transforms, experiences vital to the consciousness of his listeners. A
20-year-old college girl says of Dylan: "I just feel, when I hear
one of his songs, like he has been everywhere and he is sending
us back pictures, but there is no one message for everybody; it's
like clues, but clues to something that if it's pinned down, it'd be
destroyed."

The Beatles and Dylan make light of any suggestion that they
are poets, thus endearing themselves to their young audiences.
But Jim Morrison, lead singer of the Doors, is an active candidate
for simultaneous election to "Best Rock Poet" and "Biggest Sex
Symbol" (no longer an incongruous combination).

A former Berkeley drama student, Morrison writes lyrics loaded
with references to classical drama, which of course does not necessarily qualify them as poetry. In the Doors' second album, however, Morrison intones a short lyric called "Horse Latitudes" that
since it is spoken and unaccompanied by music, qualifies either
as a poem or as nothing:

> *When the still sea conspires an armor*
> *And her sullen and aborted*
> *Currents breed tiny monsters,*
> *True sailing is dead.*
> *Awkward instant*

19. Copyright 1968 Dwarf Music, N. Y., N. Y.
20. Copyright 1968. Publisher Gideon Music Inc. Writers M. Jagger
and Kieth Richards. All rights reserved. Used by permission. International
copyright secured.

> *And the first animal is jettisoned,*
> *Legs furiously pumping*
> *Their stiff green gallop,*
> *And heads bob up*
> *Pause*
> *Delicate*
> *Pause*
> *Consent*
> *In mute nostril agony*
> *Carefully refined*
> *And sealed over.*[21]

Intoned with pseudo-Elizabethan grandeur, "Horse Latitudes" conveys perhaps the desire of Mr. Morrison to have written a "real" poem more than it does an experience vital to him or anybody else.

If critics choose to elevate bad rock to the status of poetry, and to misinterpret rock lyrics in general, that is annoying but irrelevant, except insofar as it influences rock writers. But the rock lyricists seem to be catching on. Even Paul Simon, of whom Robert Christgau wrote, "He is the only songwriter [who] . . . writes about . . . the Alienation of Modern Man, *in just those words,*" recently has come to realize that he writes better songs, and perhaps better poetry, when he stops worrying about Poetry.

At the height of his pretentious phase, Simon described alienation like this: "You read your Emily Dickinson/ And I my Robert Frost,/ And we note our place with bookmarkers/That measure what we've lost." [22] More recently he expressed the same thought with less verbiage and a lot more style: "No good times/No bad times/There's no times at all/Just The New York Times." [23]

Interestingly, as rock lyricists turn away from official poetry, many younger poets are now being seduced by the power of rock as a medium of communication and persuasion. Foremost among these poets, certainly, is Leonard Cohen, whose poetry sells better than most novels and whose rock record "The Songs of Leonard Cohen" is a best seller on both underground and campus circuits.

Cohen sings of a strange interior world where men and women really love each other but leave each other, often self-consciously relishing the pain of parting (it's still the men who do most of the leaving) and where sexual and Catholic images are intermingled. Throughout, there is a terrible ambivalence between the ringing deadness of one-night stands and the boring temptation of monogamy, a constant protesting that it is *perfectly healthy* to leave someone you love, which probably explains why Cohen is so popular with the ambivalent young.

One of his most affirmative songs, "Suzanne," has already achieved the status of a classic because it perceives a way out of this ambivalence. The narrator achieves a commitment to Suzanne (commitment has replaced orgasm as a status symbol) but hardly to domestic drudgery: Suzanne "gets" him mystically (she touches his "perfect body *with her mind";* since the physical is so accessible, the mystical has become the sought-after goal). Notice how (see box, pages 218–219), as in most of Cohen's songs, religious and sexual images are cheerfully combined.

Like Cohen, Rod McKuen uses a persona whose essence is to wander forever solitary despite a real ability to love deeply. Apparently, McKuen manages to deal with the dichotomy that splits young people in a way that is meaningful to them, for with Cohen he is the most popular poet on college campuses all over the country. Unlike Cohen, however, McKuen makes no attempt to face, let alone reconcile, complexities; nor does he worry much about language. A typical McKuen insight: "Just the simple gift of giving/Makes you warm inside." [24]

Of the relationship between lyrics and poetry, Cohen says: "There is no difference between a poem and a song. Some were songs first and some were poems first and some were simultaneous. All of my writing has guitars behind it, even the novels."

Eric Cheyfitz, who writes poetry for Stand, The Review and Per Se, and lyrics for the jazz/classical-oriented rock group This Week Only, says: "The difference between writing rock lyrics and poetry is that eventually you can make much more money writing lyrics. Also, when you write rock lyrics you are formally limited by the melody and beat, and some phrases have to be changed because some words can't be sung in succession."

24. Copyright 1966 Stanyan Music Company.

"Suzanne Takes You Down"

Leonard Cohen is a best seller on campus and underground circuits as both published poet and recorded rock singer. Here is a song—or poem—by Cohen that in some circles has become a minor classic. The text is the recorded version ("Songs of Leonard Cohen").

Suzanne takes you down
to her place near the river,
you can hear the boats go by
you can spend the night beside her.
And you know that she's half crazy
but that's why you want to be there
and she feeds you tea and oranges
that come all the way from China.
And just when you mean to tell her
that you have no love to give her,
then she gets you on her wave length
and she lets the river answer
that you've always been her lover.
    And you want to travel with her,
    and you want to travel blind
    and you know that she will trust you
    for you've touched her perfect
        body with your mind.

And Jesus was a sailor
when he walked upon the water
and he spent a long time watching
from his lonely wooden tower
and when he knew for certain
only drowning men could see him

How do rock lyrics as a whole stack up against today's poetry? It would be easy to point out correlates in rock for many of the distinguishing characteristics of contemporary American verse: John Ashbery's surrealistic image sequences, Kenneth Koch's

he said, "All men will be sailors then
until the sea shall free them,"
but he himself was broken
long before the sky would open,
forsaken, almost human,
he sank beneath your wisdom like a stone.
 And you want to travel with him,
 and you want to travel blind
 and you think maybe you'll trust him
 for he's touched your perfect body
  with his mind.

Now Suzanne takes your hand
and she leads you to the river,
she is wearing rags and feathers
from Salvation Army counters.
And the sun pours down like honey
on our lady of the harbour
and she shows you where to look
among the garbage and the flowers,
there are heroes in the seaweed
there are children in the morning,
they are leaning out for love
and they will lean that way forever
while Suzanne holds the mirror.
 And you want to travel with her
 and you want to travel blind
 and you know you can trust her
 for she's touched your perfect
  body with her mind.

breezy humor, the projectivists' striving for a natural rhythm which reflects the patterns of American speech, the confessional poets' fascination with autobiography and personality.

Such a comparison would also reveal that nowhere in rock

lyrics does one find anything to rival Robert Lowell's complex diction, Charles Olson's awesome erudition, Allen Ginsberg's vatic howl, Robert Creeley's limpid directness, or LeRoi Jones's Catullian bitterness.

But rock lyrics have some things, quite different but equally potent, going for them. First, the music. Ezra Pound said that music rots when it gets too far from the dance, and poetry atrophies when it gets too far from music.

Music can "carry" a lyric that has no logical meaning in itself and which might have no emotional meaning if it were simply printed instead of sung. This is true of the Beatles' "Walrus." Van Morrison's "Brown Eyed Girl" contains the lines: Whatever happened/To Tuesday and 'so slow'/Going down the old mine with a/Transister radio." [25] Somehow, within the context of the song, these lines are transformed into a poignant evocation of the things we remember of a lost lover.

Rock is nothing if not song, and rock lyrics shrivel when torn out of their musical context. Considered as a word/music whole, however, the range and depth of rock challenge the best of contemporary poetry, and certainly excel the work of routine Department of English poets-in-residence.

Because it hits with a musical punch, then, and because it is completely continuous with everyday life rather than a departure from it, rock lyrics get through to millions of kids and adults for whom conventional poetry is a closed book.

The hunger of the young for words to match the fervor, complexity and tone of their sensibilities has been fed not by poets in the usual sense, but by the rock lyricists. Whether or not rock lyrics are "really" poetry is not, after all, more than a matter of definition. What matters is not their verse techniques but their force and relevance.

Critic Donal Henahan cut to the core of the matter when he wrote: "In their own ways, the better popular and serious composers today are addressing themselves once more to life as it is actually lived, and if up till now one must admit that there has been a coarsening of sensibility, there has been a heightening of reality to compensate. The truths that Dylan rasps, that is, are for

25. Copyright 1967 by Web IV Music Inc. All rights reserved. Used by permission.

the moment more valuable for us than the truths that a less con-
vulsed society found in Brahms. The truth-teller, in whatever
guise, serves his own time well; listen, next time you have a
chance, to the words of Dylan's 'The Times They Are A-Changing,' and admit what a clear prophecy they were of the last five
years in America."

A heightening of reality, a telling of the truth, an utterance of
prophecy—these, after all, are what poets have traditionally as-
pired to. To the degree that contemporary verse falls short of
these ideals, and rock lyricists achieve them, the latter may be
doing even more than taking their place in "real poetry." They
may be reinventing it.

Why the Girls Scream, Weep, Flip

by David Dempsey

WITH THE predictability of a plague of locusts, teen-age America is swept to its feet every few years by the newest craze in popular music. Although symptomatic relief of this seizure is not difficult for most young people—they can dance all night—the side effects are disturbing to say the least. In the presence of their latest folk hero, many admirers often stand in one place and jump up and down. Usually this is accompanied by incessant screaming and, on the part of girls, by protestations of undying love.

Sometimes this hero worship takes a violent form and the singer is mobbed by his fans. At other times, the kids go into a Zen-like trance. The pupils of their eyes dilate, a rapt expression comes over their faces, and they achieve a state of teen-age Nirvana. (In this condition, they are given those posthypnotic suggestions that send them all out to buy crazy-looking wigs, photos of their heroes on laminated buttons, toss pillows and tight, very tight, pants.)

The newest outbreak of this madness, as everyone knows, was occasioned by the Beatles, four young singers from England who have, indeed, brought a new kind of love to millions of females

From the *New York Times Magazine,* February 23, 1964, copyright © 1964 by The New York Times Company.

between the ages of 10 and 30. The chant of "Yeah! Yeah! Yeah!" follows them everywhere and their travels have inspired the largest mass following since the Children's Crusade.

What is happening here is significant. Although idolatry in popular music is nothing new, the method of expressing this idolatry seems to be changing. A generation of youth that shrieks at the sight of a Fabian, or packs the Cotton Bowl to cheer Elvis Presley, seems 100 years removed in spirit from the generation that tuned in on the Ipana Troubadours or settled back to the nasal tones of Rudy Vallee. As our singers get progressively more frantic, their followers become increasingly frenzied, and an audience that once swooned in the presence of its favorite singer, or at best squealed, has given way to a mob that flips.

The cause of this malady is obscure—so obscure, in fact, that modern scholarship, in its quest for an etiology, has expanded its investigations into four major fields: the anthropological, the psychological, the socio-economic and the moral. All appear to play a part, at one time or another, in influencing the mass behavior patterns that sweep the country from time to time when a new type of music—or musician—appears on the scene. If you are of the opinion that youth today is simply out for fun and excitement, skip it. This is much too simple an explanation. (In fact, let us pretend that this possibility was not even mentioned.)

To begin, first, with the anthropology of rock 'n' roll. It is generally admitted that jungle rhythms influence the "beat" of much contemporary dance activity. Every man, according to this theory, is instinctively aboriginal in his feet, if not in his heart; much of today's jazz-dancing—as anyone knows who has seen it—is strongly reminiscent of those tribal dances performed to the tune of a nose flute and the beat of a tom-tom. Aboriginal society being collective, however, the group catharsis that takes place is not only highly ritualized, but is frequently carried out as a supplication to certain mythic beings—the god of the hunt, or of fertility—that are lacking today. The idolatry in this case is totemic.

By comparison, contemporary rock 'n' rollers lack a social focus for their energy, which is thereby visited on the godlike individual. According to this notion, modern society, with its emphasis on decorum, suppresses a need in man for uninhibited kinetic self-expression. Today's music is a throwback, or tribal atavism, made endemic through mass communication. It is probably no coincidence that the Beatles, who provoke the most violent response among teen-agers, resemble in manner the witch doctors who put their spell on hundreds of shuffling and stamping natives. Far-fetched? Not for some anthropologists. At any rate, it is a theory worth thinking about.

The aborigines, of course, have no monopoly on fancy footwork. Nor are they the only ones who dig the music. An example closer in spirit to our own times is Orpheus, who, except for the fact that his lyre was not an electric one, might easily pass for the Elvis Presley of Greek mythology.

You may remember that Orpheus could charm the stones right out of the field. What is sometimes forgotten is that he, too, was set upon by screaming females who were determined to devour him. His music alone held them at bay until, finally, ". . . the wild shouts which they . . . raised deadened the sound of the notes and so left Orpheus helpless. So great was the rage of the Bacchantes that they actually tore him limb from limb," reports Prof. Frances E. Sabin in her aptly titled book, "Classical Myths That Live Today."

It is clear from this that the problem of modern teen-age behavior was not altogether different, with respect to popular musicians, from that of the classical world, although the Greeks had the good sense to keep the whole matter decently in the lap of the gods.

A more fashionable line of inquiry into the mob response so prevalent in popular music today is psychological. At its simplest, this view holds that the young are undergoing a hysterical reaction to a craze. Whether dancing, or merely listening and jumping, those taking part are working off the inner tensions that bedevil a mixed up psyche. For these young people, the singer performs a healing role.

Nor is there anything uniquely modern in this behavior. Parents concerned about such dances as the Twist or the Slop can draw some consolation by thinking back to the wildest and strangest dance of all, the tarantella. A product of rural Italy, where it achieved its peak popularity in the 16th and 17th centuries, the tarantella comes even closer to simulating insanity than that now-famous drug, LSD.

It has been described by the Sicilian scholar Ernesto de Martino, in "The Land of the Bad Past," as "an instinctive experiment in madness." The dancer goes into a frenzy in order to kill frenzy; she is finally "cured"—or at least exhausted, for the tarantella is said to "reintegrate the people after the collapse of psychical balance."

Would this not indicate that a fairly recent counterpart, jitterbugging, was possibly a deliberately induced outer frenzy aimed at staving off the inner frenzy that threatens young people during a difficult period of adjustment? Such an idea is suggested by a lengthy study of the jitterbug addict in an article by Dr. T. W. Adorno, with the assistance of George Simpson—it takes two to write on jitterbugging—that appeared in the scholarly journal Studies in Philosophy and Social Science at the height of the jitterbug movement in 1941.

Adorno and Simpson distinguish between two major types of mass behavior toward popular music, the "rhythmically obedient" type, and the "emotional" type. The latter are likely to get a crush on a movie star and let it go at that; in general, they remain passive, and give little trouble. The "rhythmic obedients," on the other hand, make up the vast, noisy and clamorous mob of adolescents whose star has been in the ascendant ever since the onset of Frank Sinatra. They like to keep time to the music, and the crazier the music, the better they like it.

But they are not just letting off steam; in fact, although they may not know it, they are expressing their desire to obey. They are products of a conformist, and sometimes authoritarian, society, and their obedience to the beat "leads them to conceive of themselves as agglutinized with untold millions of the meek who must be similarly overcome."

Here again, such activity, no matter how eagerly participated in, should not imply joy. The jitterbug can't help himself. He is not really having a good time; he only thinks he is, since the craze for a particular fashion, in the Adorno-Simpson view, contains within itself the latent possibility of fury.

"Likes that have been enforced upon listeners [by press agentry, mass media and an age of conformity] provoke revenge the moment the pressure is relaxed." The Bacchante syndrome? Possibly. The authors add that "the whole realm of jitterbug fanaticism and mass hysteria about popular music is under the spell of a spiteful will decision." It is based on such superficial enthusiasm that it must be continually reinforced by repetition and the safety of numbers if it is to survive. Hence its mass character.

The conclusions reached by Adorno and Simpson are, at first glance, discouraging. These "rhythmic obedients," they believe, will inherit the earth. Yet this prospect is not as deplorable as it may seem. "To become transformed into an insect [i.e., a jitterbug] man needs that energy which might possibly achieve his transformation into a man."

Here again, the parallel with Beatlemania is apparent. Beatles, too, are a type of bug; and to "beatle," as to jitter, is to lose one's identity in an automatized, insectlike activity—in other words, to obey. Do not underrate this hypothesis in trying to understand your teen-age daughter.

Let us turn now to the socio-economic interpretation of the present craze over pop singers. This can be summarized as follows: hero worship, such as that conferred on Fabian, Johnny Mathis and the Beatles, is ultimately the product of an affluent society which, for the first time in history, has made possible a leisure class of professional teenagers.

Out of this new class has come a culture which, in turn, constitutes an enormous market of consumers. One of the products sold to this market is the hero, along with all the ikons of worship (records, rings, pin-ups, Beatle clothes, etc.).

"The religion of teen-age culture, as such, may be said to be the cult of popular personalities, singers, actors and performers of all kinds," writes Prof. Jessie Bernard, of the Pennsylvania State University, in The Annals of the American Academy of Political and Social Science.

A unique feature of this religion is the insistence by those who practice it that the gods be approximately the same age as the worshipers. The day when young people "looked up" to their heroes is gone; instead, for the first time they now have a self-identifying culture which they need not transcend in order to find the values that reflect their own aspirations. The hero is not only an idol but an image.

Most contemporary pop singers get their start at 16 or 17. As they grow older, their popularity with the bandstand set wanes and their places are taken by new idols. Presley, for example, at 29, is a comparative oldster, as is the once fan-ridden Pat Boone, who is also 29 and has a family. The 19-year-old Paul Anka, and the 21-year-old Bobby Rydell typify those who now hold down the tabernacle.

All of this makes it easier for the female members of the cult to go berserk. This is especially true of those who, for one reason or another, are alienated from their peer group. Fabian has observed that many of the young girls who besiege him are lacking in physical attractiveness, and it has been noted that membership in the screaming and jumping societies includes a high proportion of the homely, and of those who are lonesome, or ill at ease in social situations. They can act out their feelings most easily in a group.

Moreover, by "mobbing" a singer, they are thus able to reverse the boy-girl roles, in fantasy at least, for in a sense they are saying, "I wish the boy would go after me, but because he won't, I'll go after him; and since there's no danger that I'll get him, the whole charade is safe." For these teen-agers, such a troupe as the Beatles is made to order—four young men instead of the customary one.

As long as teen-age culture remains an entity in itself, a large percentage of its members will continue to jump with joy—or what they think is joy. Such a prospect raises the fourth, or moral, line of inquiry, namely, that youth today has found a new, and perhaps a last remaining, excuse for being young. In this sense, young people are rebelling against an adult world that pretends to higher standards of entertainment. Much exhibitionism among teen-agers is carried out in a spirit of defiance. This is the "last fling" theory, and it proves again that rock 'n' rollers are rather desperate even in fun.

Paradoxically, however, this rebellion is taking place against a society that has shown no real indication that it really cares about the standards of teen-age entertainment. Upholders of this view point out that young people today are exploited by popularity "ratings," payola-taking disc jockeys, press-agent ballyhoo, sponsored fan clubs and a communications industry that panders plainly to the "kookie" interests of the teen-age group. The violent and spectacular diversions of the young are taking place in a moral vacuum caused by the abdication of their elders. If this vacuum is filled with tin gods, it is largely because the adult world has not offered them a valid religion.

Such criticism, to many psychologists and others who work with teen-agers, is unduly harsh in that it ignores the fact that the tin gods are highly temporary, to be worshiped only until the real thing comes along.

"The teen-ager, after all, is entitled to be young," states Dr. Jane Vorhaus Gang, a psychiatrist in the New York area who works with this age group. "You can't expect girls of 15 or 16 to have a mature set of values. They are trying their wings at this age, and hero worship is a fairly normal and harmless way to go about it. The bobbysoxer, with all her silly behavior, often turns out to be the responsible P.-T.A. chairman of tomorrow."

Even assuming that parents have abdicated in the face of the insect invasion, there is evidence that youth is taking the problem into its own hands. The increasing popularity of folk music and the hootenany, which appeals to the same rhythmic instincts as pop music, yet requires a more creative participation, and in a somewhat higher cause, is an encouraging trend. Although a craze in its own right, the movement can be said to represent a step upward by drawing on certain indigenous American values; in any case, the vapid banalities of much of pop music are discarded.

Moreover, an influential segment of teen-age America is now throwing its rhythmic energies behind the Freedom Rider Movement. Possibly most of these young people were never serious candidates for rock 'n' roll, but in any case they have shown that the generation to which they belong is not the monolithic stereotype that has been pictured. Seized by an equally strong desire for the beat, they are keeping step to a different breed of guitar, while singing another kind of song, "We Shall Overcome."

As for those who remain obedient—who are waiting to *be* overcome—it is well to remember that they exhibit a form of madness that has baffled mankind for centuries. The compulsive shuffle of the aborigine, the rage of the Bacchante, the frenzy of the tarantella dancer and the hysteria of the Beatlebug are all expressions of a common, and complex, demon. No wonder the jumpers can seldom explain what makes them jump. And no wonder that they have such a miserably happy time doing it (Yeah! Yeah! Yeah!).

Part 5

ART

WHEREIN LIES the fascination of pop art, which came into prominent view in 1964? John Canaday, the noted art critic of the *New York Times,* questioned the relevance of this "new" art with its blend of commercialism, Dadaism, and realism. In his article, Canaday points out that pop art has been called neo-realism and neo-social consciousness, but it might also be a gigantic put-on more properly called the New Fake.

There is a kind of irony in the success of pop art, which takes as its point of departure the most common of arts that surround us—comic strips, billboards, magazine advertisements, bargain window displays, or, in Canaday's words, "any other mass-produced vulgarity." Millions upon millions of cans of Campbell's Tomato Soup were opened and discarded without further thought until Andy Warhol made this the object of his artistic probing. Warhol eventually tired of painting and became a film-maker of even uglier subjects than he had painted. In Warhol we come to the *reductio ad absurdum* of popular culture—yet he is the darling of the super-sophisticated critics.

Another, less pretentious, form of pop art is, of course, the comic strip. Although the "funnies" have been an important aspect of popular culture throughout this century, none has surpassed the popularity of Charles Schulz's *Peanuts.* This strip, which appears in more than nine hundred newspapers throughout the United

States and one hundred or more in Europe, South America, and elsewhere, has extended its influence far beyond the comics page. Barnaby Conrad, in his article on the *Peanuts* phenomenon, notes that it has become a $20-million-a-year industry. Charlie Brown, Lucy, Linus, and Snoopy can also be seen in a long-running musical, heard on millions of records, and viewed on some of the highest-rated television specials. In fact, a full-length cartoon movie of the *Peanuts* family was the 1969 Christmas program at the *sanctum sanctorum* of movie houses, the Radio City Music Hall. Charles Schulz is truly one of the great humorists of the twentieth century—nobody knows this better than the people.

Pop Art Sells
On and On—Why?

by John Canaday

THE 1963–64 ART SEASON in New York, which began on schedule after Labor Day and, on schedule, will soon droop into summer hibernation, definitely belonged to something new called "Pop art."

"Something new" is a description that not everyone would accept. Some of Pop's critics think it is really just something old (commercial art) dusted off and jazzed up, while others think it is just something borrowed (the Dada movement of the nineteen-twenties) without much change. And undeniably, Pop can get pretty blue—in the showbiz sense of designating an off-color gag.

But whatever Pop art is—its patrons and practitioners are still haggling over definitions—it has arrived and gives every sign of staying around at least for a little while. Whether or not Pop is a new art, and whether or not it can last, it has supplied a new bandwagon. And in the art circus as it operates today, that is the final accolade of success.

As the 1960's dawned, Pop was not much more than a rumor up and down Madison Avenue. But during a series of kittenish feints with the established *avant-garde,* it suddenly bared fangs that scared the living daylights out of the most quick-eyed members of a group of artists who until then had felt firmly entrenched as the Latest Thing. By 1963 it had demonstrated that even those fangs had been only its baby teeth, and during the 1963–64 season it had things pretty much its own way, becoming a staple on the market.

Pop's list of converts is impressive, at least in numbers. Collectors who used to say "It's fine as entertainment, but who could ever live with it?" are now buying it, although from the looks of their apartments they may soon have to move out. Chronically advanced critics, who at first just couldn't see Pop, are making the shift (as quickly as dignity will allow) to a more sympathetic second look, rather than stay behind with their formerly *avant-garde* protégés who have become has-beens overnight. And the two artists who seem most to have anticipated the movement —Robert Rauschenberg, only 39, and Jasper Johns, only 34— have already been canonized in massive retrospectives as Pop's old masters.

In 1964, the American section of the Venice Biennale, which is the established barometer for that combination of sales market and critical market that dictates current esthetic values, was heavily loaded with Pop art. The New York State pavilion at the World's Fair, potentially the most influential piece of architecture in the place, included Pop art among the decorative murals and sculpture on the exterior of its theater wing, implying that Pop is as legitimate to our situation as the statues of saints on the exteriors of Gothic cathedrals were to that of our ancestors.

Pop is bulldozing its way through the groves of academe. Teachers teach Pop. Graduate students write theses on the origins and development of Pop. Long, dull seminars headed by venerable professors discuss the esthetics and, for goodness' sake, the history of Pop. On less astral planes, Pop has also got it made. Mass circulation magazines and TV love Pop for its novelty value. The same value brings Pop the largest and most fascinated (if not always the most appreciative) audiences in the galleries along 57th Street and Madison Avenue. And finally, perhaps indicating that the end is already in sight, Pop has replaced abstract expressionism as the thing for easy-come artists to imitate and for easy-go intellectuals to prattle about.

In the smoke from this grass fire, Pop has been called the New Realism, the New Romanticism, the New Social Consciousness, the New Landscape and the New Fantasy—as a beginning. It has also been called, less admiringly, the New Fake and the New Tragedy. What it does is to take the commonest arts, or non-arts, that surround us—comic strips, billboards, magazine advertising, bargain window displays and any other mass-produced vulgarity that this list may suggest—and use them as a point of departure.

The point of departure may be virtually indistinguishable from Pop's point of arrival. "EAT" signs by Robert Indiana, not much different from those that hang outside roadside restaurants except for the price tag, may now be contemplated at leisure in the perfect illumination and sanctified hush of high-class galleries and museums. If it is a lucky day, you may also find a classical rendition of a can of soup by Andy Warhol nearby, or a toothpaste face (seven feet from chin to hairline) by an ex-billboard artist gone legit (or the other way around), James Rosenquist, and some comic-strip characters, true to comic-strip style, but Michelangelesque in dimensions, by Roy Lichenstein.

"Pop" is short for "popular," in the sense of "of the people" or "of the common herd," and by definition Pop is thus opposed to fine art created for the cultivated few. But perversely, and with a perfectly dead pan, the Pop artist addresses his "EAT" signs, soup cans and so on to the most precious echelon of the art-conscious public. As a working definition, we could say that Pop is an art that introduces variations of debased commercial and industrial art into the social, financial and intellectual circles where such art and design have always been regarded with a natural shudder of horror.

As a preliminary explanation of Pop art's vogue, we may say that for this jaded audience, with its insatiable appetite for surprise, Pop is surprising. Its unexpectedness transforms the natural shudder of horror into the artificially induced *frisson* of pleasure that, by one standard, is the first test of a work of art. But even for an audience of this kind—a fairly limited one that finds its amusements in specialized areas—a vogue of such dimensions is not self-generative. So the compound question remains: Why were any critics interested in Pop in the first place; what induced dealers to take it on, and where did the dealers find the first purchasers to crack a market that seemed cornered by exactly the opposite type of commodity—abstract art?

In all three categories—the writer-promoters, the salesman-distributors and the collector-patrons—a large element of opportunism is mixed with more admirable stimuli. Many a young critic, coming on the scene within the last decade, found himself stuck with the job of sizing up forms of art that had already been staked out by older critics who were in at the birth of such movements as abstract expressionism and had said all there was to say—and a lot more. The appearance of Pop art was equivalent to the discovery of a critical Klondike. New claims could be staked, and new areas mined for interpretation.

Aside from critical opportunism, there is the more creditable fact that art is so much talked and written about today that any hint of a new movement stirs genuine excitement among people whose profession, or avocation, it is to keep an eye on what is going on. The rapid swing from boredom to excitement and back to boredom and then to new excitement may be unhealthy, tending to give disproportionate attention to new movements and also to overfeed them so that they die before they have a chance to develop naturally, but it is a process that explains the extreme receptivity of critics to anything that takes a new turn.

No turn since the early years of this century has been quite as startling as the turn Pop took. For 50 years, the most persistent thread in new art movements has been progressive abstraction, and Pop was the first movement in the direction of literal realism that looked revolutionary rather than reactionary. Pop, as a result, may have been argued pro and con out of all proportion to its potential significance, but the argument nevertheless has established it in the spotlight. And once the spotlight is focused on one part of the stage, the main action goes on there until somebody gets up and shifts the beam again.

Among dealers, who are businessmen, the Klondike analogy is too obvious to need much explanation. When one market is at its peak, a good merchant, knowing that it must decline, casts around for a new one. As a businessman, the merchant of contemporary art is in the same position as the clothing merchant. He depends on new styles to keep the customers coming, and his job is to anticipate the new styles, or even to originate them, while keeping his old line moving. It is worth noticing that Pop art, although widely exploited, is being most successfully exploited not by new, adventurous dealers, but by well-established galleries who yesterday were pushing yesterday's styles.

More idealistically, a dealer gets satisfaction out of creating a name for an unknown artist. He likes the feeling that he is more than an art broker, that he is a perceptive arbiter of taste. If a critic he respects finds a new product, such as Pop art, worth attention, then the dealer can argue that turning it into a readily available commodity is a cultural, indeed a humanitarian, duty. When he sends up a trial balloon, more critics get interested even if their interest lies in puncturing it. The spotlight is getting focused. More dealers come in, then more critics and so on in a spiral that leads directly to the man who ultimately makes or breaks a movement in the system as set up—the collector, who foots the bill.

Some Pop art is bought just for fun by people who can afford to follow a fad. Many a cocktail party that would otherwise have died a natural death has been saved by a piece of Pop art hanging on the wall (or lying on the floor, as much of it does). But that Pop has found serious collectors indicates how the nature of art collecting, which for centuries meant the gathering together of rare and beautiful objects, has changed in recent years. Pop is the opposite of rare, and although there may be collectors who are attracted to it for its own lovely self, this is difficult to believe since few collectors are totally blind.

But Pop is a natural for the type of adventurous collector who is eager to be in on the newest thing and is willing to take first crack on the chance that today's questionable item will supply tomorrow's basic collection of early works in a new school. The possibility of increased value is also there for the investment collector, with the cushion of income tax deductions at worst, if the movement begins to die and the stuff is given in time to an amenable museum. But, most important, there are the collectors of modern art who try to build historically complete collections.

For such collections, examples of Pop art are now imperative if the collection is to be comprehensive. For Pop, having happened, is now history, no matter how curious and lamentable the way of its happening. It is still current history, but if it should die tomorrow it is already part of the story, however brief and flashy its life may prove to be. All esthetic values aside, the fact that Pop can have happened to the extent that it *has* happened is in itself an ineradicable comment on what the art situation is today.

If Pop is only a novelty, it is as good as dead already. At its present pace, its staying power or its vulnerability to that sinister question, "What next?" should be proved within the next art season or two. The question can be staved off only as long as Pop can keep us wondering about the basic question of its validity as art or answer that question affirmatively. Is there really anything, beneath the novelty, to give it an audience interested in more than vaudeville? Even if it is vaudeville, how long can it find new stunts that keep it from repeating itself too badly? And if it fails as itself, what are its chances of producing sports that, stemming from it, may prove Pop's importance by proving its generative fecundity?

Taking these questions one at a time, we might look first at Pop as the New This and the New That—in some of the terms already listed.

As the New Realism, Pop owes its attraction to its satisfaction of a widespread feeling that it is high time for art to return to some reference to life instead of staying off in a corner and indulging the splatter esthetic that had all but starved out everything else five years ago. But Pop, in abandoning abstraction for a form of realism and declaring itself anti-esthetic in opposition to hyper-estheticism, has hardly taken the course hoped for by a public that still thinks of realism in the terms of the art history books.

Instead of cultivating the good, the true, the beautiful or the socially significant in understandable terms, Pop art has tied its wagon to a curious star, indeed—the bad, the false, the ugly and the socially deplorable, in terms that are all too understandable (although sometimes it is difficult to believe that Pop really means what it seems to be saying).

The New Realism is a rangy term that also applies to any art that, rather than using drawing and painting as its medium, employs actual objects and materials and sticks them together. Pop art does this, too, and visitors to a recent exhibition were offered spiritual elevation in the form of a life-size nude, painted by Tom Wesselmann, in a painted bathroom that included such real accessories as a towel rack with towels, a laundry hamper, a door and a wall telephone rigged up to ring every few minutes.

The reaction of people to Pop as the New Realism parallels the punch line of the old shaggy dog story. A public yearning for an art in which things are recognizable has greeted various tentative returns toward realism, one after another, with the objection, "Not realistic enough." But faced with Pop's offerings, people cry out, "Oh, no, not *that* realistic!"

A few defenders argue that when you come down to it, Pop isn't really realistic—it just looks that way. Deep down it's just the opposite—romantic. This would have to mean that Pop is a form of soul-searching. The search for beauty in ugliness, pleasure in pain, enlightenment through innocence and purification through debauchery have all been methods of romantic exploration from time to time, and it is quite possible to argue that Pop's glorification of the banal, by artists who of course are fully aware of the horrors of banality, is comparable to the romantic hero's taking up with a degraded prostitute in order to find his own salvation.

The trouble with all this is that Pop doesn't give much sign of interest in salvation. Perhaps because of its extreme youth, it seems more interested in just having a good time, although it does amuse itself in some perverse fashions.

The fact remains that some explanation must be found for Pop's decision to occupy itself with all the ugliness, the cheapness and the shoddiness of the most routine aspects of the man-made world that surrounds us. One way out has been to call Pop the New Landscape, since it deals with our omnipresent environment. An early virtue claimed for Pop was that it creates a new awareness of ordinary objects and hence makes for an intensification of experiences to which we have become calloused through exposure.

There is something to this. As the New Landscape, Pop is proving once more that nature imitates art. Where Pop used to look like comic strips or highway restaurant signs, highway restaurant signs and comic strips are now beginning to look like Pop—which is an improvement of sorts.

"But Pop is not interested in externals. It is at the very heart of life," some of its defenders say. "It doesn't present our world as a landscape—it presents it with a New Social Consciousness."

A theory is that Pop art is the artist's solution and, through him, ours, to living in the world as it is. All the horrendousness of contemporary life—the mass-produced objects devoid of taste, the degraded images produced serially by the hundreds of thousands—must be not only accepted but embraced. By accepting and even by exaggerating these horrors, we have at least the form of escape involved in the adage, "If you can't lick 'em, join 'em."

But a philosophy of escape through resignation to the inevitable is an odd form of social consciousness, and Pop too frequently suggests horseplay for this interpretation to hold. As a more conventional form of social consciousness, Pop has been called protest by satire, social comment by parody.

Satire and parody, however, can easily drop into fantasy, and here, for one reason or another, Pop plops right over on its reverse side and enters the world of unreality. Pop likes to blow things up to enormous size, which cancels out imitation and realism. A hamburger, an ice cream cone, a tube of toothpaste or a slice of pie, sculptured and realistically colored but executed in a scale of feet for inches, transforms the banal into the grotesque. From here, at hop-skip-and-jump tempo, Pop gets into a no-holds-barred area with a dozen peripheral variations still based on the vulgarity of the motif but transmuting this motif in dozens of ways.

George Segal, classified as a Pop artist but more truly a member of this periphery, is one of the most unnerving artists at work today. His appellation of sculptor brings howls from more conventional members of the breed, but there is nothing else to call him. Segal's dead-white plaster figures have an uncanny lifelikeness, not entirely explainable by the fact that they are actually a form of casting from life, made by covering live models with plaster-soaked rags that are allowed to harden and are then removed for assembly as hollow dummies. Their eerie reality is made doubly real and infinitely more eerie by their placement in or on actual objects, which is their Pop connection.

Adding a Segal to your collection is like adopting a new member of the family, according to collectors who should know, and a Segal, once acquired, is likely to be given a name for easy reference. ("Darling, the maid didn't dust Dave yesterday. Will you ask her to?") If you own a Segal, you have to find room in your house for, say, a nude plaster woman who sits on her own real honest-to-God bed, all messed up; or a woman who stands in a real bathtub, perpetually shaving her plaster legs; or a bus driver behind the wheel of a real bus; or a group of bus riders on real bus seats; or a man who gives the impression of being ready, at any moment, to crack the plaster film that covers him and reach for the next letter on a full-scale mockup of a theater marquee.

Segal's race of ghosts are partly amusing but largely disturbing, and about equally grotesque and literal. Inhabiting their own little corners of the world, they are examples of an interest that Pop shares with some other *avant-garde* movements—the idea that art should not be dedicated to the production of isolated works but to the creation of an environment. Claes Oldenburg, the Pop chef who created the transmutedburger, has also done an entire bedroom of wee-wawed furniture, complete with lamps, ashtrays and radio, that achieves the impossible by making mass-produced pseudo-modern interior decoration even uglier than it is.

Because of its deadpan and frequently mechanical look, Pop art at its purest can be just about as impersonal as art can get, although each Pop master has his gimmick trademark. But in Pop-related developments, there are hints of more personal, expressive directions in which the movement may eventually discover its true realization. Leading the list is a young woman who uses only her first name professionally, Marisol.

Marisol may offer us, lifesize, an entire jazz band, or a family out for the day in the automobile, or three women, a little girl and a dog out for a walk, executed in a combination of sculpture, squared blocks of wood, life casts, drawing, painting and real articles of clothing, in some of the wittiest and most inventive—what's the word? Concoctions?—being turned out at the moment.

But Marisol differs from straight Pop artists in that she is not looking objectively at the world around us, or even pretending to. She looks into a world of her own, the kind of world that Pop theoretically rejects. But as Pop develops, there are more and more frequent signs that its artists have not so much rejected the inner world as rejected the old paths by which it was explored. The hope for Pop as a significant art movement rather than as a running gag is that it may end by beating out a few such paths, even if it does so in spite of itself.

You're a Good Man, Charlie Schulz

by Barnaby Conrad

"CARTOONING IS A *fairly* sort of a proposition," said Charlie Brown's creator recently. "You have to be fairly intelligent—if you were really intelligent you'd be doing something else; you have to draw fairly well—if you drew really well you'd be a painter; you have to write fairly well—if you wrote really well you'd be writing books. It's great for a fairly person like me."

For an only *fairly* person, Charles (Sparky) Schulz bids fair to becoming the most successful newspaper cartoonist of all time. "Peanuts," which appears in some 900 newspapers in the U.S. and Canada, plus 100 abroad, has endeared the characters of Charlie, Lucy, Linus, Schroeder and Snoopy to an estimated 90 million readers. Records, films, advertisements, sweatshirts, dolls, books, cocktail napkins and other "Peanuts" paraphernalia have capitalized on the craze to make it a $20-million-a-year industry. The statistics of the triumphs of the strip and its various offshoots are so staggering that its millions of fans—and even its creator— are wondering how the original quality and simplicity of the product can be maintained. As I was interviewing him in his studio— an unexpectedly over-decorated and plush office—near Sebastopol,

From the *New York Times Magazine*, April 16, 1967, copyright © 1967 by The New York Times Company. Reprinted by permission of Harold Matson Company, Inc.

Calif. (an hour north of San Francisco), the telephone interrupted constantly: A Hollywood producer wanted to talk about a big "Peanuts" musical movie; a caller wanted to know something about the London opening of the hit play "You're a Good Man, Charlie Brown" (now running Off Broadway in New York), another wanted information on his new paperback, "The Unsinkable Charlie Brown." And then there were all the calls from people who wanted him to paint posters for charities, make personal appearances or donate money to this or that cause. Each time Schulz—who, with his crew cut and serious boyishness looks like every freshman's senior adviser—hung up the phone with a sigh. It was not a sigh of exasperation, but rather regret—regret that he was not always able to do the many things that people demand of him.

"I usually get between 400 and 500 letters a week and for years I've managed to answer all of them personally, but I don't know." He leafed through some of the letters. "Most of them are so nice and their requests are so polite and worthwhile—a drawing for a crippled kid, a poster for a special high-school dance. 'Just do a quick sketch of Snoopy,' they ask; 'it'll only take five minutes.' And they're right—it *would* only take five minutes. But they think their letter is the only one on my desk. The five minutes have to be multiplied by hundreds." He looked mournfully at the heap of mail. "Thousands. They forget that I not only have to do some drawing, I occasionally have to do some thinking."

He looked out of his studio window and studied a clump of trees beyond an artificial pond. "It's hard to convince people when you're just staring out of the window that you're doing your hardest work of the day. In fact, many times when I'm just sitting here thinking and therefore working like heck I hear the door open and I quickly grab the pen and a piece of paper and start drawing something so that people won't think I'm just goofing off and anxious to have a little chat. But I like visitors when I'm drawing. It gets lonely up here all day, not like an office or a dentist or somebody who has company around him all the time." Schulz has been termed a recluse but he says: "Oh, we go to San Francisco about once a month, see friends, go to a play. But we aren't nightclubbers or cocktail types. Neither of us drink, never have, just isn't part of our life and our friends just have to accept us like that."

He picked up some more letters. "Lots of people write in ideas. Some are good, but I don't seem to be able to use other people's suggestions. Here's a pretty good one—'Why not make Snoopy pretend he's a Grand Prix racing driver?' Now that's not a bad idea, and I guess it would work. But first of all, I didn't think of it, and secondly I'd be imitating myself—sort of copying the Snoopy and the Red Baron business. It's always dangerous to copy yourself. Al Capp had a great success with the Schmoos, so then he had to try to repeat with the Kigmies and it wasn't as good. The Red Baron was a good idea but let's not imitate it. My son says he gave me the idea for that—he was working on a World War I model and claims he suggested the Red Baron business, but I don't remember. People think I'm a World War I nut and send me these"—he gestured at shelves of flying books.

I asked him about the hit record "Snoopy and the Red Baron," based on the dog's flights of fancy and aerial encounters with The Red Baron, the king of World War I skies. "I based the Baron on Richthofen because he's sort of the Beethoven of flying. Incidentally, I never heard about this record by the Royal Guardsmen until a friend said, 'Great song you wrote.' I checked with my lawyer the next day and we put a stop to that right away. Or rather we threatened to put a stop until we were included in the success. I understand they've sold two and a half million copies of it already. [Schulz gets a varying percentage of two other hit records as well—Vince Guaraldi's "Jazz Impressions of Charlie Brown" and "Charlie Brown's Christmas," put out by Fantasy Records.]

"Speaking of records, have you heard this?" He picked up the album of "You're a Good Man, Charlie Brown," and played the overture. "I'd like to see the show, but haven't really had time. Maybe next month we'll get to New York, but first I'm taking my wife and four of our five kids and four kids of friends of ours to Sun Valley for our first real vacation in two years. I hear it's a good show—love the music."

The Off Broadway play, made up of prose taken from "Peanuts" strips, opened on March 7 at Theater 80 St. Marks. In his ecstatic review Walter Kerr wrote: "They [the people of 'Peanuts'] have marched clean off that page of pure white light . . . and into forthright, fuming, explosively funny conversation without losing a drop of the ink that made their lifelines so human."

When Schulz talks he is every bit as modest and unassuming as one could want the progenitor of "Peanuts" to be, yet there is a pride of profession in his voice. "Hollywood wants to make a movie of the play and I guess some day we'll do something. There was a nice fellow up here recently who produced 'To Kill a Mockingbird,' and we talked pleasantly. But the moment they start talking about 'their writers' I kind of get chills. I want it to be my words in everything I do. Just as I guess I'm the only cartoonist who doesn't have a helper to do the Sunday strip or fill in backgrounds and stuff. I even do my own lettering. I've thought of it—hiring someone to help. Sometimes I think it would be nice. But then—what would be the point? I don't do this for the money"—he gestured at his big drafting table with several half-inked-in strips on it. "People think I do, but I don't. I do it because I love to draw.

"The things I like to do best are drawing cartoons and hitting golf balls. Now if I hire someone to do my work for me what fun would I get? It'd be like getting someone to hit the golf ball for me. But maybe I'll have to." He glanced balefully at his secretary as she brought in a new stack of mail. "Life magazine said I was a multimillionaire—heck, no cartoonist can become a millionaire—but that's what the magazine said and now I'm getting requests for money from all over the world."

Whether or not he is in the millionaire bracket yet, Schulz lives like one. On his 28-acre estate, Coffee Grounds (on Coffee Lane), he has two elegant houses besides his big studio. Then there are stables, a cat, dog and horse per child, a tennis court, a baseball diamond and a four-hole golf course. He is an excellent golfer, 5 handicap, and shoots consistently in the 70's. The highlight of his year is the coveted invitation to the Crosby golf tournament in Monterey. He tries to play golf once a week, but as his success mounts and the work load increases he has to forgo more and more games.

Schulz begins his day at 9:30 by walking the quarter mile from his sprawling one-level house across the lawns of his golf holes, past the big swimming pool to his studio. With a secretary in the outer office and a plush living room before you arrive at the place where he actually draws, it could very well be the office of a successful real-estate broker or a pre-need cemetery-lot salesman.

Clinically neat and organized, Schulz sits at the drawing board and begins by playing around on a scratch pad with a pencil, doodling situations and ideas. He tries to conceive of the week's work as a whole; six separate days' drawings which will somehow make a unity. When he has the ideas fairly well set in his mind he takes a 28-inch illustration board, which has the margins of the four panels printed on it already, and inks in the dialogue. When he has all six days' strips "dialogued in," he begins to draw the figures and the action, preferring to draw directly with the pen with a minimum of penciled guidelines.

One day's strip takes him about an hour to draw. The Sunday page takes the whole day. He is required by the syndicate to be five weeks ahead on the daily and eleven weeks ahead on the Sunday. When I called on him he was just finishing up the strips for the week of May 8 to May 13, the theme being "Be Kind to Animals Week." (In one sequence, Snoopy is holding a sign with that legend on it, and as Lucy goes by he shuts his eyes and puckers up for a kiss. "Not on your life!" bellows the dear girl, bowling the dog and his sign over backward. Another day ends with Snoopy's saying: "This was a good week—I didn't get kicked.")

Right now Schulz is also busy preparing an hour-and-a-half film, plus another TV special. (He writes every word, and supervised the animation of the other three TV specials.)

The books are a further drain on his time. Since the first one, called plain "Peanuts," Holt has published some 4,493,000 copies, and they are all in print. After Holt has had a year or two to sell a "Peanuts" book at $1, the rights are turned over to Fawcett, which takes the Holt volume, splits it in two, and sells each copy for 40 cents. To date Fawcett has sold 12 titles to the tune of 10 million copies. But the publishing doesn't end there. A few years ago an enterprising San Francisco woman named Connie Boucher persuaded Schulz to do a book for her Determined Productions company. It turned out to be "Happiness Is a Warm Puppy," and it was on The New York Times best-seller list for

45 weeks in 1962 and 1963. This was followed by more "Happiness Is—" books, plus a Peanuts Date Book, totaling around three million copies in all. In 1965 the John Knox Press published "The Gospel According to Peanuts," being the theological thoughts extracted from the strip, which has been that firm's best seller of all time at more than 635,000 copies.

Which brings one to another consuming interest of Charles Schulz: religion. A member of a Scripture-oriented Protestant nondenominational organization called the Church of God, he keeps 12 Bibles, plus a set of the dozen volumes of the Interpreters' Bible, in his studio. On Sundays he teaches Sunday School in Sebastopol ("to adults only—I could never teach other people's children"). A pushover for charities and organizations designed to help people, he recently consented to accept the chairmanship of the National Aid to the Visually Handicapped and set about organizing a huge golf tourney, to be known as the "Charlie Brown–Lucy Tournament," the proceeds of which went to the aid of partly blind children. He brooded for weeks over a request to do a poster for Aid for Retarded Children, tried dozens of ideas, and finally had to give up. "There was simply no way to do it without the danger of seeming to mock them."

So this is the hectic world that was created by Charlie Brown Schulz (he confesses that they are one and the same person). How did it come about and how did it snowball into these proportions?

Charles Monroe Schulz, as every good "Peanuts" aficionado knows, was born 44 years ago in Minneapolis, Minn. When he was two days old, he was nicknamed "Sparky" by his family for Barney Google's horse Sparkplug, and is still called that by his family and friends. From almost the beginning he wanted to become a cartoonist, thinking it among the noblest of the artistic professions.

"It's a great art," he says now. "I'm convinced it's much harder and more important than illustration. Look at that"—he points to a framed original cartoon page of "Krazy Kat" by George Herriman—"that's art. It was done around 1912 and its humor is every bit as fresh today as then."

Sparky's early life was very Charlie Brownish. "People read

a lot into the strip, and I guess what people see in it, that's what's in it. But actually the strip is just about all the dumb things I did when I was little."

In fine Charlie Brown fashion he was the goat on the baseball field, once losing a game 40 to nothing, and even his drawings were turned down by the high-school yearbook. In the Army he was similarly unsuccessful. After being trained as a machine gunner, he discovered he had forgotten to load his weapon the one and only time he was confronted by members of the enemy forces.

"It was the last week of the war and we were going along a road in Southern Germany in a halftrack and somebody said, 'Hey—look over there, there's somebody in that hole over there in the field, shoot him.' So I swung the gun around—50 caliber— pressed the butterfly trigger, and nothing happened. Before I could load he came out with his hands up and I was sure glad I hadn't been able to shoot him."

After the war he got a job lettering a comic magazine, then taught in a Minneapolis art school of the "Draw-me-and-win-a-scholarship" mail-order variety. A fellow instructor was named Charlie Brown, and later unwittingly lent his name to posterity. Another had a pretty blue-eyed sister named Joyce Halverson, and Schulz married her. In 1948 he sold his first cartoon, to The Saturday Evening Post. Then he did a weekly cartoon for The St. Paul Pioneer Press called "Li'l Folks." Within a year it was dropped. After many rejections from other syndicates, it was picked up by United Features in Manhattan. Over Schulz's protests it was renamed "Peanuts." To this day he is still indignant.

"What an ugly word it is," he says disgustedly. "Say it: *Peanuts!* I can't stand to even write it. And it's a terrible title. Now 'Peppermint Patty' is a good title for a strip. I introduced a character named that into the strip to keep someone else from using it. Funny, people don't tell you how to draw or write but EVERYBODY'S an expert on titles."

The first month Schulz made $90 with his newly titled strip. A few months later it was up to $1,000 a month. Now, 17 years later, it is close to $1,000 a day.

"Funny," Sparky muses, "I never set out to do a cartoon about kids. I just wanted to be a good cartoonist, like, say, Herriman or my boyhood idol, Roy Crane, who draws 'Buz Sawyer'—a fine cartoonist. I always dreamed of some day coming up with some permanent idea or phrase that would pass into the language, like Snuffy Smith's 'bodacious' or some of Al Capp's gimmicks. I guess maybe 'Good grief' has made it. And perhaps the Great Pumpkin. And the 'Happiness Is . . .' title.

"There are a lot of good cartoonists around. I read all of 'em. Capp, Caniff, 'Miss Peach.' It pleases me that my children seem to like 'Peanuts' as well as any of the others. They know all the books by heart and have favorite strips on their walls and play the records. It's all very gratifying."

When asked about Snoopy, who is my family's favorite character in the strip, he said, "Snoopy's not a real dog, of course—he's an image of what people would like a dog to be. But he has his origins in Spike, my dog that I had when I was a kid. White with black spots. He was the wildest and smartest dog I've ever encountered. Smart? Why, he had a vocabulary of at least 50 words. I mean it. I'd tell him to go down to the basement and bring up a potato and he'd do it. I used to chip tennis balls at him and he'd catch and retrieve 'em." Schulz's sensitive face clouds at the memory. "Had him for years before he died."

Many psychiatrists who charge a good deal more than Lucy van Pelt's 5-cent consultation fee have tried to analyze the special appeal of "Peanuts." My pedestrian conclusion is that Charles Schulz feels the loss of his dog Spike today as deeply as—or more deeply than—he did a quarter of a century ago, just as he feels the loss of his childhood. Happily for the readers, he is able to translate this long memory and deep feeling into words and pictures. It seems to be universal, either because we had a childhood like that, or wish we had. There's a little Charlie Brown in all of us males and, Lord knows, we've all known, and maybe even married, a Lucy van Pelt, a girl who shouts: "I don't want any downs—I just want ups and ups and ups." Certainly there's been *someone* in each one of our lives ready and eager to pull away the football just as we're about to kick it.

So very often the strip touches chords that remind us of things and homely events we thought we had forgotten. As the catalogue for the recent Whitney exhibition of Andrew Wyeth (Schulz's favorite painter, along with Picasso) stated: "But art arises in the human spirit beyond the reach of words from the levels of deepest memories. We are creatures who need the near and the familiar as well as the exotic."

Emerson wrote in 1838: "A man must have aunts and cousins, must buy carrots and turnips, must have barn and woodshed, must go to market and to the blacksmith's shop, must saunter and sleep and be inferior and silly."

Another factor in the strip's popularity with all ages is his sublime handling of how far the fantasy should go. For example, Snoopy's dog house is always shown in profile; we never see it three-quarters view or actually go inside it. We just accept the fact when it is said that Snoopy has a Wyeth and a Van Gogh and a pool table in there, but if we actually saw inside and discovered an unbelievable dog house we would cease to believe in Snoopy as a dog and his relationship with the children. Another all-important factor in Schulz's astonishingly good batting average is his unfailing sense of what is subtly funny.

"I get letters all the time," he told me, "from optometrists saying, 'How come you're always talking about ophthalmologists'— Linus wore glasses, you know—'why not give us a break?' It's hard to tell them that ophthalmology is somehow funny and the word optometry just isn't. Like Beethoven. My favorite composer is Brahms—I could listen to him all day—but Brahms isn't a funny word. Beethoven is, so I gave him to Schroeder. Like names: Linus is a good name. I borrowed that from a friend, Linus Maurer. Funny, the other night I was trying to think of a good last name for Pigpen—he hasn't got one—and I fell asleep and I dreamed of a new character named José Peterson. That's a good name, isn't it? But I only put him in the strip for a week —he was a baseball player—but he just didn't belong, so out he went, along with some others I've gotten rid of. My strip is not like the kind that depends on variety or new characters. I've got pretty much the same characters and basic idea that I had 17 years ago. I want to keep the strip simple. I like it, for example, when Charlie Brown watches the first leaf of fall float down and then walks over and just says, 'Did you have a good summer?' That's the kind of strip that gives me pleasure to do.

"I liked one I did that I got from one of my children—the only idea I've ever gotten right from something they did or said. We were at the dinner table and Amy was talking away on a real talking streak and finally I said, 'Can't you *please* be quiet?' and she was silent for a moment and then picked up a slice of bread and began to butter it, saying, 'Am I buttering too loud for you?'

"I gave the line to Charlie Brown after Lucy yelled at him. And I like the violent action ones, kids getting bowled over and such things that cartoons were born to do. Too many of these new strips are not cartoons—they're imitations of films, and the movies can do it so much better, beat them at their own game. But I like the quiet ones too. I like it when Linus says, simply: 'Sucking your thumb without a blanket is like eating a cone without ice cream.' I like it when Charlie Brown gets all excited about a big spelling bee and then goes out on the first word because they say, 'Spell "maze," ' and, being the good baseball fan he is, he spells it 'Mays.' I like to keep it all simple. For instance, it seems to me that Snoopy's been getting pretty fantastical lately. I think I'll simplify him, let him just be a dog for a while.

"Incidentally, Snoopy wasn't in the most popular strip I ever did, the one I've had the most mail on. That was the one where the kids are looking at the clouds and Linus says, 'See that one cloud over there? It sort of looks like the profile of Thomas Eakins, the famous portrait painter. And that other group over there—that looks as though it could be a map of British Honduras. And then do you see that large group of clouds up there? I see the stoning of Stephen. Over to the side I can see the figure of the apostle Paul standing.' Then Lucy says, 'That's very good, Linus. It shows you have quite a good imagination. What do you see in the clouds, Charlie Brown?' And Charlie says, 'Well, I was going to say I saw a ducky and a horsey, but I've changed my mind.' "

The phone rang and he talked for a while. When he hung up he said, "That was something about having a helicopter be attacked by the Red Baron. Over Chicago. They've got a real German World War I plane. Publicity stunt of some kind." He shook his head incredulously, and a little sheepishly, at the world he had created. "Where's it all going to end?"

Where, indeed, is it all going to end? Last Thursday I came home from work, hungry for dinner, to find the entire kitchen given over to the making of a two-foot birthday cake for my daughter. It was in the shape and color of Snoopy. Like any other red-blooded male of this generation, I could only look straight out of the panel at the reader and say, "Good grief!"

Part 6

BOOKS

THE SINGLE article in this section deals with the impact of paperback books on a typical American city. Muncie, Indiana, was the scene of two famous inquiries by the sociologists Robert Lynd and his wife, in 1929 and 1937. "Middletown" supposedly is the home of the "average" American, and Richard Lingeman visited it in 1967 to determine what kinds of books were being sold and read. The city's three book stores relied mainly upon paperback sales. About 200,000 copies of paperbacks were received that year by the Muncie News Agency, and some 80,000 were sold. The big hits: *Valley of the Dolls, Candy,* and *The Carpetbaggers.* Lingeman concludes that the real function of paperbacks in Middletown may be to replace the "sex-adventure" magazines that people were reading in the twenties and thirties when the Lynds were doing their study.

The world of popular culture coexists with the actual world of Americans as we enter the 1970's. The same newspaper that brings us the endless details of our tragic misadventure in Vietnam also gives us a moment of surcease with the philosophy of Snoopy. Women who cannot cope with their own family problems continue to seek guidance and guilt-release by watching soap operas on television every day. The Young Audience, many of whom are in protest against American commercialism, are ironically the best customers of RCA and Columbia records, and the major hope that Hollywood will find a viable audience. The world of popular culture is often like a trip to a carnival's crazy house, with mirrors that distort and mock us. It may be as close to reality as we can tolerate.

Middletown Now

by Richard R. Lingeman

MUNCIE, IND.: *Current population:* 71,000. *Principal industrial products: automotive parts, storage batteries, power transformers, gear transmissions, meat products, TV tubes, hammer and upset forging, glass products, tools. Colleges: Ball State University,* 13,000 *students. High school students:* 9,000. *Elementary school students:* 11,000. *Median family income:* $8,040 (1960: $5,-806). *Unemployed: approximately* 3% (1960: 5.4%). *Around* 40% *of employed are in manufacturing, compared with* 35.9% *in white-collar jobs. Foreign born:* 0.6% *Non-white:* 5.3%. *Indiana born:* 72%. *Number of churches:* 89 (83 *Protestant,* 2 *Catholic,* 1 *Jewish,* 1 *Christian Science,* 1 *Seventh Day Adventist and* 1 *Mormon). Muncie was subjected to intensive sociological study by Robert S. and Helen Merrell Lynd in their books "Middletown" (1929) and "Middletown in Transition" (1937). In that decade the principal industry was the Ball Brothers Glass Co., makers of glass "Ball jars" used in canning, and according to the Lynds, the Ball family ruled the town like a "manorial system." But by 1962 the brothers had all passed on and the company had moved most of its glass manufacturing elsewhere; now only a research division remains in the city. Currently the city fathers are preoccupied with stemming decay in the central city; a "mall" type of renovation is planned, whereby streets will be closed to*

*traffic, converted to grass walkways, and some older buildings
torn down. It will get under way in a year, they hope.*

OUT IN MIDDLETOWN, U.S.A., which, as everyone knows, is the
fictitious name for Muncie, Indiana, coined by Robert S. and
Helen Merrell Lynd for their sociological studies, the people are
trying hard to think up a new descriptive slogan for themselves.
Back in the early part of the 20th century, Muncie was known as
"Magic Muncie" or "Magic Town." Then, along came those two
Middletown books and Muncie decided that it obviously was the
"Typical American City."

But now, in its ceaseless quest for identity, Muncie has decided that merely being typical is not enough, and is trying on
a variety of new names for size. Mayor John V. Hampton sees
his constituency as the "Mainspring of the Midwest." The people
who put out "Spotlight on Muncie," which lists the city's night
spots and restaurants and runs articles on things like the Sudlow
Potato Chip Company, call it "The City of Pride." But Richard
A. Greene says in his pamphlet on the history of Muncie that
"The Friendly City" is preferred these days.

Whether proud, friendly or mainspringlike, Muncie is still suffi-
ciently typical for the Census Bureau to designate it a Standard
Metropolitan Statistical Area, and for many market-research
firms to use it as a testing point for a variety of new products
ranging from soap to dog food. Having learned that many publishers regard the Middle West as their largest market for paperback books, I recently made a pilgrimage to this oracle of
Americana, to see what I could learn about what Muncie is reading, and, more specifically, what effect, if any, the mass market
paperback (which did not exist in the Lynds' time) has had on
people's reading habits.

In "Middletown in Transition" the Lynds wrote: "Middletown
is not a book-buying city. . . ." To a degree this is less true
today; the people of Muncie do buy books; unfortunately they
don't buy terribly many of them. The city has three bookstores;
one is housed in the Ball Department Store, the other two are the
City Bookstore and Penzel's. Penzel's has been around since
1906, when it was founded by C. A. Penzel Sr. His son, C. A.
Penzel Jr., carried on with the store after his father's death until

five years ago when he moved to Puerto Rico after making John Landes manager and part-owner.

John Landes, who styles himself "a hardware man," can recall when Penzel's was the only place in town where students could buy textbooks, but about 10 years ago, the schools took over textbook sales, and the bookstore part of the Penzel operation shrank accordingly. Still, Landes regards his book trade as quite satisfactory, by which he means that he sells 4,000 to 5,000 trade books a year, with sales on a steady upward trend since he took over. He sells no paperbacks because he just doesn't have room and doesn't think the paperback business is very profitable anyhow.

The main paperback store in town now is the City Bookstore, a small and reportedly marginal operation. The owner, Kenneth Foltz, who has been at his present location across the street from Penzel's for two years, says he sells mainly paperbacks now and has let the hardback operation run down.

Together, these two bookstores appear to be selling about 5,000 hardcover books a year. Add, say, another 5,000 sold at the small bookstore in the basement of the Ball Department Store (from which figures were not available). Not counting book-club members in Muncie or sales at the college store, which has the largest hardback department in town but whose clientele consists mainly of students and professors, that makes about 10,000 trade books a year being bought by Muncie's 80,000 people. A satisfactory number, perhaps; but certainly not a cultural revolution—in case you were expecting one.

Sales of mass-market paperbacks are of course much more sizable; yet, somehow, not what one would expect. The paperback (and magazine) wholesaler in Muncie is the Muncie News Company. Jack Sorenson, manager there for 12 years, says his dollar grosses have been going up steadily the past few years, but he attributes this to rising cover prices; he is not selling as many copies as he used to. Last year, he received a total of 202,748 books and sold 83,137 of them, or 41 per cent. The Muncie News Company services about fifty dealers—and this is full servicing: tending the racks, culling out the non-sellers and keeping the hot titles replenished—located mostly in drugstores, supermarkets, candy stores and the like. His best outlet is a drugstore located in one of Muncie's ubiquitous shopping centers; and his biggest expansion recently came when he added a chain of supermarkets to his dealer list. With his rising costs, his rather static sales and the inelastic percentage of the book's price he rakes off for himself, Sorenson feels somewhat in a squeeze. He would like to do more business with the schools, but says that market has slipped considerably in the past few years because teachers can't be counted on to assign the same book every year and it is difficult to fill orders from the schools at short notice.

Sorenson's biggest problem, though, is that perennial (and progressively louder) plaint of the mass paperback business—too many titles and not enough space to display them. To Sorenson, it seems that the New York publishing leviathan is bent upon inundating him with titles, at the rate of approximately 200 a month. He objects to what he calls this "numbers game" and feels that the law of diminishing returns is setting in. Or, as he succinctly puts it: "We could have sold more, if we had received less." So glutted is Muncie News with books that many boxes that come in are returned unopened, to make room for still more boxes in the warehouse. A typical dealer serviced by Muncie News will have a rack with 80 slots for books; try getting 200 titles in *that*. Sometimes, Sorenson has regrets about those books in the boxes in his warehouse that never see the light of day. "I just don't know how many good books we don't see," he says. He also confesses he doesn't do much reading. "I get so I don't even want to look at a book," says the Middletown cadre of the paperback revolution.

Kenneth Foltz doesn't think his City Bookstore needs any more rack space. It would "mess up the store," and increase his pilferage problem, by turning some racks away from his watchful eyes (he has a lot of high school students coming in). Of course he could take out the greeting-card bins . . . but that is obviously inconceivable. Foltz estimates, "conservatively," that he sells 1,000 paperbacks a month. With the tight margin he is working under, that is barely enough and expansion would probably be out of the question. (Another source told me that Foltz would like to sell out.)

A listing of the hardcover and paperback books most popular in Muncie contains few surprises, and no books of unusual artistic

or cultural merit. Not surprisingly, the folks in Muncie are reading a sort of abridged, somewhat dated version of the national
best-seller lists. Jack Sorenson lists as his recent best-sellers such
titles as "Mandingo" by Kyle Onstott, "To Kill a Mockingbird,"
dictionaries, Dr. Spock, "Candy," "Flying Saucers—Serious Business"—any book on flying saucers, for that matter ("can't keep
in enough of them"), "Peyton Place" (still), "The Carpetbaggers,"
"Gone with the Wind," Dennis the Menace, Snoopy of the Peanuts gang and the Perry Mason mysteries, whose publisher Sorenson praises as knowing precisely just how much of the Erle
Stanley Gardner traffic Muncie will bear. Among his newest titles,
in addition to Harold Robbins' "The Adventurers," "In Cold
Blood" and "The Source" are taking off nicely.

Kenneth Foltz offers "Valley of the Dolls," "Phyllis Diller's
Household Hints" and Sam Levenson's "Everything But Money"
in hardback; and, among the paperbacks, Kyle Onstott's titles, the
various progeny of the Harold Robbins stud farm, "In Cold
Blood," "A Gift of Prophecy," "Candy," "Fanny Hill," "Flying
Saucers—Serious Business," with the mystery and spy genres
always doing well. Foltz's best sellers, though, are what he calls
"risqué"—the Times Square school of literature, with the sexy
covers and titles like "I Was a Slave in a Lesbian Love Factory."

At Penzel's, "Valley of the Dolls," of course, is the front runner.
("A lot of people bought it as a last-minute Christmas present,"
Landes said. "Respectable women in their 50's, who said they
were going to give it to their husbands.") Not far behind were
Adela Rogers St. John's, "Tell No Man," Irving Stone's "Those
Who Love" and Allen Drury's "Capable of Honor."

These best sellers aside, John Landes thinks there is, in general, more interest in what he calls "serious books—books such
as those that increase your knowledge of world affairs." (There
were no books on Vietnam on his racks.) Still, some of his
strongest sellers are what he calls "thrill books"—"Candy," "Valley of the Dolls" and Mrs. Robbins' *oeuvre*—books which "give
you a thrill while you read them but don't leave you with anything." Somewhat similarly to Jack Sorenson, who simply receives
the books publishers send him, many of the books John Landes
stocks are what he calls "automatic orders," that is the publishers
send him books they think he can sell, without his requesting

them. This works out well for him; he simply pays for the books, and if he can't sell them, returns them for a refund. When Landes orders books on his own, he does so with an eye on The New York Times and The Chicago Tribune best-seller lists. "I have to depend on something," he says.

Jack Sorenson thinks people are reading more "good books"— by which he would mean best-selling novels and non-fiction, as opposed to Westerns and mysteries. Kenneth Foltz says that most of his clientele are the kind of people who would prefer to wait until the paperback edition of a book they want to read comes out. Those who buy hardbacks do so when it is "something special, something they really want to read," or else they have a personal library which they like to supplement with hardbacks from time to time. Some of his customers, though, are accumulating paperback libraries. In this category, he offered the example of the man who collected James Bond books, and who preferred to wait for the paperback edition of Fleming's last book, "The Man with the Golden Gun," rather than close out the collection with a clothbound anomaly.

In Muncie, the burning question of obscenity in literature is sputtering rather fitfully at the present time. Foltz probably needs his risqué book sales to keep going, and makes no apologies for them. The more prosperous Penzel's, whose book business is practically a sideline compared with its line of office furniture, bookends, manicure sets, ash trays, stationery, clocks, lamps and greeting cards, neither pushes nor withholds any of the steamier novels that come in. John Landes' attitude is that there is no one definition of obscenity: what one person might see as obscene, another will not. His feeling is that any customer who comes into his shop—kids excepted—is entitled to ask for and get any book he wants. "If somebody asked me to order the filthiest book in the world," Landes says, "I would do so without hesitation. He has *honored* me by coming into my shop, and I'm here to serve him."

Only once did a representative of the local censorship forces bother him. The store had received, without ordering them, six copies of "Candy." As is often the case, he put the book out without having read it and not knowing what it was about. Zoom! The first six disappeared before you could say Maxwell Kenton. So Landes ordered a dozen more, then a dozen more after *that,* and displayed the book prominently in his window. Then one day he happened to pick up a copy and take it back to his office for a little spare-time reading. He opened it to a particular passage . . . well, it was the passage about . . . anyway, that was going too far. So he promptly removed the book from prominent display, but continued to sell it. Then somewhat later, a church lady came in and asked if he had "Candy." "Yes, I do," he told her. "Would you like a copy?" The church lady blanched. "Oh, no! That trash! How can you sell such a book!" Landes explained his policy, that he was in business and had no cause to offend his customers by telling them they couldn't have something they asked for. The church lady, though disapproving of the book, admitted he had a point, and there were no further complaints about "Candy."

To Jack Sorenson's mind, obscenity is something that exists for some people and not for others. Still, he doesn't want his dealers to have any trouble, and will remove forthwith any book about which there are complaints—"Last Exit to Brooklyn" being the most recent example. In his view, it is the publishers of the "obscene" books who should be arrested, rather than the sellers. He draws an analogy to a druggist who unwittingly sells a bottle of aspirin containing arsenic. The druggist wouldn't be liable; it would be the manufacturer who put the arsenic in by mistake. Since he reads very few, if any, of his books, Sorenson's analogy is delightfully apposite.

Such is the book business catering to the general public of Muncie. Probably the main vendor of paperbacks in the city, however, is the bookshop of Ball State University. This state-owned, red brick university is in the throes of the biggest expansion in its history. Its student body has quadrupled in the space of 12 years, and the present enrollment (13,055) is up 13 per cent over last year. Ball State only achieved university status in 1965; now there is talk of snaring a new medical school.

For this large market, the college bookshop has only one competitor, the College Book Exchange, which is located across the street from the campus. The exchange deals mainly in used textbooks—buying and selling—but opened up a paperback department last year, which is cautiously being expanded. The exchange carries no hardbacks, however, other than textbooks, because, says Manager David Myers, "the publishers won't give you any protection."

The present college-owned store has been in its current location in the basement of the L. A. Pittenger Student Union Building for only five years, and already its paperback stock is threatening to overflow all available shelf space. Mrs. Dorothy Bailey, the petite lady directly in charge of the paperbacks, estimates that in the last year or so the store's paperback volume has tripled. Four years ago, some professors didn't use any paperbacks in their courses; now some professors use only paperbacks. Mrs. Bailey has no idea how many paperbacks she has in stock, but in variety and intellectual range, the store's collection compares favorably with any of the largest paperback stores in New York—perhaps exceeds most.

The store has also a fairly extensive stock of trade books, and Mrs. Mabel Ross, in charge of the trade books, hums to herself as she leafs through The Times Book Review, looking for new books to order. A full-page ad for "The Man Who Knew Kennedy" by Vance Bourjaily catches her eye. "That will be a good seller," she says. Another full-page ad for "Thomas Woodrow Wilson" by Freud and Bullitt elicits a similar response. The hardback department here seems more current and offers more nonfiction titles than that at Penzel's. Mrs. Ross says she doesn't do a large business and that about half-and-half students and professors buy the books. Lots of professors are buying "Valley of the Dolls," she chuckles: "They say there's *something* in it that's good." "Human Sexual Response" sold 10 last week and 10 more were ordered and are on display. Otherwise, her other strong sellers ("How to Avoid Probate," "Everything But Money," "Capable of Honor," "The Secret of Santa Vittoria") are all familiar tenants of the national lists.

In the Muncie public school system, paperback usage is also widespread, says William Lyon, director of instruction. Textbooks officially adopted for class work, however, are all hardback; and the school libraries are generally "very choosy about paperbacks. Since they don't hold up, it's a better investment to spend the money on hardbacks." The increased availability of paperbacks has had little effect on the curriculum, though; their "accessibility" is their chief virtue. When a student can do his reading in his own copy of a paperback, rather than in a library book, **the** course is made more "realistic" to him, Lyon said.

The Muncie Public Libraries largely steer clear of paperbacks, purchasing only a small number, simply as a convenience, to duplicate books on the high school reading lists, for which there will be a brief flurry of demand.

Library Director Leon Jones attributes one change in library usage in part to the appearance of paperbacks on the Muncie scene. They (along with TV and magazines) have taken over much of the "escape-reading" function the library used to perform, Jones thinks. Now people are to an increasing degree using the library primarily for what he calls "purposeful reading." This has resulted in a falling off in borrowings of mystery, Western and light romantic fiction, and an increase in nonfiction and technical reading.

In "Middletown in Transition," the Lynds noted that nonfiction reading rose in Middletown in good times, but decreased in the depths of the Depression, with a concomitant rise in "escape" reading, what the Lynds called the "anodyne of fiction." Recent figures show that adult nonfiction reading in Muncie is over twice the highwater mark recorded by the Lynds in 1929, when 20.1 per cent of all books borrowed from the library by adults were nonfiction. In 1966, 45 per cent of all books borrowed by adults were nonfiction.

Jones sees the present role of the main library as a sort of central depository for reference, technical, historical and other informational matter, rather than the morale builder and "anodyne" dispenser it tended to be during the Depression. The library is seeking to encourage this trend. For example, it maintains a Business and Technical Collection and sends out a monthly mimeographed list of books thought to be of interest to the 300 or so businessmen who receive it. For February, the subject was urban renewal—very much in the Muncie air these days—and recommended titles included "The City Is the Frontier" by Charles Abrams, "Planning and the Urban Community" edited by Harvey S. Perloff and "The Making of Urban America: A History of City Planning in the United States" by J. W. Reps.

Leon Jones is a soft-spoken, thoughtful man who appears more involved with social problems than he is with bookish concerns.

He has to be, for the patterns of library use in Muncie are shaped by currents of urban change. In Muncie, the main currents are similar to those in most of our cities: people are moving to the suburbs, suburban shopping centers attract their business and the center city decays. The shops in the central business district are well stocked, yet (on a week day) almost devoid of customers, with the exception of the Muncie Central students who crowd the cafeteria in the Ball store at lunchtime.

What this means to the main library, located on Jackson Street near City Hall, is clear. "We have the same problem as the center city businessmen," Jones says. "Getting downtown and parking is a problem. It is much more convenient going to a suburban shopping center than driving downtown and bothering with a parking lot." The upshot of this is that the three branch libraries of the Muncie Public Library system now serve more people than the main branch. In fact, the relatively new John F. Kennedy Library, located in the Northwest shopping center, with plentiful parking space, last year for the first time had a higher circulation alone than the main branch (111,900 to 98,838), even though the main branch has 79,284 books to Kennedy's 19,686—plus 135 periodicals, 4,000 records (to Kennedy's 656), audio-visual materials, micro-readers and so on. As Jones puts it: "We have all our power in one place and all our demand in the other."

The Maring Branch, located in a poorer section of town, with inadequate parking facilities, and adjacent to heavily traveled streets that are dangerous for children to cross, had the lowest circulation. The population it serves is the lowest-educated in the city and hence less prone to read; still, those are the people who need a library most, and when the Library Board talked of closing Maring, Jones successfully dissuaded it.

Back in 1935, the Lynds reported that 6 out of 10 people in Middletown had library cards; now less than 1 of 3 do. Further, though population has almost doubled, total circulation is down 100,000 from what it was in 1935. True, these figures are somewhat misleading. In 1935, books could only be checked out for two weeks and each renewal was counted as one "circulation"; nowadays, books are charged for four weeks. Also, four years ago, a re-registration program was carried out which resulted in a considerable net loss in card-holders. Since that time the number registered has increased slowly but steadily; but it has a ways to go before it will reach the 1935 level. In 1933 the per capita circulation of library books in Muncie was 12.2; in 1954 it was only 4.8. Even allowing for differences in borrowing time it would appear that people in Muncie are using their library somewhat less than they did in the thirties. Total circulation declined a bit from 424,767 in 1965, to 417,176 in 1966. The Lynds noted that library circulation increased rapidly during the Depression; the converse—that it declines in prosperous times— may hold true today.

Leaving Middletown, one thinks of those thousands of paperbacks being dumped indiscriminately on the city and feels exasperated that they have worked no tangible change. The only spice they have given the bland Middletown reading diet—and I'm speaking of the town, not the University—is the sexiness of the mass-market best sellers and the "risqué" books. Even that is illusory; I think of the town's new discotheque, Woodbury's Club 67, where two girls dance beside the band with colored lights playing on them. They look nude, but they are not; it is a trick.

Perhaps the real function of paperbacks in Middletown has been to replace the "sex-adventure" magazines—the lurid True Confessions type—that people there were reading in the twenties and thirties, according to the Lynds. Still, although the popularity of the "risqué," as well as mystery and spy-genre, may reflect the tastes of the good people of Middletown, one truism enunciated by the Lynds still holds true: "Most of Middletown's reading matter originates outside the city."

Suggested Reading

OVERVIEW

Daniel Boorstin, *The Image: A Guide to Pseudo-Events in America,* New York, Atheneum, 1964 (Harper Colophon paperback).

Sebastian de Grazia, *Of Time, Work and Leisure,* New York, Twentieth-Century Fund, 1962 (Anchor paperback).

August Hecksher, *The Public Happiness,* New York, Atheneum, 1962.

H. Marshall McLuhan, *Understanding Media: The Extensions of Man,* New York, McGraw-Hill, 1964 (McGraw-Hill paperback).

William Rivers and Wilbur Schramm, *Responsibility in Mass Communication,* New York, Harper and Row, 1969.

Bernard Rosenberg and David Manning White, eds., *Mass Culture: The Popular Arts in America,* New York, Free Press, 1957 (Free Press paperback).

Gilbert Seldes, *The Great Audience,* New York, Viking, 1950.

Alvin Toffler, *The Culture Consumers,* New York, St. Martin's Press, 1964 (Penguin paperback).

TELEVISION AND RADIO

Wilbur Schramm, *et al., Television in the Lives of Our Children,* Stanford, Stanford University Press, 1961 (Stanford paperback).

Gary A. Steiner, *The People Look at Television: A Study of Audience Attitudes,* New York, Knopf, 1963.

David Manning White and Richard Averson, eds., *Sight, Sound and Society,* Boston, Beacon Press, 1968.

CINEMA

Pauline Kael, *Kiss Kiss, Bang Bang,* Boston, Little, Brown, 1968 (Bantam paperback).

Arthur Knight, *The Liveliest Art,* New York, Macmillan, 1959 (Mentor paperback).

Martha Wolfenstein and Nathan Leites, *Movies: A Psychological Study,* New York, Free Press, 1950.

POP SONGS AND POP ART

Jonathan Eisen, ed., *The Age of Rock: Sounds of the American Cultural Revolution,* New York, Random House, 1969 (Vintage paperback).

John Russell and Suzi Gablick, *Pop Art Redefined,* New York, Praeger, 1969.

Arnold Shaw, *The Rock Revolution: What's Happening in Today's Music,* New York, Macmillan, 1969.

David Manning White and Robert Abel, eds., *The Funnies: An American Idiom,* New York, Free Press, 1963.

Index

A Note on the Editor

One of our most astute authorities on popular culture, David Manning White is chairman of the Division of Journalism at Boston University. Born in Milwaukee, Wisconsin, he studied at Cornell College, Columbia University, and the University of Iowa. He has worked with newspapers, radio, television, and book publishing, and is currently editor of the *Television Quarterly*. His other books include *Mass Culture; Identity and Anxiety; The Funnies; People, Society and Mass Communication;* and *Sight, Sound and Society,* all of which he has co-edited.